The Complete Book of Fly Tying

ALFRED A. KNOPF / NEW YORK / 2000

THIS IS A BORZOI BOOK
PUBLISHED BY ALFRED A. KNOPF, INC.

Library of Congress Cataloging in Publication Data

Leiser, Eric.
  The complete book of fly tying.

  Bibliography: p.
  Includes index.
  1. Fly tying. 2. Flies, Artificial. I. Title.
SH451.L42 1977   688.7′9   77–74975
ISBN 0–394–40047–X

Manufactured in the United States of America
Published October 31, 1977
Reprinted Nineteen Times
Twenty-first Printing, April 2000

Also by Eric Leiser

FLY-TYING MATERIALS

THE CADDIS AND THE ANGLER
(With Larry Solomon)

STONEFLIES FOR THE ANGLER
(With Robert H. Boyle)

THE COMPLETE BOOK OF FLY TYING

ERIC LEISER

DRAWINGS BY DAVE WHITLOCK / PHOTOGRAPHY BY GUS NEVROS

To the trout and the salmon
and all other gamefish that take flies—
The only reason and excuse for
this beautiful obsession called
fly tying

Contents

III / SUBSURFACE FLY PATTERNS

IV / BUCKTAILS AND STREAMERS

Appendixes

Acknowledgments

Whatever the undertaking, we'd all like to think we can do it alone. Yet if we are honest with ourselves, we realize that many of our endeavors, especially such things as books, would never get done at all without the encouragement, advice, and friendship of those around us.

Here and now I extend very special and personal thanks to Ted Niemeyer, my teacher and every fly tier's fly tier: to Gus Nevros, my fishing companion, who gave up much of his free time to take and develop the photographs for this book; to Matthew M. Vinciguerra, who rushed to take some vital last-minute photographs of the whip finish knot; to Harold Campbell, a diamond in the rough but a true friend to all who know him; to Walt Dette and Harry Darbee, the renowned Catskill fly tiers who were never too busy to share a few moments or a few secrets; to Dr. Bill Priest of Saginaw, who introduced me to Michigan; to Nick Lyons, a writer's writer, who introduced me to Angus Cameron, my editor and guide through the pages of this book (a merciless taskmaster—and I love him for it), who, in turn and much more importantly, befriended me and introduced me to salmon fishing.

I am a very lucky individual. I have many friends, and I'm grateful to all of them. Thanks—and see you on the river.

Preface

Another book on fly tying? Why?

So many times while teaching at various affiliated Federation of Fly Fishermen or Trout Unlimited clinics, I have been asked, "How did you do that? Would you show it to me again? Please do it again. *Do it again.*"

In most instances the question is about the simplest of fly-tying procedures, fundamentals I assumed every fly tier, even a novice, would know. There is a great deal of material available to tiers, much of it in public libraries. There are also many clinics, classes, and individual instruction courses. And so I took it for granted, as do most of us who have gone beyond elementary fly tying, that these basic techniques were understood —that is, until I remembered my own search and attempt to conquer this fine art.

The purpose of this volume is to take nothing for granted, to assume nothing. And to do it again, and again, and again. And, as you progress in your own endeavors, to urge you, too, to *do it again.* For this reason there is justification for another book on fly tying.

I

Beginnings

1

The
Beginning

HOW TO USE THIS BOOK

Very few of us pick up an instructional or technical book and read it the way we would read a novel. Unlike novels, "how to's" usually have very boring plots, and almost no one reads them from beginning to end, retaining and actually putting to use all the information in them. Instructional books are meant to be dipped into whenever the need for a particular piece of information arises, and so it is with this book.

There are three basic forms of flies used for fishing, so this volume has been broken into three sections. The first pertains to all the types of flies that are used on the surface of the water; the second, to those used below; and the third, to those that imitate baitfish. These sections are presented in the order preferred by most angler/tiers. However, if your own inclination is not consistent with this order, by all means go directly to the section you favor. You will be able to learn to tie the fly of your choice by using only that section. However, there are parts in each section which refer you to procedures in another section. This has been done to avoid undue repetition and keep this book a reasonable size.

As you progress through the various sections, you will see that I refer to the use of certain styles and models of hooks, threads, tools, and other materials or equipment. These will be, for the most part, the tools and materials I have on hand. They are not necessarily the only brands to use for tying.

In the case of hooks you will find references to those manufactured by O. Mustad and Son of Norway. Mustad is not the *only* hook manufacturer in the world. However, its hooks are the most readily available through supply houses. Therefore, if you find a hook from another manufacturer which meets the specifications of the particular pattern you are working with, by all means don't hesitate to use it. You will also find other hooks produced by the same manufacturer which can be substituted for a given pattern. For example, if you are tying a streamer fly which calls for a Mustad model 9575 hook, you certainly can substitute a Mustad 3665A. The hooks are identical except that the 9575 has a looped eye. If you cannot locate either of these hooks, a Mustad 79580 can be used; it is also a streamer or bucktail hook, though it is not quite as long as the other two. It will make no difference to the fish which hook you use. The only minor problem you will have in the substitution is the proper proportioning of the fly you are tying, and you will learn to adjust for this after you have tied one or two patterns.

The same holds true for such items as threads and tinsels. While I prefer to use the fine Flymaster brand of thread for most of my tying, nearly any thread of an equivalent diameter will serve you for a particular pattern. All that is needed is a little common sense. If you are tying a large saltwater pattern, you will, of course, require a heavier thread. On the other hand, you will get nowhere should you decide to use a size A on a size 14 Light Cahill dry fly.

With the increasing use of the synthetic Mylar, tinsels are losing popularity in the millinery and garment industries. I suppose that eventually tinsel as we know it today will all but disappear, and Mylar will become as common as the plastic fly lines that have replaced the once prevalent silk lines.

Tools and other kinds of equipment are, for the most part, matters of individual choice. Manufacturers cannot afford to make an inferior product since it will not sell—at least not to fly tiers and fly fishermen. In that area our fraternity is a unique lot. We may be willing to pay a little more for a good product, but we rarely purchase second best. Many tools are recommended. Many more are manufactured. If they do the job they were designed for, you should have no qualms about using equipment that is not mentioned in this book.

As carefully as any author tries to write a technical book, there are still times when the reader will be confused about a certain term or the use of a particular word. For this reason I have included the section Definition of Terms (Appendix A). A brief perusal of this section now and then will answer some of your questions.

An index has also been included. It not only refers to the patterns of particular flies but also lists methods, processes, and techniques. You should be able to tie almost any pattern just by using the index, though it may refer you to many parts of this book to do so. For example, it may lead you to one chapter which illustrates the proper technique for winging a dry fly, to another which describes the method used to form a clipped deer hair body, and to yet another which instructs you in the correct process for hackling the pattern. If you wish to take shortcuts with a new pattern, consult the index. This holds true for both fresh- and saltwater species.

As you work through the various chapters, you will find lists of different types of patterns. Regardless of which pattern you tie, remember the components of each pattern are listed in the order in which they are tied to the shank of the hook. The only exceptions will be those patterns which have materials like tinsel ribs or hackles which, though tied in earlier, are wound to their destination after other processes have been completed.

In this book we have tied our flies with the aid of a tool called a bobbin because it gives better control of the thread with less wear and tear (this is explained further in the text). What then of the fly tier who has already begun to learn the art without using a bobbin? There is no problem. If you have learned to tie without a bobbin and feel comfortable or just don't want to change, there is no need to. You can still tie any of the patterns listed here by using the half-hitch and button method. That's what some of the greatest tiers used to do years ago.

I do, however, recommend that you at least try tying with a bobbin. Once you get the hang of it, you won't go back to the old method for the simple reason that a bobbin can get into tighter corners than your finger and you won't be burdened by that lumpy half hitch as you tie. Just to say, "Well, that's the way my grandfather did it," is nonsense. The fact is he probably would have used a bobbin if they had been available. Years ago they also fished with fly rods made of greenheart and lancewood. Would you give up your modern glass, graphite, or bamboo rod just to "do it the way they used to"? Common sense solves many problems.

As you work from pattern to pattern, whether a dry, a wet, or a streamer, you will notice that certain hook sizes are called for. They will generally be on the large side so you can tie the fly with as little difficulty as possible. However, if you feel the hook size specified still gives you some trouble, by all means go to a larger hook. Many beginners have trouble at first gauging the proper proportion on smaller hooks. There just does not seem to be enough room on the shank to tie in all the required materials at the right places. Always tie with the hook size you are most comfortable with, and then gradually work your way to the proper size for the pattern.

Obviously no fly-tying book can also be a complete fly *pattern* book. All fly-tying books give the patterns for *some* flies, just as this one does (123 different patterns); none can give the "recipes" for *all* flies, although some give more patterns than others. For example, the late Ray Bergman in his famous book *Trout,* which is not *specifically* a trout fly-tying book, gives recipes for 689 flies. Joseph D. Bates, Jr., gives many streamer and salmon fly patterns in his *Streamer Fly Tying and Fishing* and *Atlantic Salmon Flies and Fishing.* The books starred (*) in the Selected Bibliography may be referred to for some of the thousands of flies, streamers, and bucktails that ingenious anglers have devised over the years.

Think of this book as a friend. Go over it briefly. Get familiar with it. Learn what the different chapters deal with, and then really familiarize yourself with the sections that are of most interest to you. Pick out the little tips and hints that make fly tying easier. Refer to the book now and again, even after you feel you have learned all you think there is to learn. Strangely enough, even the things I write about, which I've learned only from others in our fraternity, sometimes have a way of receding in my mind, and it is good to refresh an old memory. And remember to use the index; it lists fly-tying processes as well as patterns, materials, and tools.

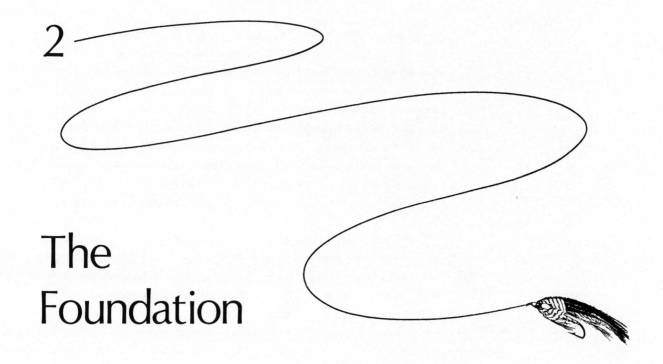

2

The Foundation

The carpenter needs his hammer and saw; the painter, his brush and canvas. These are their tools. Every artist and craftsman requires them. The quality of their accomplishment is determined to a large degree by the quality of their tools. So it is with fly tying. It is, after all, an art and a craft. A set of good tools is the foundation of good fly tying.

I cannot stress strongly enough that you should use the very best tools available. Do not skimp in this area, for it may mean the difference between frustration and achievement. You won't need many, and some mentioned later are helpful but not absolutely necessary. Your primary tools, however, are essential and should be of the highest quality.

PRIMARY TOOLS

The tools discussed below are required for good tying.

VISE: A vise holds the hook while the fly is being tied. It should do this without damaging the hook or letting it slip. The jaws of the vise itself should be made of hardened steel for a firm grasp on the softer-metaled hook. If the jaws are not well constructed, they will eventually wear, causing the hook to break with the uneven pressure or to slip during a tying operation. The jaws should also have an adjustable gap expansion device which will allow the insertion of hooks of various sizes.

The vise should come with a table clamp that allows it to be raised or lowered to the proper and desired height. Whether it is operated by a lever or tightened by a screw knob is not important, but either mechanical device should open and close the jaws correctly for a firm grip on the hook. Most tiers prefer a lever since it requires less effort and works much faster.

The angle of the barrel should be set at approximately 45 degrees for the most efficient operation. Some vises are made with adjustable angles of barrel position. I do not recommend this type because the knob screw which is supposed to lock the vise into position has a tendency to slip—usually during a critical tying operation.

It does not matter whose vise you purchase, as long as it does the job it was designed for. In my own tying I have used the Thompson model "A," which has served me in good stead for many years. Recently I have been using a vise similar to the Thompson, the Sunrise "AA," which has proved just as excellent but costs over $4.00 less, a substantial saving in our inflated economy.

When I am tying saltwater flies or large double salmon patterns, I switch over to one of Veniard's Salmo vises, which will comfortably take and hold hooks up to size 3/0. This vise will hold a 5/0, but in that range it has a tendency to slip. But what do you use when tying a very large hook? A small bench clamp, which can be purchased in any hardware store, has served me perfectly for tying tarpon or shark flies.*

Another vise, of especial interest to professional tiers, is the Universal rotating vise. It has a barrel which, by the push of a lever, can be released to rotate freely in a complete circle. The advantage of this vise is that you can perform certain operations very quickly. For example, if you were winding a wool body or a tinsel rib, all you would have to do is hold the material being wound on the shank with the fingers of one hand and rotate the vise with the other. You just guide the wool or tinsel forward as the vise is being rotated instead of having to wind it around the hook shank with your fingers.

*There is now a vise that will hold a 5/0 6/0 hook firmly. It is the Angler's Roost vise, otherwise known as the ARII.

A tier is occasionally interested in a portable vise. Two of them come to mind. One is the Croydon hand vise, a simple affair with chuck jaws that will hold hooks from size 10 to size 20. The other is a standard vise such as the Thompson "A" or Sunrise "AA" whose stem has been threaded to allow insertion into a heavy metal base. Sometimes called Porta-Vise or Anywhere Vise, this type will hold the hook sizes used in most tying and can be used literally anywhere—at a campsite, in a motel room, or on a car top. This is a great advantage when you're traveling.

HACKLE PLIERS: Usually made of stainless spring steel, hackle pliers work just the opposite of regular pliers. They are pushed open and allowed to grasp a feather or other material and then are closed by releasing the pressure. They are an indispensable tool. A pair of hackle pliers should grasp the tip of a hackle feather and hold it so firmly that if you pull on the feather, you'll break it off. The feather should not slip out while it is being pulled. In addition, the pliers shouldn't cut the hackle in any way.

Once in a while you will see a pair of good-quality pliers that *does* cut hackle. Because hackle pliers are manufactured, not made by hand, a burr of metal is occasionally left on one of the jaws of the pliers. This can simply be filed off.

Well-made pliers usually have one smooth and one serrated jaw. The kind I use were invented by the late Herb Howard and are now manufactured by the Danville Chenille Company in South Danville, New Hampshire. They are sold by suppliers throughout the country, though many will list them under their own name.

SCISSORS: Extremely fine and well-meshed points are the prime requisite for scissors. Your scissors should enable you to trim and cut the finest and softest feather hackle and fur fiber in very tight quarters. If you can locate such a pair and it has holes that conform to your fingers, you'll have an added bonus. The finger holes on many of these embroidery scissors are, unfortunately, too small for men because they are generally manufactured with women in mind.

BOBBIN: The bobbin holds your thread while you are tying. The important thing here is to find one that is both comfortable to your hand and adjustable to the tension of the thread. It should be able to hold a size 7/o thread without breaking it.

There are many models to choose from. Two I can recommend are

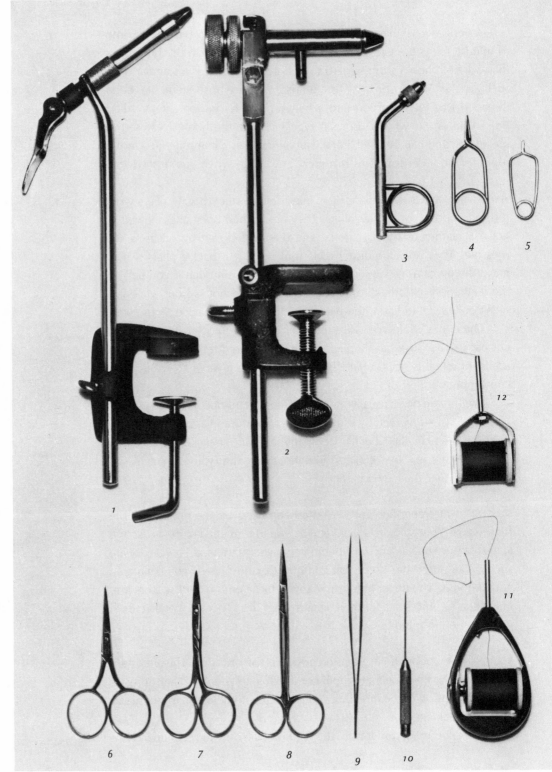

Figs. 1–2. Tools

1. Thompson model "A" vise
2. Veniard Salmo vise
3. Croydon hand vise
4. Herb Howard hackle pliers
5. Mini-hackle pliers
6. Short fine-pointed scissors (large finger holes)
7. Curved-blade scissors
8. Fine-pointed Swiss scissors (Sunrise)
9. Tweezers
10. Dubbing needle
11. Chase bobbin
12. S & M bobbin

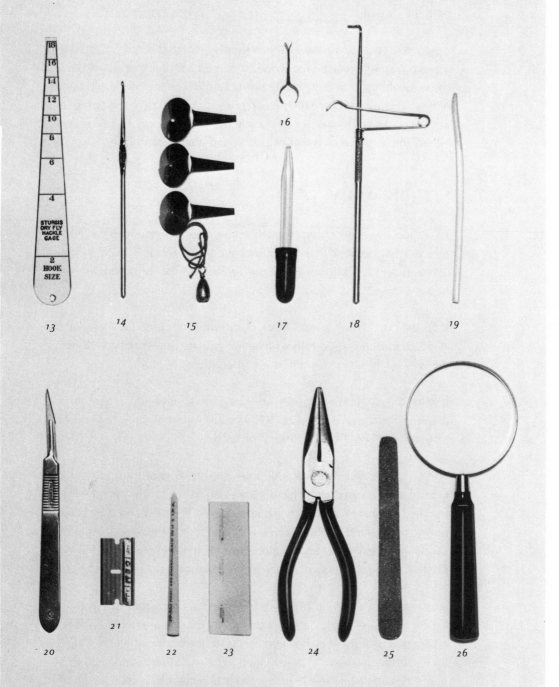

13. Sturgis hackle gauge
14. Crocheting needle
15. Hackle guard set
16. Material clip
17. Eyedropper
18. Whip finisher
19. Half-hitch tool
    (peacock butt)
20. Scalpel
21. Razor blade
22. Sharpening stone
    (pencil point)
23. Sharpening stone
    (knife edge)
24. Flat-faced pliers
25. Emery board
26. Magnifying glass

11

the S & M bobbin and the Matarelli bobbin. Both are tension adjustable by the simple expedient of pushing in or pulling out the metal sides which hold the thread.

DUBBING NEEDLE (or BODKIN): This is simply a pointed needle inserted into a piece of metal, plastic, or wood. It is used for plucking out wayward hairs, roughing fur bodies, and applying lacquers to the heads and bodies of flies. They are very inexpensive, but if you wish to save the cost of this item, you can easily make one yourself. Just insert a medium-sized sewing needle into a piece of wood or plastic and glue it into place.

SECONDARY TOOLS

TWEEZERS: Tweezers come in handy when, upon completion of a fly, you notice a hackle fiber that has misbehaved. Just reach in with a pair of tweezers and pluck it out. Tweezers are also useful for picking up small hooks.

MATERIAL CLIP: This is a small metal clamp which fits onto the barrel of any standard vise. It is used to hold material you are not working with out of the way while other operations are in progress.

HACKLE GAUGE: Hackle gauges are designed to give the proper hackle diameter for a given hook size. It is an assist to the beginner who has yet to develop a sense of proportion for his flies.

WHIP FINISHER: Whip finishers tie the whip finish knot more simply and faster than you can do it by hand. However, I do not recommend this tool for any beginner. The whip finish knot should first be learned by hand, if only to understand how and why it is done. Once the novice has mastered this knot by using his fingers alone, he should feel free to use a whip finisher. Strangely enough, many professional tiers do not use this tool.

HALF-HITCH TOOL: This tool is used to tie the half-hitch knot. The half-hitch knot is used very rarely; in fact, I use it only for one or two operations on one or two patterns. It is, however, an aid to the beginner. Here again, this tool is readily available at a nominal price though there is no need to buy one. One can be had free of charge simply by cutting a 3-inch length from the butt section of a large peacock or goose feather. Nearly all large feathers have a smooth tapered butt which ends in a perfect indentation —a natural half-hitch tool.

RAZOR BLADE or SCALPEL: Both these items have a variety of uses. I use my blade or scalpel mostly for cleaning the end of my dubbing needle when it gets coated with head lacquer.

BOBBIN THREADER: Many bobbins sold by supply houses come packaged with a piece of bent wire which can be used as a bobbin threader. Alas, the wires are so fine and bouncy that I've personally lost or misplaced a number of them over the years. I now use one which is made especially for bobbin threading. It consists of a properly shaped piece of fine spring steel embedded in an aluminum handle. It can't fly away. Whenever my thread breaks at a time it shouldn't, which happens more often than not, I simply reach for my bobbin threader, which I keep stuck in a set of Styrofoam "steps" on my tying table. If you don't use wax on your thread or a waxed thread, you can probably retrieve the broken thread end by simply sucking it through the tube with your mouth. Once the tube of the bobbin gets clogged, however, you'd better get a bobbin threader.

You'll find as time goes by that there will be an ever increasing list of gadgets and tools available to you. Most of them are designed by some enterprising fly tier—which is good. And you'll try them all—which is fun. But for now, the primary and secondary tools listed above will more than serve you well.

OTHER NECESSITIES

TYING BENCH or TABLE: Unless you wish to incur the wrath of certain members of the household, you had better get a tying bench or table which you can call your own. You are, after all, going to clamp a vise to it. You *will* have feathers and fur scattered over it most of the time. And you may occasionally spill some head cement or other liquid on it. For peace in the family, your own tying bench (and possibly area) is a must.

LAMP: Fly tying is delicate work so proper lighting is important. A combination of direct and indirect lighting is best suited for this work. I use an overhead room light and a desk lamp. The latter shines directly on my vise while the other eliminates any shadows.

A good desk lamp for the tier is the Tensor, manufactured in several sizes and found in many department stores as well as fly-tying materials houses. Tensor lamps all use high-intensity bulbs and thus cast a very bright light. Also available is the Luxo magnifying lamp, which is extremely large and heavy and requires a substantial bench or table to support it. However, the lamp itself, which has a circular fluorescent bulb 4 inches in diameter which in turn encircles a magnifying glass of the same size, is perhaps the best I have ever seen for fly tying. Both lamps rotate, swivel on their hinges, and can be placed into almost any position required by the fly tier.

A little trick I learned from Harry and Elsie Darbee of Livingston Manor, New York, is to surface a desk or tying table with green blotter paper. Green is a relaxing shade that doesn't give off the harsh reflection you would get from a white or shiny surface.

WAX: Though not a tool or material, a cake of wax is nevertheless a necessity. You will need it to coat the thread on which you spin the fur to make your fly bodies. It will also prevent your thread from slipping when it is first wound onto the smooth shank of the hook.

There are two kinds of wax, the very sticky (which will adhere not only to your thread but also to your fingers) and the nonsticky sticky (which will stick to the thread but not your fingers). I prefer the latter. You will learn what I mean if you do use a liquid wax or the Thompson tinned wax. Don't misunderstand. The very sticky type does have a use, especially for making bodies on which the material is not only coarse but very smooth and glassy. Seal's fur and polar bear dubbing are good examples. When you use the sticky sticky wax, try to make all your bodies before proceeding to the other parts of the pattern. This way you can wash the excess off your fingers and proceed normally.

The best all-round wax is the kind Herb Howard used when he made his prewaxed thread. It coats the thread well, is tacky enough so that all but the coarsest materials adhere to it, and does not stick to your fingers. This wax contains just the proper amount of resin to do the job. It comes in cakes of about half an ounce which will last you for at least the next 10 or 15 years. It never seems to run out or lose its strength.

There are also some liquid waxes on the market. In my opinion they are more trouble than they are worth since the two waxes just mentioned will do all the work you will ever require of a wax.

LACQUERS AND CEMENTS: You will find a variety of lacquers and cements in a host of types and colors listed in every supplier's catalog. All of them have particular uses, and each of them is preferred by certain tiers. Let's take a look at some of them.

The simply labeled head cement is the most commonly listed and sold. This is a clear lacquer, usually with a Celluloid base. It is used on most parts of the fly and always at the head after a whip finish knot has been applied to a pattern.

Another clear lacquer is vinyl cement, which dries very quickly and is excellent for wing cases on nymphs and the bases of dry fly wings, among other things. It can be used in place of regular head cement.

Plio cement is a newcomer. It is made by diluting a glue called Pliobond. It penetrates the thread deeply, which is what many tiers prefer. It acts something like varnish, which also penetrates but takes much longer to dry. Spar varnish is hard to beat for certain things, especially preshaping large stonefly nymphs like those created by Ted Niemeyer of New Canaan, Connecticut.

Lacquers come in a variety of colors. They are used mainly for painting the eyes on streamer flies and the bodies of popping bugs. They are usually made with an enamel or Celluloid base.

THREAD: This is the material with which you attach all your feather and fur to the hook. Always try to tie with as fine a thread as you can handle and the hook will allow. For most of my tying I use Flymaster prewaxed thread. This is size 7/0, though its diameter is slightly larger because of the wax. This was also developed by Herb Howard and is manufactured by the Danville Chenille Company. Most supply houses carry it.

Usually I would advise any novice to use a thread slightly heavier than the pattern or hook size calls for, but because the Flymaster thread *is* as strong as a standard 3/0 thread, there is no need to. The thread will hold up even for inexperienced fingers. This thread can be used for hook sizes 2 through 28.

For the larger saltwater or bass bug patterns, a size 2/0 is recommended. It is stronger, will hold the materials more securely, and does not require as many turns to achieve the proper taper for a head.

As far as fly tying goes, thread sizes are indicated by the number of zeros they carry. The more zeros, the smaller the size. In other words very fine threads are oooooo, ooooooo, and so on; a size 6/o thread should actually read oooooo. To save space, however, the thread manufacturers use the slash system. On a scale of 2/o to 8/o, the finest would be 8/o and the largest 2/o. Sizes larger than 2/o are designated by letters—A, B, C, D, and so forth, with A indicating the finest thread. Larger threads are used mostly for rod winding.

Always pick a thread whose color is as close as possible to the fly being tied, one that blends in well. Remember, the thread is not really part of the fly; it only holds the components together.

HOOKS: Hooks should be used for the purpose for which they were intended.* While you can tie a dry fly on a hook that is designated for a wet fly, you will be defeating your purpose because a wet fly hook is heavier and will not support your fly as well as a lighter hook. The same holds true for hooks designed for streamers or bucktails. These are longer in the shank so that they will imitate baitfish. Each style of hook has a purpose.

When I began fly tying, hook designations had me thoroughly confused. There were so many styles, types, and models. Some were short, some long, some heavy, some light. The shape of the eyes and gap widths varied. Let's see what we can do here to simplify the hook situation.

The length of a hook is standard unless otherwise indicated. For instance, you may have noticed that some hooks are listed as 1XL, 2XL, or even 8XL. These abbreviations mean, respectively, "1 extra long," "2 extra long," or "8 extra long." Each of these hooks has a slightly longer than usual shank. The shank of a 6XL hook is actually half again as long as a standard shank. The actual size of the hook (gap, bend, and point) is the same.

The same holds true for hooks marked 1XS, or 2XS—they are shorter than standard (the 2X is shorter than the 1X and so on). Wire diameters also vary, and you'll see designations of 3X fine or 2X stout. This only means lighter or heavier wire.

*There are manufacturers of hooks other than O. Mustad and Son of Norway. The only reason Mustad is listed so consistently throughout this volume is that its hooks are readily available and usually the only ones carried by most of the supply houses in the United States. These companies, however, also make excellent hooks for fishing and fly tying: Alcock, Wilson, Eagle Claw (the trade name of Wright and McGill), Partridge, and Veniard.

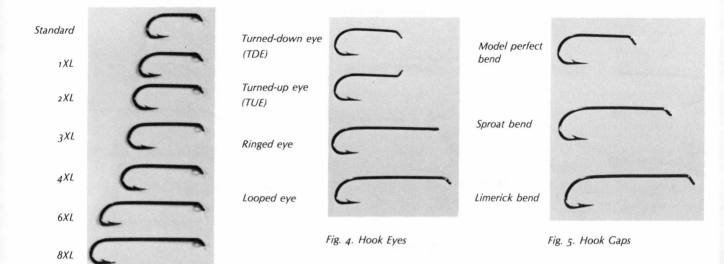

Standard

1XL

2XL

3XL

4XL

6XL

8XL

Fig. 3. Hook Lengths (Size 10 Hook)

Turned-down eye (TDE)

Turned-up eye (TUE)

Ringed eye

Looped eye

Fig. 4. Hook Eyes

Model perfect bend

Sproat bend

Limerick bend

Fig. 5. Hook Gaps

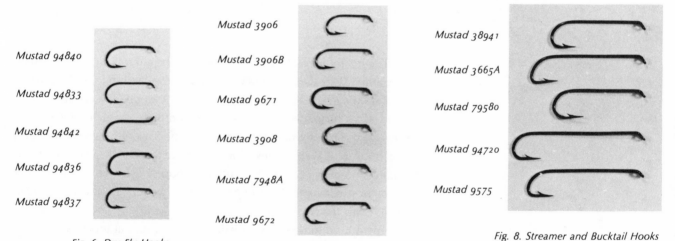

Mustad 94840

Mustad 94833

Mustad 94842

Mustad 94836

Mustad 94837

Fig. 6. Dry Fly Hooks

Mustad 3906

Mustad 3906B

Mustad 9671

Mustad 3908

Mustad 7948A

Mustad 9672

Fig. 7. Wet Fly and Nymph Hooks

Mustad 38941

Mustad 3665A

Mustad 79580

Mustad 94720

Mustad 9575

Fig. 8. Streamer and Bucktail Hooks

Hook size is less difficult. Starting with 1, 2, you work your way up by twos for the smaller sizes: 1, 2, 4, 6, 8, 10, 12, 14, 16, 18, 20, 22, 24, 26, 28. The higher the number, the smaller the size. Hence, size 1 is the largest hook, and 28 is the smallest. For larger hooks you again begin with 1 and simply add a slash and a zero: 1, 1/0, 2/0, 3/0, 4/0, 5/0, and so on. The smallest hook here is 1, and the largest 5/0.

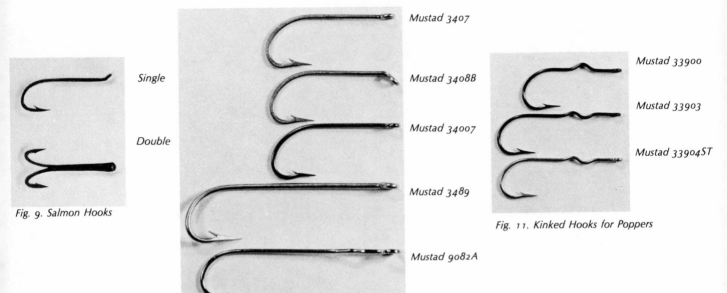

Fig. 9. Salmon Hooks

Single

Double

Mustad 3407

Mustad 3408B

Mustad 34007

Mustad 3489

Mustad 9082A

Fig. 10. Saltwater Hooks

Mustad 33900

Mustad 33903

Mustad 33904ST

Fig. 11. Kinked Hooks for Poppers

The matter of hook eyes is also simple. The abbreviations here usually go like this: TUE, TDE, or looped eye, ringed eye, and so forth. TUE means "turned-up eye"; TDE, "turned-down eye." A looped eye is one in which the wire has been forged to double back onto the shank, forming a loop or eye at the point where the wire was bent. This, incidentally, is a very good hook to tie with because you don't have to close the eye with thread to prevent leader cutting while fishing. Looped eyes are made only for salmon or streamer hooks. A ringed eye is neither up nor down, but evenly aligned with the hook shank.

There used to be many varieties of hook gap, but today we need be concerned only with three: model perfect bend, sproat bend, and limerick bend. The model perfect is almost completely round; the sproat has a bit more of an oval taper. The limerick breaks sharply from its bend into the point.

You will find one other hook mentioned now and then. It is the kinked shank hook, and it is used for poppers. There is a kink, or hump, in the center of the shank so the hook can be inserted into a piece of cork or plastic and not twist once the popper has been completed.

All Mustad boxes are well marked, as are the suppliers' catalogs where these hooks are listed.

MATERIALS

There are so many materials available today in addition to feathers and furs that it would be impractical to go into all of them here. They will be covered as they are required in the chapters where they are to be used. Briefly, however, I would like to mention just a few important points about some materials.

FURS: In tying dry flies, the most desirable fur you can use is that of a water animal, especially in forming the body. Water animals have a protective oil in their fur which resists water and thus makes for a higher-floating fly. All furs can be used for wets or nymphs, but when tying dries it is always best to take every possible advantage.

Besides fur the down of all waterfowl can also be used for dubbing material. Again, it is highly water-resistant and extremely suitable for dry flies.

HACKLE: When the word "hackle" is mentioned, fly tiers generally think of rooster necks or capes. Hackle does have other meanings, as we shall later see, but rooster necks are probably the single most important item in any fly tier's supply chest. They are sought after, collected, and hoarded. Some are considered so superb by their owners that they are never even tied with, only admired. It is almost like Midas counting his gold.

Good-quality rooster necks are expensive, as you will learn once you have tied for a while, so here is a good rule to follow: *If you find a rooster neck of exceptional quality, purchase it, regardless of color, if the price is reasonable.* This is one way to start a good collection. However, as a novice, you can save a bit by purchasing second-grade, or "sale," necks. After all, your fingers have not yet become educated. Why waste a good-quality neck in the process of learning? By using second-grade necks, you will still be able to tie, and tie well, *and* have flies to fish with. Once your ability has improved and you are an accomplished tier, by all means use the finer grade of neck hackle found on the expensive capes.

A question I am often asked, especially by beginners, is, "How do you determine the quality of a rooster neck? What makes one cape grade A and another grade B?" There are a few things you can and should look for.

1. Overall appearance. The neck should be full, with enough usable hackles to warrant the price. The hackle neck itself should also be in

prime condition. If it contains many pinfeathers (small immature feathers just beginning to grow out of the skin), the rooster has been killed before the prime season.

2. Overall color. Color should be uniform throughout or at least in the area of the neck you will be plucking your most usable hackles from. If it is a badger or furnace neck, the black center marking should be distinct on all of the feathers on the neck, up through the nape, where the very small midge hackles are to be found. Whatever the color, it should have a luster and not be drab or dull. Dullness is often a sign of poor diet, resulting in inferior-quality hackle or a dehydrated cape.

3. Resiliency. You can pick up a rooster neck and by bending the skin just a little raise the feathers. Stroke them or poke them back and forth with your fingers. They should be bouncy, resilient. The faster they come back to their original shape, the better the hackle is for a dry fly.

4. Stiffness. The individual fibers of each feather should stand out from the center stem as straight as possible. They should not bend or feel soft. Some tiers like to take a single hackle feather, bend it, and poke their nose or lips with the tips of the fibers. These are sensitive areas, and I suppose if you do this enough you can feel the difference between soft and stiff hackle.

You should also look for the amount of web a hackle feather has, though this is not necessarily a crucial criterion. I have found good stiff hackle feathers with an excess of web. In a badger hackle the black center is *all* web. Web, incidentally, is the softer center on any hackle feather. On some hackles the web runs all the way to the tip. On good stiff dry fly hackles this webbing terminates approximately halfway down the feather.

5. Use. What you want to use the neck for should also be a determining factor. For a salmon tier a large neck with stiff hackles that will tie a number 4 or 6 White Wulff will appear superb. For the trouter, who must pattern his imitations in 14's, 16's, and 18's, the same neck is useless, except for tailing.

As you see, there are a number of considerations. However, don't be upset if you don't get the hang of it at first. It will come to you. The more necks you handle, the better you will get. So don't ever miss the opportunity to sort through a collection of them should you get the chance.

Rooster necks are the one item not sold in packets or by the ounce. They are sold individually, unlike all other materials.

FLY-TYING KITS: I do *not* recommend kits. I would rather see you spend a bit more money on a good solid basic set of tools and enough material to properly dress only one fly pattern. When you have learned to tie that one pattern properly, purchase the material for the next one, and so on. Most fly-tying kits are an assortment of odds and ends that you will rarely use.

If you must have a kit or want to purchase one for a friend or relative as a gift, at least try to ascertain the contents. Make sure the supplier lists all the materials that are in the kit and the flies it will tie. Then you will know exactly what you are paying for.

Incidentally, fur and feather materials need not always cost you money. The furs and feathers of all animals and birds can be used some-time, somewhere, in fly tying. Therefore, if you hunt or have a friend who does, you can begin collecting on your own. There is also another way to get materials—"road hunting." Animals that have been killed by passing automobiles are a good source. Keep a knife, a pair of pruning shears, and a large plastic bag in your car. You will be able to salvage much of what will only be wasted. Do, however, check your local game laws before you pick up any road kills. In some states possession of certain species is prohibited.

You may also be able to pick up some fur and feather at no cost or at a minimal charge from your local taxidermist. He may have a few scraps and cuttings he intends to discard. Fly tiers, of course, never discard anything.

FEATHER AND FUR MATERIALS

Perhaps a brief word about the colors and uses of some of the most commonly used feathers and furs would be in order. In the case of feathers substitutes have also been listed where applicable.

Feathers
BRONZE MALLARD: Feathers from a drake mallard duck just above the point where the wing merges with the body; similar to mallard flank, except that

much of the feather is brown/bronze. Like the mallard flank it is barred with fine black stripes.

Substitute: Dyed mallard or teal flank feathers.

DUCK BREAST: Small fan-shaped feathers from the breast of any wild (various shades) or domestic duck. White duck breast feathers are used in making fan wings, cut wings, and no-hackle flies.

DUCK QUILL. *See* Mallard Quill.

GOLDEN PHEASANT CREST: Topknot of a golden pheasant. It is a very smooth, fine, curved feather with a brilliant yellow/orange sheen.

Substitute: None.

GOLDEN PHEASANT TIPPET: Orange feathers banded with black bars. Found on the neck of the golden pheasant.

Substitute: Lady Amherst tippets dyed orange.

GOOSE QUILL: Flight feathers of a Canada goose, which is gray or black/gray, or flight feathers of a domestic white goose. The latter are dyed various shades.

Substitute: None required.

GUINEA HEN: Body feathers, which are black or grayish black dotted with white spots. The natural feather is also dyed green, brown, blue, red, and orange for certain effects. The wings, which have a similar marking, are also used occasionally.

Substitute: None required.

JUNGLE COCK EYE: Waxlike black feathers with yellow/orange spots and bands from the neck of a jungle fowl. Feathers are very narrow. No longer available.

Substitute: Starling body feathers, quail neck feathers, Lady Amherst body feathers. All of these substitutes should be lacquered to give them the firmness of the original. There are also some fair synthetic substitutions available.

LADY AMHERST TIPPET: White feathers with black bands from the neck of a Lady Amherst pheasant.

Substitute: None.

MALLARD FLANK (SIDE FEATHERS): Pearl gray feathers very finely barred with black stripes. Found on the side, or flank, of a drake mallard. These feathers are often dyed brownish yellow to be used as a substitute for natural wood duck flank. They are also dyed various shades of yellow, green, and bronze.
Substitute: Teal flank.

MALLARD QUILL: Sometimes referred to as mallard pointer quill; slate gray feathers from mallard wings (see above). Primary use is the winging of many standard wet and dry flies.
Substitute: Wing quill feathers (pointers or flight feathers) from ducks of similar coloration.

MALLARD WING: Entire pair of mallard wings. Slate gray.
Substitute: Other wild duck wings of similar coloration, such as pintail, widgeon, gadwall, or teal.

MARABOU: Originally from a marabou stork; now gathered from a domestic white turkey. Marabou shorts, or blood feathers, are undeveloped feathers with no center stem. Marabou is dyed various shades for a variety of patterns.
Substitute: None required.

MOTTLED BROWN TURKEY WING QUILL: Inner flight feathers of a brown turkey. Color runs from a light to a rich dark brown and has a speckled, distorted marking throughout. Very scarce since this breed of turkey is no longer raised for food in the United States.
Substitute: The same wing feathers from a wild turkey, ringneck pheasant tail, or golden pheasant tail; peafowl secondary feathers.

OAK SPECKLED TURKEY. *See* Mottled Brown Turkey Wing Quill.

OSTRICH HERL: Individual fibers from an ostrich plume.
Substitute: None required.

OSTRICH PLUME: Entire tail feather of an ostrich. Occurs in natural black, gray, and white. Shorter body feathers, with very fine herl, are called mini-ostrich. The white feathers of the ostrich are dyed various shades.

Substitute: None required.

PARTRIDGE HACKLE: Body feathers of the European grouse; feathers are speckled gray or brown and finely barred with black stripes.

Substitute: American ruffed grouse, sharp-tailed grouse, blue grouse, and certain other game birds. Occasionally similar marking is found on the neck or body feathers of a domestic hen.

PEACOCK EYED TAIL: Tail feather from male peafowl. Fibers are iridescent green with a hint of bronze. "Eyed" portion is banded in a circle of bronze, green, bronze, blue, and purple.

Substitute: None.

PEACOCK HERL (STRUNG): The loose iridescent green fibers from a peacock tail which have been sewn together to form a string. Since most of these fibers are from the lower portion of the tail, they are long and suitable only for topping on streamer flies.

Substitute: None.

PEACOCK STRIPPED QUILL: Fiber from the "eyed" portion of the peacock tail from which the flue has been removed.

Substitute: Stripped starling wing quill stems, fibers from the flight feathers of a peacock.

PEACOCK SWORD: Side tail feathers of a peacock with broken or separated green fibers on one side of the stem.

Substitute: None.

RINGNECK PHEASANT: Sometimes called English ringneck or Chinese pheasant. The cock pheasant is truly a multicolored bird, ranging from light tan through speckled blends of blues, greens, and browns. The head is a deep metallic green with a white band. The hens are tan/brown but have some interesting barring which can be used for many patterns. Hen pheasant wings are used by some tiers for the March Brown wet fly.

Substitute: None.

RINGNECK TAIL: Center feather from the tail of a cock ringneck pheasant.

Substitute: Golden pheasant tail.

SILVER PHEASANT BODY: Body feathers of the silver pheasant; white with very fine black barring.

    Substitute: None.

SPECKLED TURKEY WING QUILL. *See* Mottled Brown Turkey Wing Quill.

STRIPPED PEACOCK. *See* Peacock Stripped Quill.

TEAL FLANK: Feathers from the flank, or sides, of a drake teal duck. They are white/gray and have very distinctive black barring.

    Substitute: Mallard flank, well marked.

TURKEY TAIL, WHITE-TIPPED: Long feather from the tail of a brown turkey. It has a very dark brown mottled coloration. The tip of the feather is off-white. This feather is becoming fairly scarce.

    Substitute: Tail feathers of a wild turkey.

WOOD DUCK FLANK: Sometimes referred to as "fly tiers' gold"; side, or flank, feathers from a drake wood duck. Approximately half the feathers are a lemon/brown in color with fine black barring; in addition, the other flank feathers have broad bands of black and white at the tips.

    Substitute: Dyed mallard or teal flank. However, the substitution is used only for those wood duck feathers without the black and white bands.

Furs and Hides

ANTELOPE: The body of the antelope has coarse gray, brown, and white hair fibers. Used primarily for spinning bodies or heads (bass bugs, Spuddlers, Sculpins, and the like).

BADGER: The primary use is winging bucktail patterns. This is done with the guard hairs, which are barred white, black, and brown. The underfur, which is light beige, is used for dubbing.

BEAVER: The light to medium gray underfur has glossy highlights and is an excellent dubbing for dry flies. Guard hairs are dark brown.

BLACK BEAR: The hair that shades from dark brown to coal black is the most frequently used. It is an excellent winging material for bucktails and streamers.

BUCKTAIL: Bucktail usually refers to the tail of an eastern whitetail deer, though tails from the western mule deer and blacktail deer are also used. The hair is a natural white on the underside and brown to black on top. It is fairly long, sometimes running 4 to 5 inches. Used for streamers and bucktails. The tail is dyed a variety of shades.

CALF TAIL: Sometimes called kip or impala, today a calf tail is what its name says it is—the tail of a calf. The hair, which is used for winging and tailing, is usually natural white, though a few brown and black tails are available in the natural state. The white tails are dyed various shades.

CARIBOU: The fine hair of this animal is natural gray to white. The fibers are used for spinning bodies.

COYOTE: Coyote guard hairs are occasionally used for the wings and tails of bucktail and streamer flies. Color varies with animal, but it is generally brown, beige, and black. Underfur, which can be used for dubbing, is a tan/gray.

DEER BODY: This hair is taken primarily from the back or underside of a whitetail deer, though mule deer and blacktail deer hair is also used. Color is gray/brown to white. Hair fibers are coarse and hollow, making them an excellent material for spinning the bodies or heads of such flies as the Irresistible or Muddler. The white hair is dyed various shades for bass bugs.

ELK: The firm and stiff fibers of this animal are used primarily for wings and tailing. Mostly brown, shading off to tan and gray.

ENGLISH HARE'S MASK WITH EARS: The short tan/gray guard hairs are mixed with the softer tan/gray underfur to form the body of the famous Gold-Ribbed Hare's Ear pattern. It is often blended with other furs to create certain effects for specific patterns.

FITCH BODY: The underfur is used for dubbing. It runs from rich cream to beige.

FITCH TAIL: The tail has excellent guard hair material shading from brown to almost black. Used very often for winging salmon flies.

FOX TAIL: Fox tails come in a variety of natural shades of white, tan, gray, and mixed colors and are used primarily for winging material on bucktail and streamer flies. The underfur is also usable.

GRAY FOX: The gray and black guard hairs are used by salmon tiers for winging the fly in a number of patterns. Underfur is gray.

GROUNDHOG. *See* Woodchuck.

HARE'S EARS. *See* English Hare's Mask with Ears.

MINK: The underfur from mink bodies is available in a variety of natural shades—white, beige, brown, gray, black. The white is dyed various colors. An excellent dubbing for the bodies of several dry fly patterns. Mink tail is also to be had in numerous natural shades. Tail guard hairs provide an excellent stiff material for winging a number of patterns, especially caddis imitations.

MOLE: The soft gray fur of the mole is used only for dubbing.

MOOSE HIDE: The coarse dark brown to black fibers are used for tails.

MOOSE MANE: By alternating strands of the long light and dark gray fibers from the mane of a moose, you can form flies which give the impression of segmentation. Also used for tailing.

MUSKRAT: The underfur is light to dark blue/gray. It is one of the most popular dubbing furs. Guard hairs are dark brown and rarely used.

NUTRIA: The underfur is a lustrous tan to brown. Excellent for dubbing. Brown guard hairs are too short for most practical uses.

OPOSSUM (AMERICAN): The underfur is a lustrous white; guard hairs are dark brown to black. It is strange that the fur and hair of this animal are rarely used.

OPOSSUM (AUSTRALIAN): The fur is a rich creamy yellow on the underside gradually merging into a beige and finally a gray over the back of this animal. The yellow/cream portion is a favorite for the Light Cahill pattern. Guard hairs from the tail are dark brown to black. They are fairly silky and make fine winging material on bucktail and streamer patterns.

OTTER: Otter is used primarily for its underfur, which ranges from light tan to brown.

PECCARY: Known also as javelina or wild pig, the peccary has hair of an almost brittle stiffness in mottled black and tan. It is used to make the legs and feelers of nymphs, especially stonefly nymphs.

PORCUPINE: The skin of the porcupine is covered with quills and bristles. The bristles are dark brown for the most part, though occasionally you come across one with white bristles on certain portions of the skin. The quills are white, brown, or a combination of both and hollow. They are used for some dry fly patterns, such as the Coffin Fly. The bristles are used as feelers and legs on nymphs.

RABBIT: Used for their underfur, rabbit skins come in natural blue/gray, black, brown, and white. Natural white is dyed various shades. It is used mostly for the bodies of wet flies.

RACCOON: The underfur is a light brown, often bleached to shades of ginger for such light-colored flies as the Light Cahill. Guard hairs are a combination of brown and black.

RED FOX: The underfur, which is the most frequently used part of the fox skin, comes in a variety of shades suitable for various patterns. Colors range from cream through beige to gray. The belly strip of some foxes is urine-stained, resulting in a pinkish cast; this particular shade is highly sought after for the Light Hendrickson pattern as described by Art Flick.

SABLE: The underfur is natural brown and used for dubbing. Guard hairs, also brown, are fairly long and soft.

SEAL: Fur from two kinds of seal* is commonly used—the coarse cream

*Seal fur is now prohibited from importation. An excellent substitute, which dubs much more easily, is a product manufactured by Poul Jorgensen, called SEALEX.

fur of the baby hair seal and the soft silky brown fur of the fur seal. The hair seal fur is dyed a number of shades for forming rough bodies for many flies.

SQUIRREL, GRAY: The underfur, which is gray, is used for dubbing. The guard hairs, gray with a white tip, are occasionally used for very small flies. Sometimes both the guard hairs and underfur are blended to form rough, coarse bodies.

SQUIRREL TAIL, GRAY: The long hair fibers, approximately 1 1/2 inches in length, are speckled gray terminating with a black band and a white tip. They are used for wings on many bucktail and streamer patterns.

SQUIRREL TAIL, RED FOX: The reddish brown and black barred hairs are used for bucktail and streamer patterns.

STONE MARTEN: The guard hairs on the tail of this animal are fairly long, usually 1 to 1 1/2 inches. They are brown to dark brown and very fine, yet firm, making them an excellent winging material for larger salmon and bucktail patterns. The underfur is soft and smoke gray.

WOODCHUCK (GROUNDHOG): The guard hairs on the back of this animal are barred black, tan, and black and terminate in a white tip. The guard hairs on the tail range from a medium light brown to dark brown. On some animals the tail fibers also have a speckled effect or terminate in a white tip. One of the finest materials for wing and tailing of both dry flies and bucktail patterns. The underfur, which is sparse, is a soft dull black.

RECOGNIZING TYPES OF ROOSTER NECKS—NATURAL AND DYED

Rooster necks, hen necks, and saddle capes range in natural color from white to black. The obvious colors, are, of course, fairly easy to recognize, but others can at first glance present a problem in identification, especially to the uninitiated. This is a list of the most commonly used colors in fly tying.

Natural Colors

WHITE: Hackle quality generally fair.

CREAM: Off-white. Hackle quality generally good to excellent.

CREAM GINGER (DARK CREAM): Rich creamy neck, sometimes with a hint of yellow in the fibers. Necks like this are sought for the Light Cahill pattern. Hackle quality generally good to excellent.

GOLDEN GINGER (BUFF): True ginger. Very rare in good-quality hackle capes. Many companies bleach brown necks to get this shade because of the scarcity.

DARK GINGER: Light brown neck with ginger highlights; sometimes called red game. Fairly common. Hackle quality good to excellent.

BROWN: Most common of all rooster necks. Hackle quality good to excellent.

COACHMAN BROWN: Rich dark mahogany. While the color is common enough, good hackle quality is not. Generally these necks run from poor to fair. A good-quality neck in this shade is an exception.

NATURAL DUN: Often referred to as blue dun, bronze dun, or rusty dun, depending on the shade. It is most unfortunate that the name blue dun ever came into being since it creates a picture in the mind of the tier. There is no such thing as a natural blue/gray rooster neck. Most of the necks you see will be gray with a bronze cast. They will be flecked or dotted with a lighter or darker shade, making the hackle fibers look very much like insects. This is why they are in such demand. They are very expensive since roosters with good hackle quality are bred and raised just for fly tying.

NATURAL BLACK: Appears to be black but is not a true black (very few things in nature *are* a true black). If you look at the underside of the hackle feathers, you will see that the shading is much lighter. Hackle quality generally poor. In fact, a good-quality black neck is a rarity. For this reason most tiers use a neck that has been dyed when black is required.

BADGER: White through golden cream with hackle feathers that have a black center stripe. The stripe, which runs the length of the feather, is actually the webby portion of the feather. Pure white (silver) badger is relatively scarce yet in much demand for such patterns as the White Wulff and the Silver Darter. Hackle quality generally good to excellent.

FURNACE: Brown with black center stripe. Here again, the stripe is actually the webby part of the hackle feather. Hackle quality generally poor to fair.

COCK-Y BONDHU: Same as furnace except that the tips of the hackle barbules are also edged in black. Hackle quality generally poor to fair.

VARIANTS: Any neck with color variation in the barbules of the hackle feather.

GINGER GRIZZLY (VARIANT): Ginger with hackle feathers barred with reddish brown. Hackle quality generally good to excellent.

RED GRIZZLY (VARIANT): Brown with light ginger barring; opposite of ginger grizzly. Hackle quality good to excellent.

GRIZZLY OR BARRED PLYMOUTH ROCK: Any black neck with white barring is called grizzly. Barred Plymouth Rock is a species of domestic chicken that has this particular color. However, the shading is also found among imported necks, though not as commonly. Grizzly rooster necks are among the most expensive for the simple reason that this type of rooster is not grown for food as much as it once was. In addition, labor costs on any domestic neck are much higher than those on an imported neck. In certain cases Barred Plymouth Rock are raised solely for fly tying, which can bring the price of a prime grizzly neck upward of $25.00. It is one of the most frequently used necks in fly tying. Hackle quality fair to excellent.

CHINCHILLA: White with black or gray barring; opposite of grizzly. Since there is not much call for this type of shading in the known fly patterns, chinchilla necks are often dyed, especially to shades of dun. Hackle quality good to excellent.

CREE: Sometimes referred to as instant Adams since in one hackle feather it has all the colors of the Adams dry fly. Three distinct shades should be present to qualify a rooster neck as a Cree—black (or dark gray), brown, and pale ginger. Fairly scarce. Hackle quality generally good to excellent.

Dyed Rooster Necks

Besides the obvious colors such as red, yellow, blue, green, black, and orange, rooster necks and hen and saddle capes are dyed subtle shades to imitate living insects.

DYED DUN: This, of course, is by far the most important of all the dyed colors since it is used to imitate the coloration of the majority of mayflies and caddis flies. Colors range from light to dark gray and light to dark bronze-gray. Bronze dun is gray with a brownish cast.

OLIVE: What is olive to one tier may be a completely different shade to another. I standardize on the actual olive that is found in a martini. From there you can figure light or dark olive.

SILVER DOCTOR BLUE: You will see this color listed in many of the streamer or salmon fly patterns. I doubt whether anyone knows for sure what it should be since the color was originally taken from a protected bird called the blue chatterer (not to be confused with the imported kingfisher, which is a substitute for this species). Silver doctor blue is a light blue—not pale, as some have been led to believe, but a solid yet light blue.

INSECT GREEN: This is a light green with a hint of yellow. Chartreuse would be a very good word for describing insect green.

SUPERVISOR GREEN: Also a light green but without the yellow. Something like the color of newly grown spring grass.

CLARET: Sometimes referred to as dark wine, claret is just about that color. A good burgundy is the same color.

Tiers probably use hundreds of colors in their flies. Some will tell you that it is absolutely critical to hit just the right spot on the spectrum or you will not take any fish. That's nonsense. Yes, fish do see color or, rather, may prefer one shade to another, but color is not as vital as are certain other things in fishing a fly. In order, the most important things in tying a fly that will imitate a living insect or baitfish are size, shape, and, lastly, color. Color is important, but you shouldn't be obsessed by it.

One final word about your foundation. While there are many excellent books on patterns and tying them, I strongly urge you not to rely on any of them, including this one, *entirely*. There is no substitute for firsthand experience. Learning to tie flies is best accomplished by having a teacher, perhaps a friend or professional tier who will take you under his wing. If there is a fly-tying class available to you, by all means attend it. Many chapters of Trout Unlimited and other organizations give these instructions free of charge or for a nominal fee. There are also many inexpensive adult education classes. If at all possible, do take advantage of these lessons. You will then find the reading and understanding of this and other books on fly tying just so much more meaningful.

Once you are on your way, then I do recommend you read as much on the subject of fly tying as you can afford. Each author/tier has his own special something to offer, and if you pick up only one or two tricks or procedures from each book or article, it will have been worth the price.

II

Flies That Float

3

The Conventional Dry Fly

Most of the food eaten by trout, bass, and other fish is taken under the surface of the water, but most of the materials and flies sold are for the dry fly or other top-water patterns. I have also found that most fly tiers or would-be fly tiers prefer tying this type of pattern, even though some of the other types may be simpler to master. For this reason we are going to begin the actual tying of flies with the dry fly.

One of the most difficult ideas to get across in fly tying is proportion, especially in a dry fly. Actually it varies with the type of fly you are tying and the type of hook it is being tied on (you may recall the description given to hook designations in the previous chapter). However, as a generalization and as a generalization only, Figure 1 will give you an idea of what the proportions should be on a standard dry fly.

In all parts of the United States dry fly fishing is the most popular form of the sport. The two most popular dry flies in both the east and the west are the Adams and the Light Cahill. You and I are going to tie a Light Cahill. We are going to go through this pattern one step at a time and take nothing for granted. It may be detailed and seem very slow, but I believe that if you can tie one pattern but tie it well, the rest is smooth sailing.

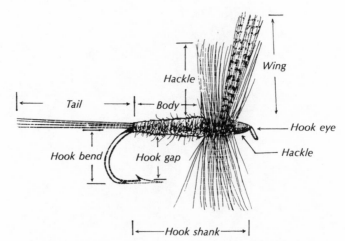

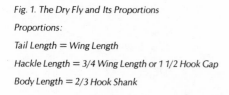

Fig. 1. The Dry Fly and Its Proportions

Proportions:

Tail Length = Wing Length

Hackle Length = 3/4 Wing Length or 1 1/2 Hook Gap

Body Length = 2/3 Hook Shank

The materials you will need for the Light Cahill are:

Hook: Mustad 94840, size 12

Thread: 6/o; yellow (Herb Howard Flymaster is perfect for all dry flies)

Feathers: Yellow/brown barred wood duck flank fibers or mallard flank dyed that shade; listed in most catalogs as mallard dyed wood duck or wood duck substitute

Fur: Cream-colored, preferably fitch, mink, or opossum

Hackle Neck: Dark cream

The pattern description for the Light Cahill is:

LIGHT CAHILL

    WING: Wood duck flank

    TAIL: Dark cream hackle fibers

    BODY: Cream

    HACKLE: Dark cream

In addition to the primary tools, you will also need a jar of head cement (clear lacquer) and a cake of wax. Now we're ready to begin.

Clamp a size 12 hook in your vise so that the point and barb are completely covered. Incidentally, we are using this size here and through most of this book for the simple reason that it is a substantial-sized hook to work with. Once you become adept, you can move down to the smaller sizes.

Some tiers prefer to leave the point and barb of the hook exposed, but if you cover them with the vise, you will remove the possibility of cutting your thread on the point. The weakest part of the hook is the barb, which has been formed by a machine cutting into the metal. If you were to clamp a smaller hook, say a size 18 or 20, entirely into the vise, you might break it at this section of the barb. Hooks size 14 and larger are not affected.

Once the hook has been fixed, it is time to lay a foundation of thread with the bobbin. Some of you may wonder why I use a bobbin instead of wrapping and tying the thread with my fingers, as some well-known tiers do. Any time your fingers touch thread or floss, they will to some degree fray these materials. With a bobbin you not only avoid undue friction but also have better control of your thread. The fine barrel of the bobbin will act as a slim finger and allow you into very tight corners.

The bobbin itself is held in the palm of the right hand with the thumb and fingers enclosing the thread spool and the outer portion of this tool.* To feed more thread through the bobbin tubing, the spool of thread is rotated with the thumb and forefinger of the hand that is holding it. You can set the bobbin tension so precisely that you can actually unravel more thread just by pulling on it while the thread is taut against the hook shank; I don't recommend this procedure, however, when a very fine thread is being used. You are just as likely to pop the thread—and you'll have to start over. Always feed the thread through the tubing by rotating the thread spool with the thumb and forefinger.

We lay a foundation of thread on the shank of the hook so that the materials tied to it will not slip off easily. The foundation is laid by winding six or seven turns of thread over itself onto the hook shank, beginning about one-sixteenth of an inch from the hook eye and winding to the rear. Upon completion of the foundation, spiral the thread forward again so that it rests in the center of the foundation you have just laid. Check Figure 2 for detail.

THE WINGS

As with most dry flies you tie in the wings of the Light Cahill first. That's to your advantage, since the wings are the most difficult to master. If you don't tie them correctly, you can start over again at this point instead of having to take down the entire pattern.

While there are other methods of tying in the wings from such feathers

*All tying procedures are reversed if you are left-handed.

A.

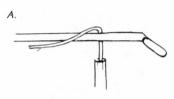

B.

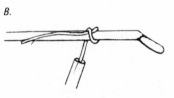

C.

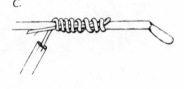

D.

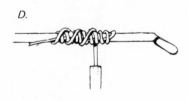

Fig. 2. Laying of Thread Foundation

Fig. 3. Flaring Wood Duck Feather

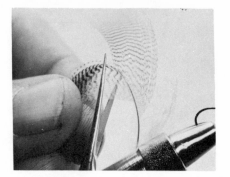

Fig. 4. Cutting Flank Feather

as wood duck or mallard flank, we will start with the simplest method. If you are a beginner, I strongly urge you to use mallard flank dyed to imitate wood duck, at least until your fingers have become trained. Natural wood duck is too expensive to experiment with. Once you have mastered the tying of wings, do, of course, use the real thing if it is available. Natural wood duck is preferred to mallard not only because of its truer color but also because of its stiffer fibers, which make for a more pronounced division in the wings.

Take the dyed mallard flank feather between your right thumb and forefinger. With your left thumb and forefinger flare the curved feather so that the tips are on an even plane (Figure 3). Grasp the feather by the aligned tips with your left hand, and with your right hand cut a section of fiber approximately one-half inch wide from the whole flank feather. Make sure that while you are cutting out this section with your scissors, you keep a firm grip on the feather so you don't lose the alignment of the tip ends (Figure 4).

Manipulate the section of fibers which you have just cut from your left to your right thumb and forefinger and then back again. What you want is one solid clump of fibers, held between the left thumb and forefinger, whose tips are aligned. The rest of the flank feather can be put aside for use on another fly (check Figure 5 for cut section and clump of fibers). Take the clump of fibers and hold them in position along the top of the hook shank so that the tips extend beyond the eye of the hook and the butts are toward the bend (Figure 7).

Now comes a part that may be a bit difficult at first, but I'm sure the ensuing illustration will help you. While holding the clump of fibers on top of the hook shank, take the bobbin in your right hand and pass the thread up along the inside of your thumb, over the shank of the hook, down the far side and against your forefinger, and under the hook shank, and *pull straight up*. Do not pull down. I cannot emphasize strongly enough the little trick of *pulling up*. It will keep the wing section, just tied in, from being pulled down the far side of the hook. This technique of *pulling up* should be used whenever it is applicable (Figure 8).

While the thread is passing between your fingers and around the hook shank, remember to keep a constant, firm, yet flexible pressure on the clump of fibers being held in place on top of the shank. The lower part of both your thumb and forefinger should just pinch, or rest, on the hook shank. Without losing control, you must loosen this pressure just enough

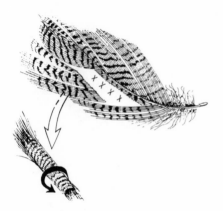

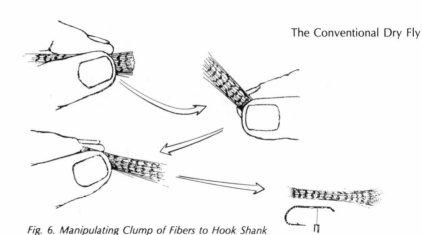

Fig. 5. Cut Section and Clump of Fibers   Fig. 6. Manipulating Clump of Fibers to Hook Shank

to allow the thread to pass through. It sounds difficult, but with a little practice you'll be able to do it without giving it any thought at all.

Once you have secured the clump by *pulling up,* you should take two or three more turns around the area for added security. From that point on the weight of the bobbin will keep the thread taut enough to hold the clump in place.

The clump of flank fibers has been tied down. Now we want to prop it up so that it stands erect. Grasp the clump of fibers with your left thumb and forefinger and bend them backward, leaning toward the bend of the hook. With your right hand take the bobbin and wind enough turns of thread immediately in front of the clumped fibers so that when you let go of them, they stand up by themselves. Figure 9 shows what I mean.

Fig. 7. Tying Position

Fig. 8. Passing Thread Between Fingers and Tying Down Wing

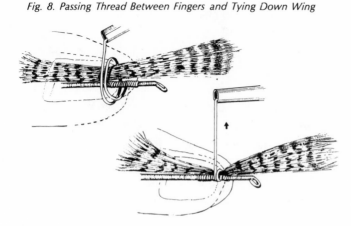

Fig. 9. Propped-up Clump of Fibers

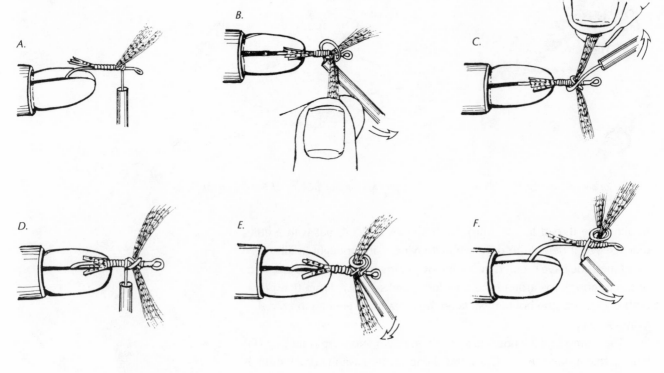

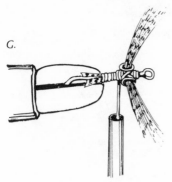

Fig. 10. Steps in Figure 8 and Reverse Figure 8

Take a break. Relax. Have a cup of coffee if you want, or just take a walk around the room. I'm going to ask you to give me all the concentration you can for the next procedure because it is one of the most important in fly tying. Once you've mastered it, you'll never have any trouble with upright divided wings, whatever they are made of.

We are going to divide that solid clump of fibers into two equal parts so that it looks like a set of wings. This means making a figure 8 and a reverse figure 8 with your tying thread. We'll take the figures one at a time. Follow the steps in Figure 10.

With your left thumb and forefinger, take half of the fibers in the clumped section (those nearest you) and separate them from the others by pulling them toward you. Take your bobbin and slant your thread through the division you have just made, going diagonally from front to rear over the top of the hook shank and down the far side.

Now grasp the remaining fibers (those on the far side of the hook). Hold them slightly away from you, bring the bobbin with the thread under the hook shank toward you, up, and then through the division, this time coming diagonally across the hook shank from the rear to the front.

Turn the thread once around the shank of the hook, and complete the figure. The thread should be dangling from *behind* the wings. You have just executed a regular figure 8.

At this point the wings are divided but a bit sloppy. This will be rectified by the reverse figure 8.

The important thing to remember about the reverse 8 is that the thread *never* passes under the hook shank. Though we dip and wiggle in and out, the entire procedure takes place on a horizontal plane above the hook shank.

Take your bobbin and bring your thread, which has been hanging behind the wings, in a circular movement around the outside of the far section of fibers, through the division, again around the outside of the far section, and again through the division of fibers. What you've actually done is encircle the far section of fibers with a full turn of thread.

When the thread is coming through the division toward you for the second time, encircle the fibers nearest you in a counterclockwise motion. When the nearest section has been encircled, continue threading through the division and down the far side of the hook shank. Take one more complete turn around the hook shank *in back* of the wings. The reverse figure 8 has been completed. Check all the illustrations carefully.

Using the reverse figure 8 method will also allow you to place your wings at almost any angle—in the spent position, at 45 degrees, or completely upright. It is especially useful for hair-winged flies, which have a tendency to misbehave.

Now you're really entitled to a breather. You've just completed the most difficult tying operation a beginner—and for that matter some advanced tiers—encounters. So take another break.

At this point we have a little trimming to do on the butt section of the wing fibers we've just tied in. Turn your thread around the butt section, just behind the wings, three or four more times. Do not cut the butts off near the thread—at least, not until you have determined the length of your tail. We want to allow the butts of the tail, which is the next component to be tied in, to connect with the butts of the wing in one smooth taper. We'll then be fashioning a natural taper on which to build the body.

Now then, if your tailing is on the short side, you want to leave a longer wing butt section, and vice versa. This way you'll keep the fly in

Fig. 11. Staggering Wing Butts

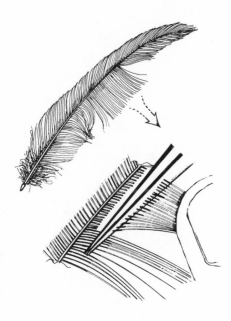

Fig. 12. Tail Preparation

proper proportion. It's little tricks like these that make fly tying much more enjoyable and, of course, simpler.

I also use the stagger method in clipping wing butts. I cut the butts a section at a time, each cut a little closer to the bend. This is another way to create the taper. Check Figure 11 for clarification.

THE TAIL

The tail on a dry fly keeps the hook resting on the water, just barely touching it. Tying in the tail is not difficult. A little practice and it can be mastered in a day.

For the Light Cahill you need hackle fibers from a dark cream rooster neck. Always try to use as tailing material the hackle feathers that suit the size of the pattern. It would be a shame to waste the longer fibers on a size 18 or 20 fly when some of the feathers with shorter fibers will do perfectly well. The longer-fibered hackles are not as plentiful and should therefore be saved for size 10, 12, and 14 flies. Remember that the tail should be approximately as long as the wing is high.

Check hackle size and stiffness before plucking the feather from the cape. The stiffer and longer fibers are generally on the feathers from the side of the neck.

Having selected the proper hackle feather, you're finally ready to start tying in the tail. Hold the feather at the tip, and stroke the hackle fibers downward so that the fibers extend out from the stem at an almost 90 degree angle.

Make sure that the tip ends of the hackle fibers are on an even plane for the section you intend to strip or cut off. Cutting the section instead of stripping it off will give you better alignment because you can hold the tips even while the section is being cut. Check Figure 12 for the preparation of your tail.

The number of fibers in the tail section depends on the size of the fly and the thickness of the individual fibers. The tail should be strong enough to support the hook—no more, no less. *For a size 12 hook a half-inch section of hackle feather is usually sufficient.*

Having cut or stripped the tail fibers from the stem, manipulate them so that they become one unit held between your left thumb and forefinger. At first, the tips may slip a bit and become uneven, but that problem will disappear after a little practice.

Hold the section along the top of the hook shank, butt ends connecting with the wing butts and tips extending over the bend approximately one-half inch.

As you did with the wings, bring your thread over, down the far side, under, and *straight up.* Make another turn. Your tail should be secure.

THE BODY

Bring your thread forward to the center of the hook shank. We are now ready to form the body of the fly.

As noted in the pattern description, the body of the Light Cahill calls for cream-colored fur. Australian opossum or fitch is excellent. For this fly we'll use Australian opossum belly fur. It is a rich cream color and dubs very well.

Give your thread a little extra tackiness by stroking it a few times with your cake of fly-tying wax.

Avoiding the long guard hairs which overlay the softer fur, pluck out some of the soft yellow underfur from your piece of opossum. Do not pick out too much dubbing. It is always easier to add fur than it is to remove excess. Most dry fly bodies do not require much dubbing.

Hold the bobbin tautly with your right hand. Take a small pinch of dubbing and the thread between your left thumb and forefinger (you can reverse hands for this if you feel more comfortable). Start spinning the dubbing on the thread about half an inch from where the thread hangs from the hook shank. Spin the fur onto the thread by sliding your thumb over your forefinger. *Always twist in the same direction, never back and forth.* You will find that the dubbing adheres to the thread readily. Continue spinning and twisting down the shank for about 2 inches. As you move along, add more fur, so that the bottom of the 2-inch section has the heaviest concentration and the top, where you started, has the least. This will give you a rough taper. Check Figure 13 for details.

If you recall, I earlier asked you to leave your thread hanging from the *center* of the hook shank. There was a reason for this. Too many tiers leave their thread hanging near the bend, where they have just finished the tail, and then try to wind their dubbed thread onto the shank at that point. They usually have trouble making an even taper or apply too much pressure to the tail fibers and thus force them down. By starting your dubbed thread from the center of the shank, you can work your way toward the back,

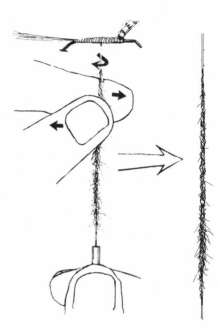

Fig. 13. Spinning Fur onto Thread

45

Figs. 14–15. Winding Dubbed Thread onto Hook Shank

approaching the bend with just the smallest and proper amount of dubbing and quickly back off. This is the easiest way to begin as fine a taper as possible and not overload the tail section.

Therefore, take your bobbin and begin winding toward the bend. Time your turns so that the part of the thread to which the dubbing fur is attached makes its first turn around the hook shank just before the bend.

Now begin working forward along the shank toward the wings. As you move forward, try to add a taper to the body so that the heaviest concentration of dubbing fur is near the wings. If you have to go over certain areas with an extra turn or two in order to fill in spaces, by all means do so. This is called cheating, but neither a trout nor a fisherman will know the difference if you use a thread which closely matches the body color. Terminate the body just behind the wings (see Figures 14–15), and leave the thread there, hanging by the bobbin.

THE HACKLE

The final step in completing the Light Cahill will be to hackle the fly. The hackle collar works with the tail to keep the fly afloat. This is one of the reasons a rooster neck with stiff hackle is desirable.

In addition to supporting the fly on the water's surface, the hackle also gives an impression of legs, just as the tail fibers simulate tails.

From your dark cream rooster neck, select two hackle feathers from the upper third or quarter of the cape. The position of size 12 hackles varies from neck to neck. The diameter of the hackle collar should be approximately three-quarters the size of the wing tied in earlier. Before plucking the feathers from the neck, you can take one, still attached, and by stroking or flaring the hackles downward, hold the stem of the feather against the hook shank and measure the length of the fibers. If it is the proper size, pluck it and its neighbor from the cape.

Ascertain approximately where the webbing on the hackle fibers ends, and with your scissors trim off the fibers from that point down to the base of the feather. Figure 16 should make this very clear.

You trim the unnecessary fibers instead of stripping them off to prevent slippage once they are tied onto the hook shank. The trimming itself should be as close to the feather stem as possible.

Place one feather on top of the other, shiny sides facing you, as they appeared on the neck of the rooster before you plucked them out, and hold them diagonally against the shank of the hook before the wing (see Figure 17). The butt ends should protrude past the eye of the hook.

Turn the thread twice around the cut stems, *but leave a small space between the point where the tying thread has secured the stem and where the actual fibers begin.* This free space, about one-sixteenth of an inch at most, will allow the hackle, when it is ready to be wound around the shank for a collar, to stand erect. The space must be there to ensure proper winding of the hackle. Take two more turns around the hackle butts in front of the wings and cut away the excess butt (see Figure 18).

The hackles are now secure and ready for winding. With your hackle pliers grasp the tip of the outer hackle feather facing you. Turn the hackle

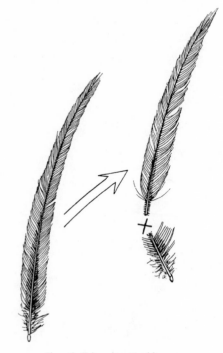

Fig. 16. Trimming Hackle

Fig. 17. Hackle Held in Position
for Tying to Shank

Fig. 18. Hackle Tied in and Excess
Butts Trimmed

A. Winding First Hackle Around Hook Shank

B. Winding Second Hackle Through First

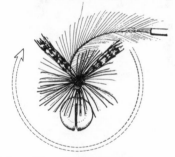

C. Front View: Hackle Wound Around Hook Shank

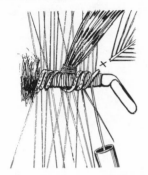

D. Close-up Side View: Hackle Fibers Tied to Shank

Fig. 19

around the shank of the hook; the motion should be away from you. You should make about five turns of hackle for each feather. The first three turns should go behind the wing and the last two in front of it.

You will have to manipulate and sometimes twist the hackle feather in varying ways to get the fibers to stand straight out from the hook shank. Don't be afraid to experiment. Most hackle feathers are tougher than you think. Remember, do whatever you have to do to make the feather behave for you.

Once you have wound the first hackle, it should be tied down with the thread, and the excess tip should be snipped off. The second hackle fiber is then wound through the first. This is accomplished by giving the hackle a wiggling motion as it snakes its way through the fibers of the first hackle. When you finish making the turns, the second hackle is also tied down, and the excess tip snipped off.

Winding the hackle for a collar is actually much easier than it appears to be. It is also fun. Many tiers enjoy winding hackle so much that they never bother with wings. All their flies are just tail, body, and hackle. In any event, the following set of illustrations should clear up any problems or difficulties (Figure 19).

THE HALF-HITCH KNOT

To actually complete the fly, you must learn the whip finish knot, or at least the half-hitch knot. For our purposes and this time only, complete the head of the fly using the simple half-hitch knot.

The principles of the half-hitch knot are demonstrated in Figure 20, which shows the sequence using only the thread and a bare hook.

The thread coming off the shank of the hook is folded over and a loop is formed (Figure 20B).

The loop is slipped over the eye of the hook and onto the shank (Figure 20C).

The thread is then pulled taut and the half-hitch knot completed (Figure 20D).

At least three half-hitch knots should be tied to secure the head of the fly. At this point the thread is clipped and a touch of head lacquer is appled to the windings. Incidentally, the head of the fly can be secured with any number of cements or lacquers. Those most commonly sold are simply called Head Cement. Whether it is head cement, vinyl cement, plio bond cement, varnish, or nail polish (every tier has his preference), the idea is to glue the head of the fly so that is will not come apart.

You will note that we have tied the entire Light Cahill pattern without using a half-hitch knot, except in completing the fly. Many established tiers prefer to conclude the tying in of each material with a half hitch, but it is not at all necessary. In fact, it only increases the bulk of the fly and the weight of the pattern, which is the one thing you don't want, especially in a dry fly.

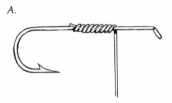

A.

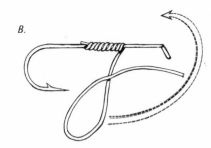

B.

THE WHIP FINISH KNOT

One of the most difficult techniques for the novice to master is the tying of the whip finish knot.* Even if it is described, photographed, illustrated, or actually demonstrated, there are certain motions requiring coordination between mind and fingers which seem to perplex and frustrate the beginner. I have given this problem more thought than any other and, I hope, have finally found a way to illustrate the basic principle of the whip finish knot, which is actually tying the thread over itself.

To learn the knot on an actual fly, such as the one we have just tied, is difficult because we are working with a fine thread and a small hook. This is the reason we completed the fly using the simple half hitch. For our demonstration we will use a much heavier thread or, better still, a line the size of cord or twine. A fly line is perfect, and I have used that for the photographs. In addition to the fly line, I have used a 5/o saltwater hook, again to magnify the process. Why go to all this trouble? Because this is the one knot you must learn and use on every fly and pattern you are ever going to tie.

The fly line used here has been attached to the center of the hook shank with a simple slipknot. You can use any knot you wish as long as it is fastened securely to the shank.

The lower portion of the fly line has been painted black (it is out of view in the first two photographs). Throughout the photo sequence you

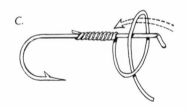

C.

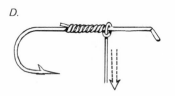

D.

Fig. 20

*The photographs on pages 51–52 showing the technique of tying the whip finish knot were taken by Matthew M. Vinciguerra.

will be looking at one continuous solid line, half of which is white, half black. This will enable you to see very clearly what is taking place.

Incidentally, for our photographs I have used a Veniard Salmo vise, which is capable of holding a 5/o hook. However, if your vise will not hold a large hook, a common bench vise, the kind used in workshops, will serve the purpose. And if you do not have a large hook, a common tenpenny nail will do just fine. The photographs show a right-handed tier. All procedures are reversed if you are left-handed.

A. Place the back of your hand against the white portion of the fly line so that you see the back of your hand with the fly line in front of it. Your fingers should be pointing past the bend of the hook (Figure 21).

B. Rotate the fingers of your right hand and take the white portion of the fly line with your right thumb and forefinger (Figure 22).

C. With your left thumb and forefinger grasp the lower portion (the black part) of the fly line and line it up parallel with and below the hook shank (Figure 23).

D. With your right thumb and forefinger and with the white portion of line, pin the black portion against the shank of the hook (Figure 24).

E. Bring white portion of line over, around and almost under the hook shank (binding black portion to side of hook shank) with your right thumb and forefinger (Figure 25).

F. Let go of black portion of line, and use the thumb and forefinger of your left hand to take the white portion of line from your right thumb and forefinger (Figure 26). (You are transferring the white portion of line from right thumb and forefinger to left thumb and forefinger.)

G. Now transfer the white portion of line back to your right thumb and forefinger; you are simply switching hands to avoid the loop which has now formed (Figure 27).

H. With your right thumb and forefinger, bring the white portion of line a-round the hook shank once more, again pressing it against the black portion on the side of the shank, to a position below the shank (Figure 28).

If you've come this far, you've all but got the whip finish knot licked. You still have to go around the shank of the hook three more times. A whip finish is usually four or five turns of thread over itself. The last two or three turns are performed in the same manner as the first two.

I. After you have made the required four or five turns of white line around

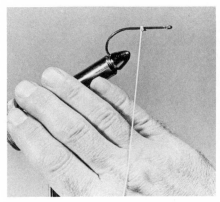

Fig. 21

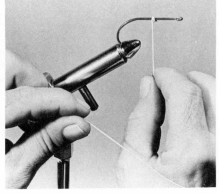

Fig. 22

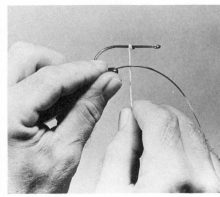

Fig. 23

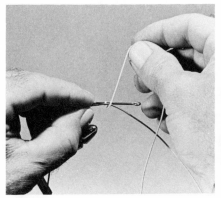

Fig. 24

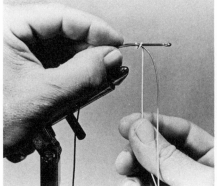

Fig. 25

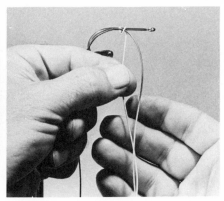

Fig. 26

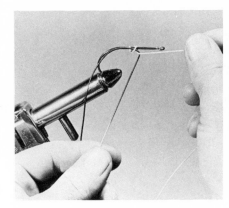

Fig. 27

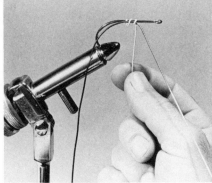

Fig. 28

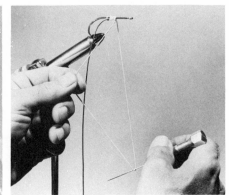

Fig. 29

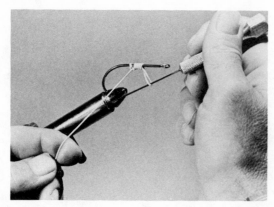

Fig. 30

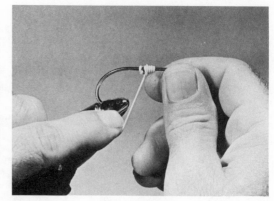

Fig. 31

the shank of the hook and the black line, hold the white line tautly with your left thumb and forefinger and insert a dubbing needle into the loop with your right hand (Figure 29).

J. Once the dubbing needle is in place, pull on the fly line to close the loop. Just before you close the loop, remove the dubbing needle (Figure 30).

K. The completed whip finish knot is shown in Figure 31. On an actual fly the excess line or thread would be snipped off and the windings given a touch of head cement for security—just a dab from the point of your dubbing needle.

That, in essence, is the whip finish knot. It should be practiced until it is mastered.

You have just completed tying your first dry fly. If it does not measure up to some of the Light Cahills you have purchased or been given in the past, don't be concerned. This happens in the beginning. Just keep tying them. Observe what you may have done wrong by comparing your fly with a well-tied Light Cahill. I would strongly urge you to purchase from a reputable firm at least one pattern of each fly you intend to tie. Then you will have an example of the proportions, color, and balance of a professionally tied fly. An actual model is far superior to a photograph or illustration while you are learning.

At this point you deserve more than a pause or coffee break. You've earned yourself a small vacation. After all, you've tied your first fly. You should really take a day off and go fishing with it, season permitting, or show the fly off to your friends. You may not be aware of it, but having tied this one fly has put you more than halfway on the road to becoming a practitioner in the art of tying flies.

Having tied the Light Cahill, you will now be able, without any further instructions, to tie such well-known patterns as the Dark Hendrickson, Dark Cahill, March Brown, and Gray Fox. They all use the same type of materials in the same places. Only the color of the body hackle or wing varies. For example, in the Light Cahill we used a cream dubbing fur for the body and a cream hackle, whereas in the Dark Cahill the dubbing is dark gray, such as is found in muskrat fur, and the hackle is dark ginger (red game). In the March Brown and Gray Fox patterns, instead of using two hackles from the same rooster neck, we use one from a brown cape and one from a barred Plymouth Rock (grizzly), thus giving us a two-toned or mixed effect. Though from different necks, the hackles are still tied and wound in the same manner.

The pattern descriptions for these flies follow; they are among the dozen most popular flies fished on the surface. If you can tie the Light Cahill, you have without knowing it expanded your mastery of dry flies to six.

DARK CAHILL
WINGS: Wood duck flank divided
TAIL: Dark ginger hackle fibers
BODY: Muskrat dubbing
HACKLE: Dark ginger

DARK HENDRICKSON
WING: Wood duck flank
TAIL: Medium dark dun hackle fibers
BODY: Muskrat dubbing
HACKLE: Medium dark dun hackle fibers

LIGHT HENDRICKSON
WING: Wood duck flank
TAIL: Medium bronze dun hackle fibers
BODY: Fox belly fur (urine-stained if possible)
HACKLE: Medium bronze dun hackle fibers

GRAY FOX

    WING: Mallard flank

    TAIL: Golden ginger hackle fibers

    BODY: Fawn fox fur

    HACKLE: One golden ginger and one light grizzly hackle mixed

MARCH BROWN

    WING: Mallard flank (dark cast) or light bronze mallard

    TAIL: Dark ginger hackle fibers

    BODY: Beige fox fur

    HACKLE: One dark ginger and one grizzly hackle mixed

ALTERNATE METHOD OF TYING A DRY FLY (FULL-BODIED)

The method shown in the preceding pages is the simplest way to tie a standard dry fly. That there are variations from tier to tier goes without saying. For your benefit I will briefly outline and illustrate one other popular method used by some expert tiers. It differs from our procedure in this way: After the wings have been tied in, the hackles for the collar are prepared and tied in, as opposed to the sequence wings, tail, body, and hackle.

To illustrate. . . . Tie in your wings. Prepare two hackles, and this time lay them back to back (shiny side to shiny side) so that they flare away from one another. Tie the hackles onto the hook shank so that the tips extend over the eye of the hook and the butts lie to the rear under the shank.

Having secured the butts, bring the thread back to the original tie-down point and lift the hackle feathers straight up so that they stand erect. In this position lock them in with your thread. Be sure to leave a bit of free space between the trimmed fibers and the point on the hackle where the barbules actually begin. Forget the hackle feathers for now.

Wind your thread to the rear, and tie in your tail in the conventional manner.

Dub your thread with fur and dub your body. *However, this time do not terminate the body just behind the wings; instead, bring it past them and in front of them toward the eye of the hook.*

If you think about it, you will realize that the body of a natural insect does not terminate at the point where its wings emerge It actually reaches its widest diameter just under the wings and then tapers off near the head. The intent here is to simulate this.

When you have formed your body, bring your thread back to a point just in front of the wings. Now you can take your pliers and wind your hackle collar. You will find that they sink into the soft fur very readily.

When you tie in the hackles shiny side to shiny side so that they flare away from each other, you will find that in winding the collar you have created a crisscross effect that may give better support.

The butt stems, which in this method have been tied under the hook shank, will also help build your thorax area. Since they are of a light pithy quality, they will also assist in a minor way in the fly's flotation.

Figure 32 lays out the procedures for the method.

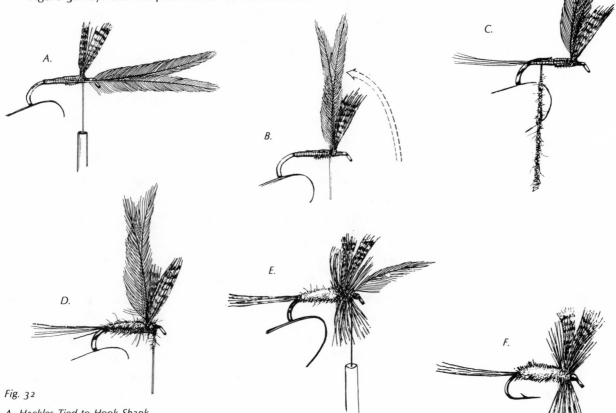

Fig. 32

A. Hackles Tied to Hook Shank

B. Hackles Propped Straight Up

C. Tail Tied In

D. Body Formed Past Wings to Eye

E. Hackle Collar Wound

F. Completed Full-bodied Light Cahill

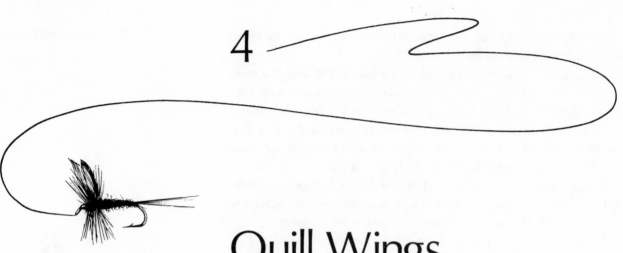

Quill Wings and Bodies

Having learned to tie the most basic form of conventional dry fly in the previous chapter, we can now turn to variations.

Quill Gordon, Red Quill, Ginger Quill, Olive Quill—these are a few flies which actually have the word "quill" in the pattern name. Other flies, such as the Blue Dun, Black Gnat, and Royal Coachman, also have a section of quill fibers for their wings. In the first group of patterns the body is made of quill; the Ginger Quill, for example, has both a quill body and a quill wing section.

You will hear the word "quill" used frequently in the course of your fly-tying education. If it seems confusing at first, join the crowd. I still recall my own problems in trying to decipher its meaning whenever it was used without explanation. Let me explain some of this word's meanings before we begin. That way you'll at least have some guide whenever you come across a new pattern description. A quill can be any of the following:

1. A complete feather, like a duck or goose quill.
2. A section of fibers. A section cut from an entire feather—goose, duck,

starling, what have you—is referred to as a piece of quill. In this instance the quill section is used primarily to make wings.

3. The outer layer of the center stem of such feathers as duck, goose, and turkey. These quills are stripped from the center stems with a knife or razor blade. The primary use here is making bodies.

4. The entire center stem of a rooster or hen hackle feather from which the fibers have been removed. Again, this is primarily body material.

5. The deflued stems of individual feather fibers from a peacock, condor, goose, turkey, or the like. These quills are usually made from the fibers of very large feathers. One of the most common is the peacock quill; here the tiny fuzzy barbules are removed either with a rubber eraser or by hand (the fuzz, or flue, can be thumbed from the quill strip). Some tiers remove this flue by immersing the peacock eye in Clorox or another chlorine bleach, which dissolves the tiny fibers, and then rinsing the stripped eye in a solution of baking soda.

6. The butt sections of such feathers as goose, duck, or turkey which have been removed whole from the main stem. These quills are used mostly for making the bodies and legs of imitation grasshoppers.

So you see the word "quill" does have its variations.

Our only use for a quill in this chapter will be in making bodies and wings for dry flies.

QUILL-BODIED FLIES

Of all of the flies with a quill body, the most popular is the Quill Gordon, named in honor of the legendary Theodore Gordon, who is recognized in the United States as the father of the dry fly. The pattern is as follows:

QUILL GORDON
  WINGS: Wood duck flank
  TAIL: Medium blue dun hackle fibers
  BODY: Stripped peacock quill (over yellow polypropylene)
  HACKLE: Medium blue dun

We'll be using a Mustad 94840 size 12 hook and a fine gray thread. Secure the hook in your vise, and spiral on your thread. Tie in the wings and tail exactly as you did in the Light Cahill.

57

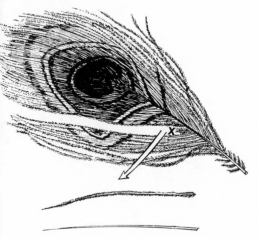

Fig. 1. Selected and Stripped Quill

Before we tie in the body and underbody, a brief discourse is in order. First, there are a few things you should know about the quill you are tying with. It comes from the eyed portion of a peacock tail. It is very fragile compared with other quills. In addition, it is also very brittle unless it is first softened. So there is a little preparation to do before we can use this material.

Instead of the conventional methods—Cloroxing or erasing the flues—I'm going to recommend a method a good friend of mine uses. His name is Ralph Graves, and he's one of the finest tiers I know—when he isn't fishing. Ralph takes a few cakes of household paraffin and melts them down. Then he immerses a bunch of selected peacock eyes, one at a time, into the paraffin, coating them with the substance. They are then dried and put away. Whenever Ralph needs a stripped quill, he simply plucks one from the waxed and solid unit and peels the wax from the quill with his thumb and fingernails. That's all there is to it. The quill comes out clean, soft, and pliable, ready for use.

If you use any other type of prepared peacock quill, you will have to soak it in water before using it. Otherwise, it may splinter.

In selecting eyes for quill bodies, choose those that are light in color but have dark segmentation. This can be done by bending and flaring the peacock eye and observing the coloration and marking on the *back* of the eye. You may have to purchase a number of peacock tails to find a few that have a distinct marking. Unfortunately, supply houses just do not have the time to go through all their tails and separate those that are suitable for stripped quills.

You may have noticed that we mentioned the use of polypropylene in the pattern description for this fly. It is intended for forming an underbody. The Quill Gordon does not normally have an underbody. It is usually tied very thinly and skimpily. And yet, the insect it imitates, the iron fraudator, has a very substantial body, as do most mayflies. We form a substantial body on most of the other imitations but neglect the Quill Gordon. Why this has been so I don't know, but we are going to remedy it here. There are, of course, many knowledgeable tiers who take this fact into account, but as far as I know, there is no literature on it.

For a dry fly, I don't usually recommend using polypropylene or any other synthetic, but in this instance it will be completely covered by quill material. Poly yarn wraps finely, tapers well, and is easy to work with. I use yellow so that when the quill is wound over it, some of the color will bleed through, giving the body a more natural appearance. Incidentally, polypropylene yarn is just barely lighter than water. It will help, not hinder, the fly's buoyancy.

After the tail is tied in, the thread should be hanging from the center of the hook shank.

Take a piece of stripped peacock quill, and with the dark edge of the quill facing left, tie it in under the shank of the hook (see Figure 2A). Spiral the peacock quill to the bend of the hook, and cover the spiral with turns of thread that also terminate at the bend. This will get your quill started in the correct direction around the hook shank and also secure it (see Figure 2B).

Take a piece of polypropylene yarn about 5 inches long, and separate a few of the fiber strands. You don't want to tie with too thick a yarn. The finer it is, the easier it is to work with and to form a taper. Tie in the poly yarn just ahead of the bend of the hook, in front of the last turns of peacock quill (see Figure 3A). The yarn is also tied in under the hook shank.

Bring your thread forward to a point just behind the wings. Now wind the poly yarn to the thread, building a gradual taper as you do so. A proper underbody is illustrated in Figure 3B. Give your poly yarn underbody a light coating of head lacquer.

Your next step is to wind the peacock quill to the thread. For this you may have to use a pair of hackle pliers, depending on the length of the peacock quill. Grasp the quill, and in an overlapping spiral wind the quill around the body of the fly to the thread. If you have tied the quill in properly, you will begin to see the body segmentation as the darker edge of the quill overlaps each of the preceding turns (see Figure 4). When you have reached the thread with the peacock quill, tie it down and secure it.

Usually all you would have to do now to complete the fly is wind on the hackle collar and whip finish the head. However, you may recall that I said peacock quill is very fragile. The very first trout to hit this fly will undoubtedly cut the quill with its teeth, and the body will unwind like a corkscrew. Not too long ago I mentioned this to Walt Dette of Roscoe, New York. Walt and his wife, Winnie, are among a select group of world-renowned Catskill fly tiers. "That's no problem," Walt said. "What you want to do is crisscross your body with some white silk thread and varnish over it."

"Won't the thread show up and distort the segmentation?" I asked.

"Not if you use *silk* thread. For some reason it seems to disappear after the varnish has dried. And it'll take a lot of trout before that body comes apart at all."

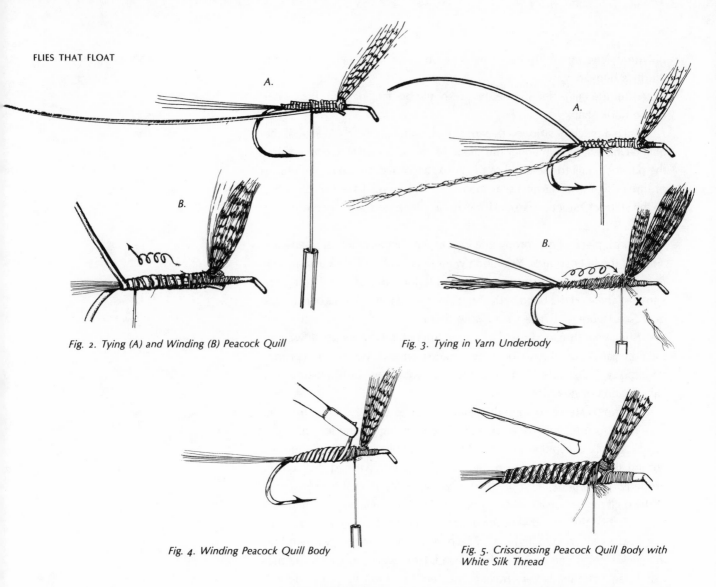

Fig. 2. Tying (A) and Winding (B) Peacock Quill

Fig. 3. Tying in Yarn Underbody

Fig. 4. Winding Peacock Quill Body

Fig. 5. Crisscrossing Peacock Quill Body with White Silk Thread

The white silk thread is tied in just behind the wings. It is then wound in an open spiral to the bend and back to the wings again. As it is being wound back to the wings, the thread will cross over itself in a series of X's. It is then tied down by the thread from the bobbin and secured. Spar varnish is applied to the entire body.

I had been tying for a number of years before I learned this little trick. And it does work. Walt Dette, incidentally, is one of those rare people who are willing to share any of their so-called secrets with you.

To *make* the body of this fly, take a 5-inch piece of very fine *silk* thread. Use size 8/0 if you have it; if not, 6/0 will do. Tie it in just behind the wings. Spiral it to the rear and then back to your tying thread, in a crisscross pattern (see Figure 5).

Once the white silk has been wound over the quill body, take your dubbing needle and apply a coat of clear spar varnish to the entire body. Using a pair of medium to dark blue dun hackle feathers, wind your collar and whip finish the head to complete the fly.

OTHER QUILL BODY MATERIALS

There are other quill materials which can be used to tie the body of the Quill Gordon. Condor quill is excellent and stronger than peacock, if you can find a supply. In addition, you may be able to use the quill strips from starling, quail, or duck, if you can find some that are the proper shade and have a segmentation effect. Quill strips from these birds are the most durable.

One other very popular quill body for dry flies is made from the center stem of a rooster feather from the neck or saddle cape. In addition to its use in many variant patterns, it is well-known for its use on Art Flick's Red Quill. Let's tie the body of this pattern:

RED QUILL
    WING: Wood duck flank
    TAIL: Medium bronze dun
    BODY: Center quill from brown neck
    HACKLE: Medium bronze dun

All the tying procedures are the same as the Quill Gordon with the exception of the body. The quill used for the body of this pattern differs from that used for the Quill Gordon in that it is larger in diameter, longer, and rounder. It used to be available in quantity when the Rhode Island Red rooster was common; today, these birds are raised primarily for breeding purposes. The Rhode Island Red is a dark brown rooster with just the right shade of reddish brown pigment in the center stem. Other breeds of roosters have this coloration, but you may have to pick and choose from a number of them to find it.

The quill we need for the body is usually found in the larger feathers near the base of the neck. Pluck one of these from the cape.

Here again, the quill will have to be prepared before it can be used as body material. The fibers must be removed from the hackle feather so all that remains is the center stem, with all of its color intact. *Do not strip the fibers from the stem by pulling them off.* This will remove the pigmentation.

The best method I have found for removing the fibers from the stem is the trimming, Cloroxing, and storing procedure. Let's take the steps one at a time. Incidentally, it takes much too long to prepare just one quill at a time. If you are going to use this procedure, I suggest you pluck a few dozen of these hackle feathers from your rooster cape and prepare them all at once for future use.

1. Trim the hackle fibers, or barbules, from each hackle feather, cutting off the fibers as close as you can to the stem proper.
2. Immerse the trimmed stems in a pure Clorox solution. This will remove the stubby ends of the fibers your scissors cannot trim. Once the stubs of the fibers have dissolved, remove the quills from the Clorox, and drop them into a solution of baking soda and water. This will neutralize the chemical action. The stems should then be given a final rinse in clear water.
3. Once the stems have been deflued and cleaned, they should be stored in a jar which contains a solution of equal parts of water and glycerin. They will keep indefinitely in this solution and are immediately usable whenever they are needed. You'll never find them brittle or hard to work with.

We will assume you have prepared a number of these quills and are ready to tie with them.

Fine gray thread and a size 12 hook are again in order.

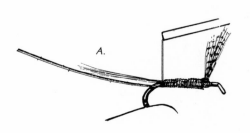
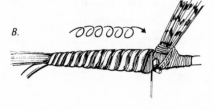
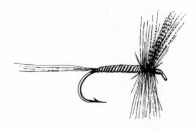

Fig. 6. Tying (A) and Winding (B) Stem Quill to Form Body   *Fig. 7. Completed Red Quill*

The wings and tail of your pattern have already been tied in. Your thread is at the midposition ready for the body material to be tied in.

Unlike the Quill Gordon, the Red Quill does not require an underbody. The quill stem for this pattern has an inherent natural taper—that is, if you use it from the correct point forward. Look at your Red Quill stem. Notice that it grows thicker as it nears the base. This gradual growth will provide the taper.

Before tying in the quill for this pattern it will be worth your while to flatten it with the soft, or rounded, edge of a pair of scissors or hackle pliers. Lay the quill on your tying table, and give it a few strokes. This will prevent any twisting or misbehaving when the quill is being wound on the shank of the hook.

Decide where on the quill the taper for the body is to begin, and clip away any excess quill stem. Place the quill under the shank of the hook with the narrow tip extending almost to the wing area. Tie it in with your thread.

Wind your thread over the shank of the hook and toward the wing, securing the tip of the quill to the shank as you do so. Wind your thread to the bend (see Figure 6A).

Bring your thread forward once more to a point just behind the wings. Grasp the butt of the quill, and wind it in adjacent spirals to the thread (see Figure 6B).

When you reach the wing area with the quill, bind it down with your thread, and snip off the excess butt. Form your medium bronze dun hackle collar, and whip finish the head to complete the fly. With your dubbing needle apply a coat of clear head lacquer to the body of the fly. Your Red Quill should look like the one in Figure 7.

QUILL WINGS

As we explained before, we are now talking about a different type of quill. For our example we will tie a pattern called the Black Gnat:

BLACK GNAT
> WING: Natural gray mallard wing quill
> TAIL: Black hackle fibers
> BODY: Black Mohlon
> HACKLE: Black

63

In this case the wing is not made of a clump of fibers divided by a thread but of two separate sections of a feather clipped as a unit from a matching pair of duck pointer quills. What is meant by a "matching pair"? If you look at a duck, it is obvious that it has two wings. The feathers on the left wing of the duck curve in the opposite direction from those on the right, just as your right hand and left hand are different. Therefore, what we need for a matched pair of quill sections is a matched pair of duck pointer quills, or one quill from a left duck wing and one from a right.

As to the duck quills themselves, the best pairs for wings are the third and fourth feathers in from the outer pointer quill on a pair of mallard wings. All of the pointer quills can be used, but these are the most desirable since they are wider and have more natural flare.

You might also take a look at the underside of a mallard wing feather. Notice that the inner part of the feather has a glossy hardness while the outer half is softer and does not appear as shiny. This difference is important. If you try to make your wings by tying on the glossy, hard part, they are liable to split on you. Always tie with the softer, duller outer edge (see Figure 8).

Now take the matched pair of mallard quills, the right and the left, and hold them in front of you. Do you see the flare or curve on the outside edge of each feather which begins about halfway from the tip? That part of the feather—from the flare almost to the base of the feathered portion—is the most desirable for making wings. The flare makes for a natural-looking wing.

Snip a section about one-sixteenth of an inch wide from each of the

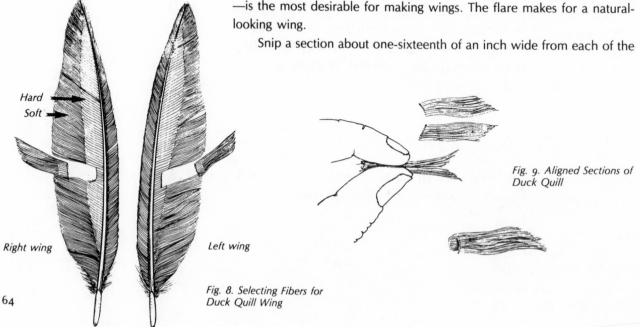

Hard

Soft

Right wing

Left wing

Fig. 8. Selecting Fibers for Duck Quill Wing

Fig. 9. Aligned Sections of Duck Quill

quills, as shown in Figure 8. If one of the sections is larger than the other, take a dubbing needle or the point of your scissors, and remove the excess fibers. The quill sections should be as close to equal in width as possible.

In your vise should be a size 12 hook (Mustad 94840) onto which you've spiraled some fine black thread, the same as you would for any of the dry flies you've previously tied.

Align the two cut sections of duck quill, one next to the other, shiny side against shiny side. Their natural tendency will be to flare outward, as they did on the feather (see Figure 9).

Grasp the duck quill sections between your left thumb and forefinger and hold them over the hook shank, as you would with a mallard flank clump, the tips extending beyond the eye (see Figure 10). As with the mallard clump, pass your thread over, between your thumb and forefinger, down the far side, under, and up. Take a few more turns of thread in the same area. Your tied-down quill section should look like the photo in Figure 11.

Grasp the tips of the quill sections, and hold them erect. Wind the thread in front of them a few more times so that they will maintain their position. Make a figure 8, as illustrated in Chapter 3, and clip the butt ends. That's all there is to it. The completed wing quills are illustrated in Figure 12.

Here's a little trick some tiers use to keep the wings in perfect position —they drop a small bead of head cement into the division of the wings where they form the V coming off the hook shank.

Once you have completed the wing, tie in a tail of black hackle fibers.

Figs. 10–12. Placing and Tying in Duck Quill Wings

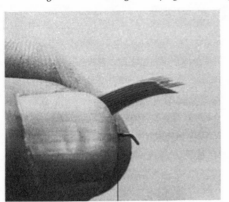

Fig. 13. Tying in Mohlon

We are now ready for the body of the fly. In this case we'll use a synthetic called Mohlon. Though not lighter than water, Mohlon is water-resistant and will float longer than wool, chenille, or peacock. It is also scraggly, thus making a body that traps tiny air bubbles and really resembles a fuzzy black insect.

Cut a single 6-inch strand of Mohlon. Lay one tip on top of the hook shank so that it almost abuts the wing. Wind your thread to the wing, binding the Mohlon to the shank as you do so. Then take the main section of Mohlon, and wind it around the shank, too, forming a gradual taper as you go. Stop just behind the wings, and secure the Mohlon with the thread. Clip off the excess (see Figure 13). The thread is left behind the wings, and the Mohlon is simply wound forward in a taper to the thread, with which it is bound down. The final step in finishing the fly is the winding of the black hackle collar. The completed Black Gnat is illustrated in Figure 14.

Having learned how to tie quill bodies and wings, you have now expanded your knowledge to such a degree that you will be able to tie the following patterns without any further instruction. The procedures on all of them are the same as those you've just mastered. Here are a few of the patterns you can now add to your collection:

BLUE QUILL

WING: Mallard duck quill
TAIL: Blue dun
BODY: Stripped peacock
HACKLE: Blue dun

BLUE DUN

WING: Mallard duck quill
TAIL: Medium blue dun
BODY: Muskrat dubbing
HACKLE: Blue dun

GINGER QUILL

WING: Mallard duck quill (light shade)
TAIL: Ginger hackle
BODY: Stripped peacock
HACKLE: Light ginger

GRAY FOX VARIANT

WINGS: None

TAIL: Light ginger

BODY: Quill from light ginger or cream cock hackle

HACKLE: One light ginger, one dark ginger, and one grizzly mixed

DUN VARIANT

WINGS: None

TAIL: Dark dun

BODY: Quill from Rhode Island Red or similar hackle

HACKLE: Dark dun tied slightly larger than usual

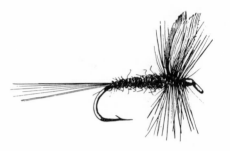

Fig. 14. Completed Black Gnat Dry

CREAM VARIANT

WINGS: None

TAIL: Cream

BODY: Quill from cream rooster neck hackle

HACKLE: Cream tied slightly larger than usual

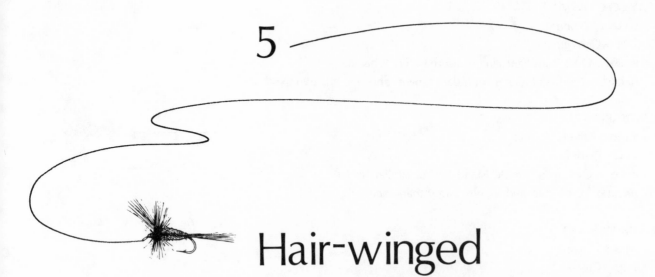

5
Hair-winged
and Deer-bodied Flies

There is a special thrill in casting a bushy White Wulff or Hairwing Royal Coachman into the rough waters spilling over a rapids and watching it bob along. When salmon or trout rise to these patterns, there is no delicate take, no hesitation. As often as not, there will be a vicious strike that will engulf your offering or miss it entirely. In either case you'll know there has been a rise. It will also take an adequate reaction on your part to set the hook.

The delicate flies like the Quill Gordon or Light Cahill will not float long, if at all, in this kind of water. Thus for such fishing we use heavy hackled, bushy winged patterns, though they are not as good copies as those we tend to match the hatch with. Their advantage is that with them we can fish turbulent streams and rough pocket water and still see the strike.

Winging and tailing of these flies is usually done with such materials as calf tail, deer tail, deer body hair, and woodchuck guard hairs, to name just a few. Calf tail is the most commonly used.

One of the more popular hair-winged flies is the White Wulff. Let's tie one:

WHITE WULFF

WING: White calf tail
TAIL: White calf tail
BODY: White wool or Mohlon
HACKLE: Light badger

Calf tail is the basic material in this pattern. Sometimes called kip or impala, it nevertheless comes from a baby cow. The hair itself is on the coarse side and is usually kinky. If you get the opportunity to search through a number of calf tails, try to pick out the ones with the most evenly tapered hairs. For Wulff flies you will not need very long hair; lengths of 1–1 1/4 inches are usually ideal.

Many tiers get a little disgruntled at having to tie hair wings. The problem is that the fibers are not straight or firm, and they don't want to behave. Yet with a little patience and, especially, some preparation, the tying of hair wings can be mastered very rapidly.

If you are fishing for trout, you should use the Mustad 94840 in sizes 8 to 14 for this pattern; size 12 is the most common choice. The White Wulff is also very popular for salmon fishing. Here you would tie this pattern on a light wire salmon hook with a looped-up eye in sizes 4 to 10.

While it would seem easier to tie this pattern on the larger salmon hooks, such as the 6 and 8, it may not be so easy to get the hackle that is used for the collar. Remember, this is a dry fly, so the hackle should be stiff enough to support it. Thus, you will need good-quality hackle with long fibers. Not every rooster neck has this quality; you may have to go to a saddle skin or the loose saddle hackle.

If you are tying for salmon, the hook is also different. Not every supply house carries the light wire salmon hook you'll need. You should look for the Wilson 1503, the Mustad 90240, or the English salmon hooks. The English hooks are not readily available in the United States, at least not from the suppliers whose catalogs I've perused. E. Veniard, Ltd., is one supplier that does carry a full line of salmon hooks (see list of supply houses in Appendix B).

For our example let's tie on a size 10 standard Mustad 94840. This will put us right in the middle of the scale. Fix the hook in your vise, and

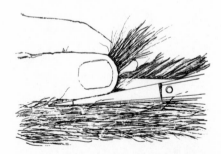

Fig. 1. Cutting Section of Calf Tail Hairs for Wing

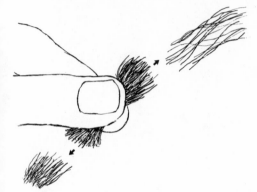

Fig. 2. Aligning Calf Tail Hairs

spiral some fine black thread onto the shank starting just behind the eye and winding away from it for a quarter of an inch. Bring the thread back to the center of the bed of thread you have just formed. Place a drop of head cement on the thread windings. This will be a great help when you're securing the calf tail fibers.

Take the calf tail, and separate a section of fiber about the diameter of a matchstick. Align the tips as evenly as possible. Holding the section firmly between your left thumb and forefinger, cut the section from the base of the tail with a pair of scissors (see Figure 1).

Take a look at the clump of fibers between your fingers. You'll notice that some of the hairs are too long and some are too short, even though you tried to align them. This is usually when you start feeling disgruntled. There was a time when I used to throw the whole clump into the air out of pure frustration after having tried to manipulate the short and long hairs into one evenly aligned tip. If you feel the same way, go ahead and throw the whole business away. When you've got that out of your system, sit back, relax, and think for a minute. What does a calf tail have more of— long or short fibers?

It is made up mostly of short and medium-length fibers. My problem —and that of many other tiers—had been bringing the short ones up to match the long. So try this: *Remove most of the long fibers at the tip end.* This very quickly gives you a fuller and truer tip alignment. Now remove the very few short fibers near the base. You won't have to do any more aligning than those two maneuvers, except for picking out the occasional strays, of course. Take a look at Figure 2. Once you have the calf tail fibers aligned, you're halfway home. The other half of the job is the actual winging.

Place the clump of calf tail fibers on top of the hook shank the same way you would a clump of wood duck flank. The tips point out over the eye of the hook. Tie the clump down onto the thread foundation you just laid, but after pulling up take a few extra turns of thread around the tied-down area. You are dealing with a bulky wing, and you need these turns for security.

Once you securely fasten the fibers to the shank, lift them by the tips to a vertical position, and wrap the thread in front of the clump to hold it upright (see Figure 3). The height of the wings, incidentally, is standard, or just as high as you would make them if you were tying with wood duck.

You must now divide the wings. This is done with a figure 8 and a reverse figure 8, as described in Chapter 3. The reverse figure 8 really pays off on this step. It will keep those scraggly hairs relatively close to their neighbors.

After you finish the 8's, take your dubbing needle, and place a liberal drop of head cement into the wing division. Don't worry—you won't lose that nice flared effect. You just don't want the two sections to start reaching out to each other. At this point your wings should look like the photograph in Figure 4.

Actually, the alignment and proper shaping of the calf tail hairs for both the wing and tail are more important to the critical eye of the fisherman than to the fish. A trout or salmon will not notice if a few hairs have gone astray. For your own satisfaction, however, and in the interest of the art, you should always do your best to make an evenly aligned and properly proportioned wing and tail. As you know, proportion will vary with the size of the hook the pattern is tied on. Thus, if you are tying a salmon White Wulff in size 4, your clumps of calf tail for the wing and tail will be relatively long and more substantial—in other words, you'll need more hair fibers in the wing and tail.

Cut another clump of calf tail fibers for the tail. Before you tie it in, make sure that it has been measured properly so that when the fibers are trimmed at the base, the butts of the tail will connect with the clipped butt ends of the wing, making a smooth taper to build the body up. Tie in your tail (see Figure 5).

The body of the White Wulff calls for a piece of white wool. Cut a single strand about 6 inches long. Lay one end of it on top of the hook shank, almost touching the wing.

Bind the wool down with your thread by winding from the bend to the wing. Let your thread dangle in its bobbin at the point just before the wing.

Grasp the wool, and moving away from you, wind it over the shank of the hook to the thread. Do not allow the wool to twist. It must lie flat. As you make each turn of wool over the hook shank, untwist it one turn. This will prevent it from turning into a rope.

Your wool body should be like any other body—very even and neatly and gradually tapered. When you are just behind the wings, bind and secure the wool with your thread. Trim off the excess wool.

Pluck two hackles from the neck of a badger rooster, the one with the white feathers and black center stripe. You may not be able to find a good-quality all white badger cape, for they are not too common. If this is the case, a light cream badger will do nicely.

Fig. 3. Clump of Fibers Propped Vertically

Fig. 4. Calf Tail Fibers Divided

Fig. 5. Tied-in Tail

71

Fig. 6. Completed White Wulff

Trim your hackle fibers, tie in the hackles, and wind the collar as you have done before. Whip finish and cement the head. Your White Wulff is completed and should look like the one in Figure 6.

Now that you've learned to tie the White Wulff the hard way, I'll give you a few tips that may make life easier if you can find the proper materials. This pattern can be tied with calf body hair as well as calf tail; body hair is finer and aligns better. Taking this one step further, if you can find some Icelandic calf skin, you've really got it made. It is truly one of the finest materials I've ever tied a Wulff pattern with. Another hair which will tie the pattern effectively and easily is mountain goat or sheep. However, you must find a piece of hide on which the ends have not been too badly broken or chafed.

Once you have tied one Wulff pattern, you can tie them all. Here are a few to try:

BLACK WULFF

    WING: Black calf tail

    TAIL: Black calf tail

    BODY: Black wool or Mohlon

    HACKLE: Black

GRAY WULFF

    WING: Brown calf tail (natural, if possible)

    TAIL: Brown calf tail (natural, if possible)

    BODY: Muskrat dubbing

    HACKLE: Medium blue dun

GRIZZLY WULFF

    WING: Dark brown calf tail

    TAIL: Dark brown calf tail

    BODY: Yellow floss or yellow polypropylene

    HACKLE: Mixed brown and grizzly

ROYAL WULFF

    WING: White calf tail

    TAIL: White calf tail

    BODY: Peacock herl divided by band of red floss

    HACKLE: Brown

AU SABLE WULFF

WING: White calf tail
TAIL: Woodchuck tail fibers
BODY: Tan opossum
HACKLE: Mixed brown and grizzly

You may have noticed that one of these patterns, the Au Sable Wulff, did not call for calf tail for the tail. This is one of the most effective patterns I've ever had the pleasure to use. Here the tail was made from woodchuck, or groundhog, tail fibers. This material, which also includes the guard hairs of the woodchuck, is excellent but much overlooked and neglected. The fibers align beautifully, behave properly, and have sex appeal—to trout. I recommend their use wherever possible.

CLIPPED DEER-BODIED FLIES

Many commercial tiers frown upon the task of tying clipped deer-bodied flies because the process is time-consuming, though it surely isn't difficult and the results are really worthwhile. These patterns are probably the highest floating and most water-resistant because deer hair is hollow. It traps air within its fibers. This keeps the deer warm in winter and a dry fly high in fast water. The best fly body hair comes from the back and the center underside of the animal. The tail and leg fibers are finer and not as hollow. They are better for winging and tailing. One of the easiest ways to determine whether a section of deer hair is hollow enough for a clipped body is to snip a small clump from the hide, lay it on top of a hook shank, and take one turn of thread around it. If it flares and bounces up almost vertically, it is the kind you want for your fly.

One of the most popular clipped deer-bodied flies in the country is the Irresistible. If you can tie this pattern properly—that is, with a neatly tapered and well-proportioned body—you can tie any pattern, including bass bugs, where clipped hair is called for.

The pattern for the Irresistible reads as follows:

IRRESISTIBLE

WINGS: Guard hairs of whitetail deer
TAIL: Guard hairs of whitetail deer
BODY: Natural gray/brown deer hair trimmed to shape
HACKLE: Medium blue dun

Now here is one pattern which is not going to be tied in the conventional order, with the wings first. If you have ever tried to do it that way, you'll have learned, as I did, that it is almost impossible to avoid cutting part of the wing while attempting to do a proper pruning on the body. It was Harry Darbee who put me wise to this when he explained the tying of one of his original patterns, the Rat-faced MacDougall, also a clipped hair affair though it is made from caribou fibers.

Our order on the Irresistible will be tail first, then body, wings, and hackle.

Place a size 10 Mustad 94840 hook in your vise. Spiral some fine gray thread onto the shank of the hook near the bend, forming your base almost around it. I like to leave the hook as bare as possible in this pattern simply because deer body hair spins much more easily over a plain shank than over a covered one.

We're going to tie this fly the hard way here—that is, according to the pattern, which calls for deer body hair fibers for making the tail as well as the wings. Once we've mastered it the way the originator intended, we'll slip in a few tricks which will save you some time and effort when you make this pattern in the future.

With your scissors snip a very small section of fiber from the hide. For a fly this size about ten fibers would be right, depending on the thickness of the individual hairs. Manipulate the hairs between your fingers until the tips are evenly aligned.

With the tips extending back over the bend of the hook, tie the fibers in as a unit. You will notice that they flare and stick out all over the place, mostly up and sideways. Don't let this bother you. Just secure the tail to the shank, and clip off the excess butts. Adding a dab of head cement to the thread windings before tying in the tail will help keep the fibers in place.

Once you have secured your tail, take a few turns of thread *in front of* the clipped butt ends, and bring your thread back over the fibers once more, almost to the bend. As you approach the bend, make a *very light* turn of thread around the tail fibers to bring them together. The turn must be light enough so that you only close up the fibers. If you bear down on the thread, you will flare them again (see Figure 7).

Once the fibers have been brought together with a loose turn of thread, carefully bring your thread forward away from the loop. Two or three turns should do it. Once you are on solid ground, let your thread dangle in its bobbin. With a dubbing needle place a liberal drop of head cement on the tail fibers where they come off the bend. This will solidify

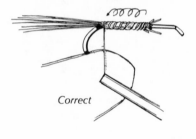

Correct

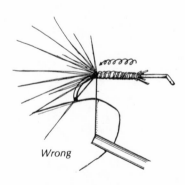

Wrong

Fig. 7. Looping Tail Fibers and Closing Them with Thread

the unit (see Figure 8). Incidentally, you can cement the tail either before or after you make the soft loop. The only reason for the cement is keeping all the fibers packed together as closely as possible.

Fig. 8

With the tail behind us, we are now ready for the fun part—spinning the deer body hair onto the hook shank. But hold on. I think I have a much better idea. Before we begin to spin the deer hair onto the pattern, let's first learn what it's all about. Let's isolate this entire procedure. Then you can use it any time on any pattern that calls for this technique.

So take a couple of half hitches on the hook you've just tied the deer hair tail on, and remove it from your vise. Place another hook in your vise, and spiral some thread onto the shank. For our practice session you can use a heavier-gauge thread if you like—perhaps a 3/0 or even a 2/0. This will let you give a little more pressure to the body hair, thus increasing its flare and minimizing the chances of breaking the thread. Once you get used to this procedure, you'll know just how much pressure will be necessary, and you'll automatically adjust to it.

Cut a matchstick-sized clump of deer hair from the hide. With the tips of your scissors remove the small amount of soft fuzzy underfur from the base of the fibers. (This should be done, by the way, whether the hair is to be used for tailing, winging, or body making.)

Trim off approximately the upper third of the tip. You won't need these hairs on this pattern, and they'll only make more work for you later. In addition, the tips do not spin as well as the hair nearer the base of the clump.

Hold the clump of deer hair between your left thumb and forefinger, and lay it diagonally across the shank of the hook. Take one turn of thread around the clump of hair and the shank, and pull the thread *toward you and slightly up while holding the hair loosely between your fingers.* The hair will begin to flare and also rotate around the shank of the hook. *Make another turn in the same area.* The hair will spin around the shank a little more and expand its flare. *Take one more turn of thread—your third— in the same area.* By this time the hair will have flared and spun completely around the shank of the hook, but the rotation will have all but stopped. After the third turn take the flared deer hair in your left hand, and stroke and pull it back toward the bend, *simultaneously taking two turns of thread in front of the flared clump.*

You have just completed spinning one section of deer body hair to the hook shank. Check Figures 9–16 for illustrations of this technique.

When you've completed the first spun section of deer hair, it's a good

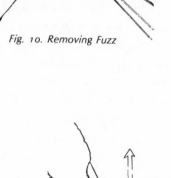

Fig. 9. Cutting Fibers from Skin

Fig. 10. Removing Fuzz

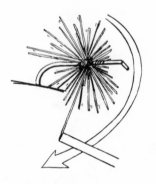

Fig. 11. Trimming Excess from Tip

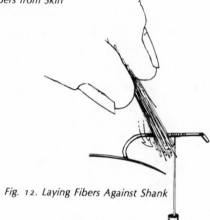

Fig. 12. Laying Fibers Against Shank

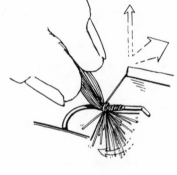

Fig. 13. Winding Thread

Fig. 14. Spinning Deer Hair

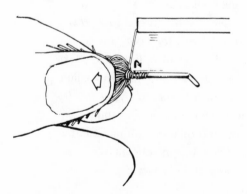

Fig. 15. Winding Thread in Front of Spun Hair

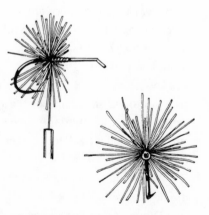

Fig. 16. Two Views of Completed Spun Clump

idea to put a small drop of clear head cement on the thread in front of the clump. If I'm doing a very large fly, such as a bass bug, on a size 2 hook, I generally add the cement only after two successive clumps have been tied in.

After the first section of hair has been spun and secured, you simply cut another clump and repeat the performance. This goes on until the entire hook shank or, in the case of this pattern, the body has been completed. I suggest, just for the sake of practice, that you spin on a few more sections as long as you still have a practice hook in your vise.

Now we're ready to go. Remove the practice hook, and insert the half-finished Irresistible, which at this point has only a tail. Spiral your thread back onto the shank to the point near the bend where you left off.

Use only a little hair for the first section to be spun on. You are going to be working over part of the tail portion, which has, as it were, enlarged the diameter of the hook shank at that point.

Turn your thread around the clump of deer hair, and make it flare. If it doesn't flare all the way, as it did during the practice session, don't be disturbed. It's only because of that tail portion underneath. Let the hair flare as far as it will go comfortably. If you have a space, just cut another small swatch of hair, place it across the open area, and fill it in. It's just like painting a ceiling. If you find you've missed a spot, you simply dip the brush into the can and paint some more.

Once you're off the tail section of the fly, you can increase the number of fibers in the clump of hair you're spinning onto the shank. Keep adding sections of hair until you have filled the two-thirds of the shank from the bend to the eye. If you get any closer to the eye, you'll have difficulty with your wings and hackle.

As you build each section, push back on the spun hair with your right hand while holding the section firmly in place with your left. This is called packing the hair. It makes for a more compact body, which, in turn, allows you to do a better trimming job later.

When you're one-third of the way from the eye, take a couple of half hitches or do a two-turn whip finish knot, and cut the thread from the fly. Remove the fly from the vise.

You are now ready to try a new skill. Have you ever trimmed a hedge or whittled a wooden duck? Well, you're going to do something like that. With a pair of scissors you're going to clip the body of the fly and shape it into a conical taper, like an ice cream cone except that the bottom is a little flat.

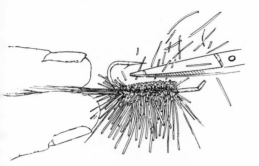

Fig. 17. Trimming Underside of Irresistible

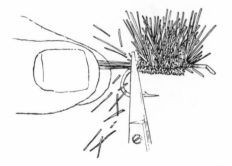

Fig. 18. Freeing Tail Fibers

I've found the easiest way to begin trimming the body of the Irresistible is to clip all the fibers on the underside of the fly. You almost can't make a mistake at this point since that is the part which has to be flattened so that it will ride properly on the water's surface (see Figure 17).

Next I work on the fibers near the tail. I don't want to cut any of the tail fibers, so I ascertain which hairs constitute the tail proper, take them in my left hand, slide my scissors along the outside of the tail, and begin trimming the fibers closest to it. Gradually the tail will emerge (see Figure 18). Once the tail fibers have been cleared and the underside flattened, all you have to do is trim the rest of the fly into a cone.

Study the figures showing the steps leading up to this point, and then take a look at Figures 19–21, which will give you a good illustration of how we formed the body of the Irresistible.

If you can tie the body of an Irresistible properly, you can tie any fly, even the largest bass bugs, without further instruction.

We are now ready for the wings. Once again place the fly, with its completed body, into your vise, and reattach the thread. It should hang from the shank just a little in front of the body. Cut another small clump of deer hair from your hide, and remove the fuzz.

Extend the tips over the eye of the hook, and tie in the clump of fibers just as you would a clump of calf tail fibers. On this pattern you will have a little more difficulty since the body tends to get in the way of your fingers. If you remember to hold the fibers securely, you can rest your left thumb and forefinger on the trimmed body and then proceed with your thread over, between the thumb and forefinger, down the far side, under, and

19

20

21

straight up. Here again, the pulling up gives you a tremendous advantage since it will actually pull the fibers down to the hook shank and thus secure them to it (see Figure 22).

Once you have pulled up and locked the wing fibers in place, turn the thread around the area a few more times for additional security. Deer hair is a little slippery. A drop of clear head cement on the thread windings before the tying in of the wing helps keep the clump in place.

Now lift the clump of fibers, and take a few turns of thread in front of them to prop them up, the same as you did with the calf tail wing.

Divide the fibers with a natural figure 8. Notice that they flare too much for a neatly tapered and bunched wing. This is where your reverse figure 8 once more becomes an advantage. Make the reverse 8, *but apply only enough tension to close and bunch the fibers for a compact, divided wing* (see Figure 23).

Once the wings are secure, you only have to tie in a pair of medium blue dun hackle fibers. Wind them on as a collar in the conventional way. A whip finish knot and a touch of head cement complete your Irresistible, which is illustrated in Figure 24.

As I mentioned earlier, you have just learned to tie the Irresistible the hard way, using the materials called for in the original pattern. You may have noticed that the spinning of the hair, though it seems difficult at first, is really very easily accomplished once the technique has been mastered. The tail and wings, however, remain something of a bother since they flare and misbehave all the time.

I no longer use deer body hair for my own Irresistible wings and tail.

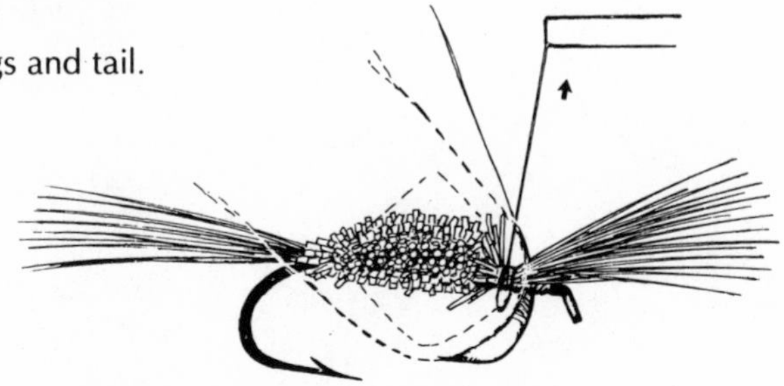

Fig. 22. Pulling up on Thread Loop to Secure Wings

Fig. 19. Compacting Deer Hair
Fig. 20. Trimming Deer Hair
Fig. 21. Deer Body Trimmed and Formed
Fig. 23. Properly Divided Wings

23

Fig. 24. Completed Irresistible

I make them from woodchuck guard hairs, which do exactly what I want them to. And they even look better than deer hair. The markings are more prominent and better defined.

Irresistibles can also be tied with calf tail, which doesn't flare. Calf tail, however, does not have the markings at the tip of the fibers that you find on deer or woodchuck. And some tiers prefer to tie this pattern with hackle tip wings, such as grizzly or chinchilla, much like that used on the Rat-faced MacDougall (see below).

There is much room for experimentation. And no matter what the wing and tail materials, the pattern will lose none of its effectiveness, for what really makes the Irresistible, after all, is the clipped deer hair body.

The Irresistible, in addition to being an important trout fly pattern, is one of the most commonly used dry fly patterns for salmon. For salmon it is usually tied in sizes 4 to 8 on a light wire salmon hook. (It is also an excellent bass and panfish fly.) In the salmon fly the hackle is sometimes changed, and a combination of brown and grizzly is used.

Another popular Irresistible, used for both trout and salmon, is the White Irresistible. The pattern description for this reads:

WHITE IRRESISTIBLE
TAIL: White deer body hair or, preferably, calf tail
BODY: Clipped white deer body hair
WING: White deer hair or, preferably, calf tail
HACKLE: White badger

The pattern for the Rat-faced MacDougall is:

RAT-FACED MACDOUGALL
TAIL: Dark ginger hackle fibers
BODY: Natural gray clipped caribou
WING: Chinchilla hackle tips
HACKLE: Dark ginger

The following two patterns were devised for salmon fishing. The Bomber is fished as a dry fly; the Buck Butt is both a dry and a wet fly. These flies also produce excellently for freshwater bass and panfish. They are listed here because they also have clipped deer hair bodies.

BOMBER: (usually tied in sizes 2 and 4)
WINGS: Deer hair protruding like feelers past the eye of the hook

BODY: Clipped natural brown or white deer hair
RIB: Brown or grizzly hackle palmered through body
NOTE: Body is clipped to a fat cigar shape. Color need not be natural or white.

BUCK BUTT   (usually tied in sizes 6 through 10)
TAIL: Fluorescent orange or green floss cut fairly short
BODY: Clipped natural brown deer hair
RIB: Brown hackle palmered through hackle
NOTE: This pattern is slightly slimmer than the Bomber.

Please note my remark that these patterns are extremely effective for bass and panfish and perhaps are used more often for them than for salmon and trout. (It may surprise the dedicated trouter to learn that the premier freshwater game fish is the largemouth black bass, not the trout.)

However, we are primarily interested in the techniques. With these techniques there is no end to the number and variety of bass bugs you can tie.

DEER HAIR MOUSE

Still, there is one particular favorite pattern of mine I would like to show you how to tie step by step. It is an old standby, the deer hair mouse:

DEER HAIR MOUSE
TAIL: Gray goose fiber
BODY: Deer hair trimmed to shape
WHISKERS: Porcupine bristles

The making of a deer mouse or any other hair bug, for that matter, consists mainly of spinning a quantity of deer hair onto the shank of a hook and trimming it to shape. Sometimes it takes a while to fill up a hook shank. It all depends on how large a bug is being made.

In this case it will take a bit of spinning and trimming. For the mouse we will need a fairly large hook, usually a 2/0, 1/0, or 1. Two good hooks to use are Mustad 7948A and 7957B.

Place a size 1/0 hook in your vise. Using a gray 2/0 thread in your bobbin, spiral some onto the hook shank beginning a quarter inch from the bend and winding toward it.

Fig. 25. Laying Deer Hair Across Hook Shank

Fig. 26. Pulling Up and Flaring Deer Hair

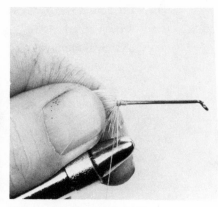

Fig. 27. Thread Wound in Front of Hair

Fig. 28. Four Clumps Tied On

Fig. 29. Deer Mouse Completely Packed

Fig. 30. Bottom Part of Mouse Trimmed

Fig. 31. Rear End Trimmed

Fig. 32. Entire Body Trimmed

Fig. 33. Neck Formed by Trimming

From the primary wing quill of a gray goose, select a single fiber, and cut it from the base of the stem. Tie it in at the bend to form the tail of the mouse.

From a piece of deer hide cut a small section of fiber, slightly less than the diameter of a matchstick, and lay it across the shank of the hook at the bend (see Figure 25).

Bring your thread over the deer hair, down the far side of the hook shank, under, and straight up (see Figure 26). When pulled taut, this simple complete turn of thread will make the deer hair flare around the hook shank. Take one more turn of thread around the hair in the same area. Now with your left thumb and fingers pull the hair back toward the bend of the hook, and take two turns of thread in front of the hair (see Figure 27). Place a touch of head lacquer at the base of the hair where you made your last turn of thread.

Cut another section of deer hair, this time slightly larger, and repeat the procedure.

After three or four clumps of deer hair have been spun onto the hook shank, place your left thumb and fingers against the hair at the bend of the hook, and with your right thumb and fingers push and bunch the hairs tightly by sliding them along the hook shank, shoving the mass to the rear (see Figure 28).

As you move forward toward the eye of the hook, you should repeat this packing of hair every turn or two. This will compact the hair, so that when it is trimmed, you will create a smoother effect. Loosely packed hair will show open spots and irregularities.

Fig. 34. Body and Neck trimmed to Overall Shape

Fig. 35. Completed Mouse

When you have packed all the hair you can onto the shank of the hook, make a whip finish knot and cut the thread. Place a touch of head lacquer on the last winding for security, and remove the bushy hook from the vise (see Figure 29; for photos fly has been kept in the vise to show steps clearly).

With a pair of sharp scissors, you can now begin your trimming. As you work, be careful not to cut off the goose fiber tail.

Begin trimming by holding the hook by the bend and the point upside down. Cut the hairs on the bottom of the hook. Here you can trim liberally, since the completed mouse will have a flat abdomen, for both imitation and the ability to float in an upright position after being cast (see Figure 30).

The next area to trim is near the bend of the hook. Locate the goose fiber tail, and let the outside edge of the scissors hug the tail as you trim the hairs in toward the bend (see Figure 31).

With the scissors now try to simulate the rounded shape of the mouse —a sort of lopsided oval with the widest part toward the rear (see Figure 32). Between the head and body of the mouse, there is a narrow band of neck. This is formed by trimming the hairs about one-third of the distance from the eye of the hook. You should make a complete circle in this area (Figure 33). Once the circular cut has been made, the hairs bordering it can be trimmed to a natural taper. The body of the mouse should curve gently into the neck area and then rise again to form the head (see Figure 34).

Upon completion of the trimming, reinsert the mouse into the vise. Spiral some black thread onto the shank just behind the eye. Our mouse is going to grow some whiskers. The whiskers can be made from porcupine bristles, peccary guard hairs, or the actual whiskers of smaller game animals such as the fox, rabbit, raccoon, or squirrel.

Lay two of the whiskers diagonally across the hook shank behind the eye, fine tips pointing off to the side and rear. Tie them down. Repeat the whiskers on the other side of the head. When they have been secured with thread, clip the excess butts, wrap a neat head with your thread, whip finish, and add a touch of head cement to the windings. Your Deer Hair Mouse is complete (see Figure 35).

6

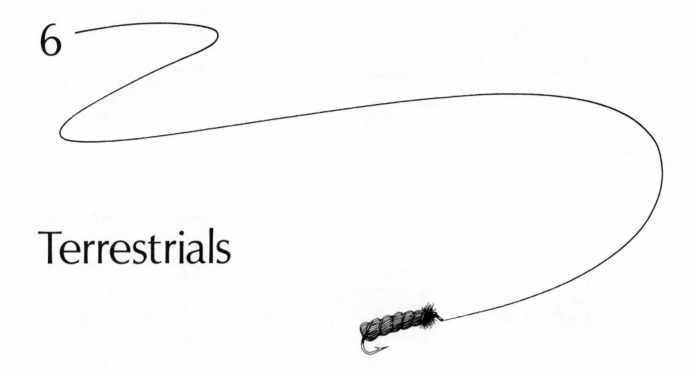

Terrestrials

Terrestrials are imitations of those land insects that either accidentally fall into streams or happen to live by them. At certain times of the year, when these insects are in abundance, trout and other fish will literally feast on them. Being at the right place at the right time, when, for instance, inchworms are falling from tree limbs overhanging a stream, can be very rewarding. In this chapter we will tie some of these imitations.

INCHWORM

Let's begin with the Inchworm, the pattern description of which follows:

INCHWORM
    BODY: Light green deer hair
    RIB: Green thread
    HEAD: Peacock herl

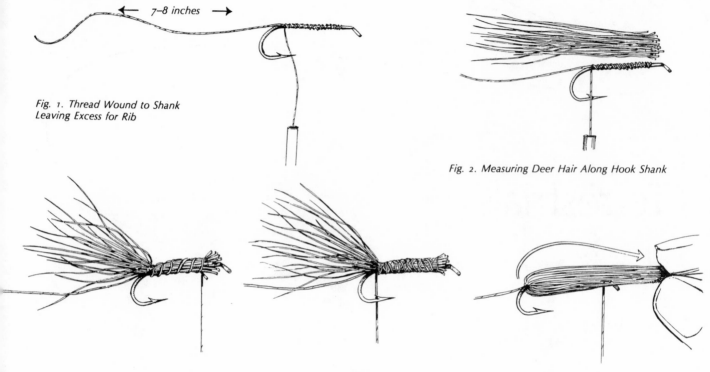

*Fig. 1. Thread Wound to Shank
Leaving Excess for Rib*

Fig. 2. Measuring Deer Hair Along Hook Shank

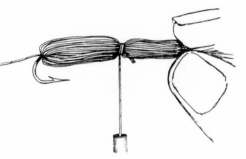

*Fig. 3. Loose Coils of Thread Securing
Deer Fibers*

Fig. 4. Securing Deer Hair to Shank

*Fig. 5. Pulling Back Deer Hair and
Surrounding Shank*

Fig. 6. Securing Reversed Deer Hair

Fig. 7. Forming Segmentations with Excess Thread

Fig. 8. Completed Inchworm

Though there are many ways to tie the Inchworm, thus far I have found this particular pattern to be the best. It is tied on a superfine wire hook with a 2X long shank; a good one is the Mustad 94831. This hook is made of extremely fine wire and is slightly longer than standard, enabling you to achieve the proper proportions for the body and at the same time

86

maintain buoyancy, which most standard dry fly hooks will not do. The completed pattern will ride right on the surface film just as a natural inchworm would.

To begin, clamp a size 12 hook in your vise. Select a medium shade of green 00 thread, and insert it into your bobbin. Run the exposed section of thread through a cake of fly-tying wax to give it a little adhesiveness. You will need about 10 inches of thread coming off your bobbin, for reasons you will see.

Spiral the thread onto the shank of the hook using only that portion of thread closest to the bobbin. Begin your turns just behind the eye, and wind to the bend. After the thread has been wound over onto itself, you will find that you have about 7 or 8 inches of it left. *Do not cut this off.* It will later be used for the rib (see Figure 1). If you have a material clip, insert the excess thread into it.

Next you will need some deer body hair which has been dyed a light green. This is the same hollow type of hair you used for the body of the Irresistible, except that it comes from the underside of the animal. It is very thick and will flare, so we'll have to be careful. The reason for using this hair is, again, buoyancy.

Clip a section about the size of a wooden matchstick from the base of the hide. Don't be concerned about aligning the tips. This is not necessary for this operation. Measure the section of deer hair along the top of the hook shank so that the butt ends come almost to the eye of the hook (see Figure 2).

With your bobbin take a loose turn of thread over the deer hair near the bend of the hook. Do not cinch down or the hair will flare. In a loose but snug spiral, wind the thread forward along the shank of the hook, loosely binding down the hair until you reach the butt ends near the eye (see Figure 3).

Once you have reached the butt ends of the deer section, near the eye, reverse your spiral, and wind to the rear again. As you spiral on the hair this time, *do cinch down* to secure it to the hook shank. Bring the thread all the way back to the bend, where you first tied in the clump of deer hair (see Figure 4).

In an open spiral bring your thread forward once more, and leave it idle in the bobbin just in front of the butt ends. You will notice that, having tied in the butt ends facing the eye of the hook, you have approximately an inch of deer hair left over, extending rear past the bend of the hook. Grasp this section of hair, and fold it forward, surrounding the hook shank

A.

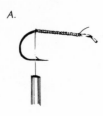

B.

C.

Fig. 9. Tying an Ant

A. Thread Wound onto Hook Shank

B. Rear Segment of Fur Ant Body

C. Hackle Tied in at Waist

as you do. Pull it taut and straight back past the eye of the hook (see Figure 5).

Keeping the deer hair taut between your right thumb and fingers, grasp the bobbin with your left hand, and bring two turns of thread over the deer hair at the point where the original butt section had ended and where your thread was left hanging (see Figure 6). Make sure the hair is secure. If you feel another turn of the thread is necessary, take it. Once more, for the moment, let your thread dangle here.

Now back to that piece of excess thread you left in your material clip earlier. Wind it in even open spirals over the deer body hair all the way up to the thread coming off the bobbin. As you spiral it forward, cinch it down by *pulling up* on the thread with each turn you make. This will form the segmentations on the Inchworm (see Figure 7). Once you have reached the bobbin thread, use it to tie down the thread you made the segmentations with. Now you may clip any excess.

To complete the fly, we just need a small head, which is made of peacock herl.

Pluck a full herled peacock quill. Tie it in. Take three or four turns of herl around the shank behind the eye of the hook so that the peacock herl fibers stand up. Tie the herl down with your thread. Whip finish and head cement. Your completed Inchworm should look like Figure 8.

ANT

Up to this point there has been something a little different or new in each pattern we have tied. The only thing different about tying an Ant, however, is the actual conformation of this terrestrial. It is small and has a unique shape. Beyond that the tying techniques are similar to those used on any conventional dry fly, such as the Light Cahill. They just occur in different areas on this fly. Nevertheless, in a chapter on terrestrials, we would be remiss if we did not at least cover this imitation in a brief discussion.

The Black Ant and the Cinnamon (or Red) Ant are probably our most important terrestrials. The natural insects that live near streams and rivers are, by any whim of the wind, potlucked into a trout's diet, so trout know them and try them. Fishermen know this and tie them.

Most imitations of this terrestrial are tied on a superfine wire hook in sizes 14–22. Though both the Black and Cinnamon patterns are very popular, the Black has a slight edge, so we'll tie that.

Place a size 16 Mustad 94833 hook in your vise. (A 16 is a good size to tie an imitation ant with; however, if you are a beginner, it may be easier to practice tying this fly on a 12 or 10 at least until you get the hang of it.) Wind some fine black thread onto the shank, terminating at the bend.

As far as a fly tier is concerned, an ant is an insect with two humps, a head, and some legs. We achieve this effect using only two materials—dubbing fur and hackle. Though many other furs can be used for the body, I prefer beaver dyed black.

Give your thread a little extra waxing. Pluck a small amount of under-fur from a piece of black beaver, and spin it onto your thread exactly as you would in forming the body of the Light Cahill.

Wind the dubbed thread forward to the middle of the hook shank, forming a rounded "humped" effect as you do.

Pluck a hackle feather from the cape of a black rooster neck. A dyed neck will do if you don't have a natural black one. The size of the fibers radiating from the stem of the hackle feather should be about three-quarters of the length of the hook shank.

Trim the excess fibers from the stem of the hackle feather near the butt with a pair of scissors, and tie it in at the center of the hook shank where you left off with your dubbing.

Take two or three turns of hackle, winding the feather over the hook shank going away from you. These turns are made right next to each other and form a collar of hackle at the very center of the hook shank. Once the required turns have been made, secure the feather with your thread and clip the excess tip.

Spin some more dubbing onto your thread, and form the front section of the ant.

All that remains now is the whip finish, which should form a tiny head, and a drop of clear lacquer to secure the whole affair. That's all there is to it.

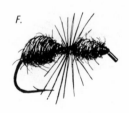

The Cinnamon Ant is tied in exactly the same manner. The only difference is fur color. Any blend that makes cinnamon will do. My own preference is cinnamon seal mixed with reddish brown mink.

D. Front Section of Fur Ant Body

E. Excess Thread Clipped

F. Completed Black Ant

There are, of course, other methods of tying the Ant patterns. Some tiers like to use deer hair, and some use lacquer for a realistic, shiny effect. None of that is necessary. None will take trout or any other fish better than the simple constructions we have just tied. Remember, most of the time realistic imitation is lifeless. Impressionistic imitation, with the accent on the appearance of movement (as in loose hairs, furs, and fibers), is lifelike.

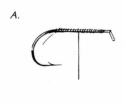

A.

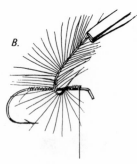

B.

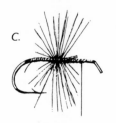

C.

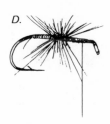

D.

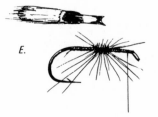

E.

In other words, you want your imitation, whatever it is, to look alive rather than to look like a live insect. Ponder that in your spare time. It will make the difference between taking trout and not taking them with your creative efforts.

JASSID OR BEETLE

Here's one more simple pattern to tie. It can best be explained by the answer to this question: When a trout views a beetle from beneath the surface of the water, what does it see? Answer: An oval silhouette with legs. That's all.

You tie it by winding fine black thread on a superfine wire hook, usually in sizes 16 to 22. At the center of the hook shank, tie in a black, brown, or gray hackle collar approximately three-quarters of the shank in length. Take three turns of hackle.

The legs on the Beetle are formed by the simple expedient of trimming the top and bottom hackle fibers at the shank with a pair of scissors, leaving only those fibers which protrude directly out from the side of the hook shank.

The Jassid calls for a jungle cock eyed feather to be tied directly on top of the hook shank to give it the shape we need. Since jungle cock is rather scarce, I suggest you use an imitation or substitute like starling body feathers, quail neck feathers, or guinea hen feathers, all of which should be lacquered and dried before being tied in as the wing of the Jassid. Actually, you can use almost any feather if you trim it to shape and give it a nice varnishing. However, leave the legs alone. They are the only thing that will give this imitation any movement.

GRASSHOPPERS AND CRICKETS

Walk through any summertime meadow or field on your way to the stream, and you are likely to kick up hundreds of grasshoppers, jumping and flying to get out of the way. They come in many sizes and a variety of shades. The most common usually have a green or yellow abdomen shading to brown on their backs and wing covers.

It's true that grasshoppers are not always taken as food by trout, but it's also true that larger trout are enticed by them. For bass and panfish they are unequaled.

Most of the grasshopper imitations tied today are of the deer hair and hackle variety. Let's tie one:

DEER HOPPER

TAIL: Bright red hackle fibers
BODY: Clipped yellow deer hair with tuft left extended at bend of hook
WING: Dark brown mottled turkey (or similar)
HACKLE: Brown

Insert a size 10 Mustad 9672 hook in your vise. Spiral a size 2/0 yellow thread onto the shank of the hook near the bend. Select 10 or 12 bright red hackle fibers, slightly more than you would normally use on a conventional dry fly, from either a neck or saddle hackle, and tie them in as the tail.

Next cut a matchstick-sized section of deer body hair that has been dyed yellow. While holding it over the shank of the hook at the bend, cinch it down with your thread so that the butt ends flare up (see Figure 11).

As with the Irresistible, continue adding yellow deer body hair until you have covered two-thirds of the shank of the hook. For a compact body remember to push the deer hair to the rear with your right thumb and fingers. Do this after each section is added. A little cement between each of the spinnings will also help.

When you have finished spinning on the body, tie off your thread, and cut it after securing. Remove the bushy half-done hopper from the vise, and begin to trim the deer hair to the shape of a grasshopper's body (the same procedure as the Irresistible, only a different shape).

When you trim, leave a small tuft of deer hair extending up at the bend of the hook. The completed body should look something like the one in Figure 12. Having completed the trimming, reinsert the half-finished fly into your vise, and switch to a brown 6/0 or 7/0 thread. The prewaxed Herb Howard thread is excellent. Spiral it onto the shank of the hook beginning just behind the eye and winding to the clipped deer hair body.

When you were still catching grasshoppers for the fun of it, you may have noticed that their wings do not lie directly on top of their bodies but

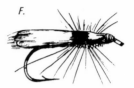

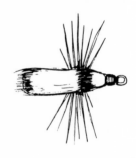

Fig. 10. Tying the Jassid

A. Thread Wound onto Hook Shank

B. Hackle Being Wound at Center of Shank

C. Hackle Collar Formed at Center of Shank

D. Hackle Trimmed Top and Bottom of Shank

E. Prepared Jungle Cock Nail Before Tying

F. Three Views of Completed Jassid: Standard, Top, and Side

Fig. 11. Tying Down Deer Hair
Fig. 12. Completed Body of Deer Hopper

11   12

along their sides. They look a little like tents. This is the way you should try to tie on the mottled brown turkey wing quill, which is the next step.

Before that, however, a brief word about mottled turkey. In recent years this material, once very common, has begun to be scarce. Brown turkeys are just not being raised for food any more, at least not in any quantity. If you cannot get any mottled turkey wing quills, use any mottled feather that is firm enough to make a grasshopper wing. A good substitute is a secondary wing quill from the peafowl. Others come from large predator or game birds; on these you will have to check local and federal regulations concerning possession. If by some chance you know a successful wild turkey hunter, another rarity, try to talk him out of some of these prized wing quills, or any other feathers, for that matter.

Unlike the wings of a mayfly, which are thin and delicate, the wings of a grasshopper are solid and firm. This is one of the reasons they are lacquered before they are tied to the body. Lacquered, they will also last through a few more trout. If you are tying a full season's supply of hoppers, the best thing to do is lacquer two entire wing quills (a right and a left). Sections are then cut from them as they are needed. A good lacquer for hopper wings is vinyl cement.

Take a left and a right turkey wing quill, and cut a section from each. The sections should be about a quarter of an inch wide (see Figure 13).

Align the wing quill sections, one along each side of the shank pointing just above the bend of the hook, with the tips extending to the rear. Make sure they also cup and cover the sides of the body. Tie the quills in with two or three turns of thread, and clip the excess butt ends.

With your scissors trim the tip ends of the quill sections so they have a slight slant (see Figure 14).

13   14

Fig. 13. Paired Sections of Turkey Quill
Fig. 14. Tied-down Turkey Wings

Once the wings are properly in place, all that remains is the hackling of the fly. Pluck a brown hackle feather from a rooster neck; the length of the fiber should be approximately half the length of the hook shank. Trim the butts, tie the feather in, and wind it as a conventional dry fly hackle collar. Clip the excess. Whip finish the head, and apply a touch of head cement to the windings. The completed Deer Hopper should look like Figure 15.

Crickets are similar to grasshoppers in shape and, in some cases, in coloration. They are generally easier to tie than hoppers because the body does not have to be clipped and the wing does not have to behave and hug the body like a grasshopper's.

One of the most popular patterns is the Letort Cricket. Though tied in sizes 10–16, it is especially effective on the smaller hook. During the few excursions I've made to the limestone streams in Pennsylvania, I've found most anglers using this pattern only in a size 16.

Since there is a slight variation in the techniques for this pattern and it is very popular, let's tie one.

Fig. 15. Completed Deer Hair Hopper

LETORT CRICKET

    BODY: Beaver dyed black (or black wool or fur)
    WING: Crow quill covered with flared black deer hair
    HEAD: Clipped black deer hair

Black thread and a Mustad 9672 hook, size 14, are again used. Place the hook in your vise, and wind the thread onto the shank, ending at the bend.

By now you are thoroughly familiar with the procedure for forming

Fig. 16. Trimmed Quill Section

Fig. 17. Tying in Quill Section

Fig. 18. Completed Letort Cricket

a dubbed body. Therefore, apply your black beaver fur to the thread, and wind the dubbed fur three-quarters of the way along the hook shank to the eye. Leave just enough room to spin on a clipped deer head.

The next piece of material you need is a section of quill from a common crow. If you don't have any crow wing or tail feathers, by all means use black dyed duck or goose, whichever is handiest.

The quill section for the Letort Cricket should be approximately one-eighth of an inch wide. Cut such a section from your wing or tail feather. With a pair of scissors round the tip of the quill (see Figure 16).

With the glossy side of the feather facing up, place the quill section on top of the hook shank so that the rounded end extends just slightly past the bend of the hook. Tie it down with your thread. Make sure before you secure it to the shank that your thread is lying partially on the dubbed body, or your quill section may tip up on you (see Figure 17).

The quill section itself should lie directly on top of the hook shank and cup it slightly around the sides. This is just a hint of a hug; it should not be exaggerated.

The outer wing covering is made from the tips of a clump of deer hair dyed black, the same type you would use for an Irresistible. Here the tips are aligned as evenly as possible. The clump of fibers, slightly less than matchstick size, is then placed on top of the hook shank so that the tips extend barely beyond the underwing. The clump is spun on in the usual manner.

The base fibers will flare up more than the tip fibers. The flare is all right but should not be excessive.

The base fibers—not those forming the outer wing—are trimmed to the size that the head should become.

Another clump of black deer hair is then cut from a piece of hide and spun onto the shank in front of the last clipped section.

The head is trimmed almost square.

The completed Letort Cricket appears in Figure 18.

We have just learned to tie some of the most basic terrestrials. There are countless others, including similar ones in different sizes and colors. I doubt, however, that you will have trouble with any of them if you just use a little thought and common sense and keep in mind that the materials should suit the purpose of the fly.

7

Parachute Flies

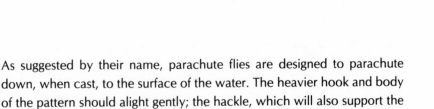

As suggested by their name, parachute flies are designed to parachute down, when cast, to the surface of the water. The heavier hook and body of the pattern should alight gently; the hackle, which will also support the fly when it lands, and the wing will act as a brake and stabilizer, creating a delicate presentation.

To make a parachute pattern, you wind the hackle of the fly clockwise on a horizontal plane above the shank of the hook and around the butt, or base end, of whatever material is being used as the wing. The wing itself can be tied either in the conventional divided fashion or as a single vertical protrusion.

Without question these flies, at certain times, are highly effective. One reason they are not used as often as they should be is that many tiers do not have the patience to tie them. There was a time I placed myself in this category; however, the parachutes are not all that difficult once you've mastered a few little tricks, and with practice you should be able to tie them as easily as any standard dry fly. Parachute flies can be tied for most

A.

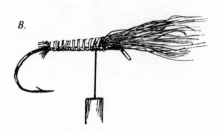

B.

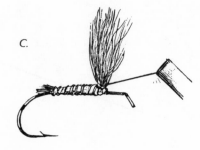

C.

of the patterns calling for the standard hackle collar, from mayflies down to midges.

Let's use the Hairwing Royal Coachman for our lesson. The various versions of the Royal Coachman are the most popular flies in the world, and they still take more than their share of trout and other fish.

HAIRWING ROYAL COACHMAN (PARACHUTE)

WING: White calf tail, clumped
TAIL: Golden pheasant tippet
BODY: Peacock herl divided by band of red floss
HACKLE: Brown, wound horizontally

Place a 94840 hook, size 12, in your vise. Spiral some fine black thread onto the shank, and form a bed on which the wing is to be tied.

Clip a clump of fibers from a white calf tail as you generally would when tying the White Wulff, and fasten it to the shank of the hook in the usual manner.

When the clump of fibers has been propped up to a vertical position and secured, you are done with the wing, which is a single upright clump. It is not divided. Apply some vinyl cement to the base of the fibers after you have trimmed off the excess butt ends.

From a brown rooster neck select a hackle feather of the same fiber -size you would use on a size 12 standard Coachman. Pull off the excess fibers from the feather with your fingers instead of cutting them off with a pair of scissors. They are stripped to the same point to which you would usually cut them.

Lay the hackle butt stem along the shank of the hook *in front* of the wing clump so that the stripped part extends beyond the bend of the hook and the fibered tip past the eye. The shiny side of the hackle should face

D.

up. In this position bind down the hackle and secure it with thread beginning in back of the wing and running almost to the bend of the hook (see Figure 1 for rundown of steps). Clip the excess butts.

The tail is tied in next. For this pattern we are using the tippet feathers from the neck of a golden pheasant. A half dozen will be sufficient. They are fairly stiff and support a fly well. Tie them on in the conventional manner.

For the body select a fairly full-bodied peacock quill with long flues. You will notice that the flues lie close to the quill. We want them to protrude from the quill stem at a 90 degree angle. To accomplish this, hold the quill by the tip, and stroke the flues downward with the thumb and forefinger of your free hand (it's something like rubbing a cat's fur the wrong way).

Place the butt of the peacock quill diagonally under the shank of the hook between the shank and the thread, and tie it in. Secure it with two or three turns of thread (see Figure 2).

Starting at the bend of the hook, wind your thread one-third of the distance to the eye. Wind the peacock herl to the thread, and tie it down with the thread.

Take a single strand of red floss, and tie it in where you left off with the peacock quill. To form the red dividing band, you only have to wind the floss around the center of the shank about four times. Then the floss is tied down, and the excess is cut away (see Figure 3).

Bring your thread forward to a point just behind the wings.

Pick your peacock quill up again, and wind it to the thread. Tie it down. Your Coachman body is finished (see Figure 4).

We've covered the tail and body on this pattern only because it differed slightly from some of those in our earlier imitations.

We are now ready to hackle our parachute fly.

Bring your thread *in front* of the wing clump and *under* the extended hackle feather. At this point make a half hitch with your tying thread (see Figure 5).

Grip the extended hackle by the tip with a pair of hackle pliers, and begin turning it clockwise and horizontally around the clump of calf tail by *pulling the hackle toward you* (see Figure 6).

Wind each succeeding turn *under the previous one* until the required number of turns have been made. Three or four turns are usually enough (see Figure 7).

After your last turn of hackle the tip should once more face out over the eye of the hook.

Now comes the toughest part. You have to switch the bobbin to your *left hand* and with it sneak the thread into the area between the wound hackle and the tip. Maintain enough tension on your hackle pliers to keep the tip facing out over the eye. With your left hand grasp the bobbin, and very carefully bring two turns of thread *over* the hackle *tip* to bind it down; remember to keep the turns of thread *under the wound hackle* (see Figure 8).

Once you have secured the tip, which can now be held in place with the weight of the bobbin, you have to get into this area with a pair of very fine scissors or a scalpel to clip the excess tip without cutting any of the hackle fibers of the wound collar.

When you have removed the excess hackle tip, return the bobbin to your right hand. All you have to do now is tie off the fly with a whip finish knot. Again, you will have to be careful not to bind down the hackle fibers of the horizontal collar. Usually I don't use a whip finisher, but for this operation it is very helpful, since it does get in there and make the knot without harming any of the other fibers. (This little trick was shown to me by Jack Mickievicz of Jack's Tackle in Phoenixville, Pennsylvania.) If you do use a whip finisher, tilt it down a bit so that you keep out of the hackle collar area..

Cut the thread with a scalpel or fine scissors. Add a touch of head cement, and your Parachute Hairwing Royal Coachman is completed. It should look like Figure 9.

What about parachute flies tied around the bases of wings made of a softer material, such as wood duck or mallard flank fibers—for example, a Parachute Light Cahill, which is made according to the description in Chapter 2 except that the hackle collar is wound horizontally? The proce-

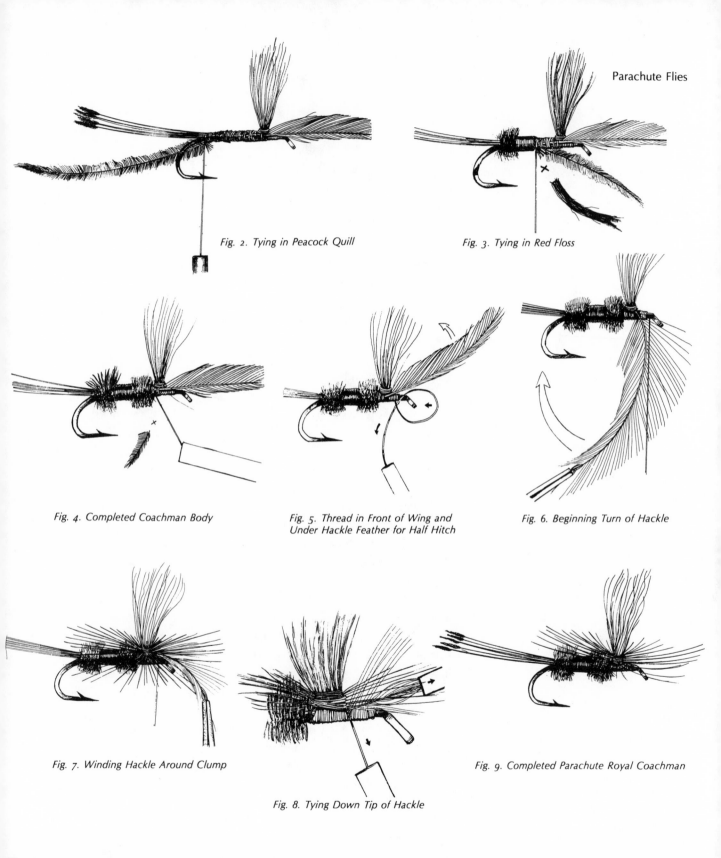

Fig. 2. Tying in Peacock Quill

Fig. 3. Tying in Red Floss

Fig. 4. Completed Coachman Body

Fig. 5. Thread in Front of Wing and
Under Hackle Feather for Half Hitch

Fig. 6. Beginning Turn of Hackle

Fig. 7. Winding Hackle Around Clump

Fig. 8. Tying Down Tip of Hackle

Fig. 9. Completed Parachute Royal Coachman

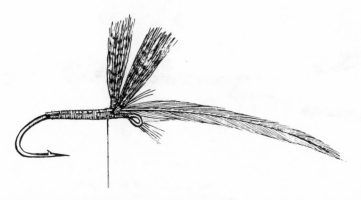

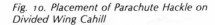

Fig. 10. *Placement of Parachute Hackle on Divided Wing Cahill*

dure is only slightly different. For an example let's quickly do the Light Cahill parachute style.

Tie in your wings, and divide them as you would normally do, making a figure 8 and a reverse figure 8 with your thread. However, as you make your reverse 8, *take two or three turns around the base of each divided section with your thread* to give each section more solidity. Here again, your wings should be absolutely vertical.

Once the wings have been secured, place a drop of vinyl cement in the center of the divided section so that some of the liquid touches the base of both wings.

Select a dark cream hackle, suitable for a size 12 hook, and strip it down from the point at which you will be using the hackle fibers for a collar later.

With the tips pointing out over the eye of the hook, lay the hackle, stripped butt toward bend, *between* the divided wing section of wood duck fibers. Remember that the shiny side should face straight up. Bind down the hackle as you did with the previous pattern—that is, almost to the bend—and clip the excess butt (see Figure 10).

The tail and body of the fly are now tied in; the hackle collar is wound in the same manner as it was on the Parachute Coachman.

You can tie parachute flies using almost any material for wings. Occasionally, however, when tying in a delicate fiber such as hackle tip wings in a fly like the Adams, you need a little more support than just the base of the wings. This is especially true of multishaded hackled flies in which, for instance, a brown and a grizzly hackle are required.

In these cases it is advisable to build a support for the collar first. This can be made from two stripped stems of hackle from the middle, or base, of a rooster neck. They are fastened to the bed of thread where you would usually tie in your wing. Prop them up, and divide them as you would a

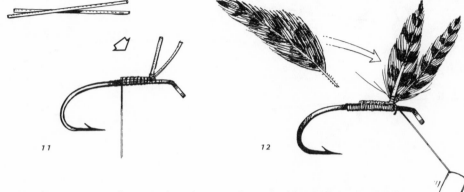

Fig. 11. Support Stems Tied into Position

Fig. 12. Hackle Tip Wings Tied to Supports

wing, but cut very short so that the actual wing of hackle tips protrudes above them (see Figure 11).

Once the support stems are in position, the hackle tip wings are prepared and tied in place inside the stems. Make a reverse figure 8 around both the support stems and the hackle tips, forming one unit. A drop of vinyl cement secures the base of both wings (see Figure 12). You now have a solid foundation with which to wind your horizontal collar when you complete the fly.

As a parachute, the Adams pattern, by the way, is usually tied with a clump of calf tail for the wing. The example above only illustrates what can be done if you wish to use hackle tips on this or any other pattern.

Now and again you will find special hooks with a vertical hump on the shank which are solely for tying parachutes. These are a fine investment if you intend to tie only patterns with very delicate wings, for the hook will support a horizontal hackle collar. The only drawback is that the hump, which is, of course, on top of the shank, weights the hook in the wrong place. Many years ago, when parachutes were first tied, the horizontal hackle collar was tied on the bottom of the hook, which is the proper place. But a parachute fly works best with the hackle wound on top of the shank, allowing the weight of the hook itself to carry the fly down and land it flush on the surface. All in all, you don't need these hooks to tie parachutes successfully.

There are other gadgets on the market designed to assist you in making parachute flies. Should you wish to experiment with them, by all means do so. But they are not necessary. You can tie most dry fly patterns using the methods just described, and that includes those with wings of mallard, wood duck, and goose wing quill sections. All you need for such patterns as the Black Gnat or Blue Quill is a good solid tie when you divide the wings and a touch of vinyl cement at the base of the division.

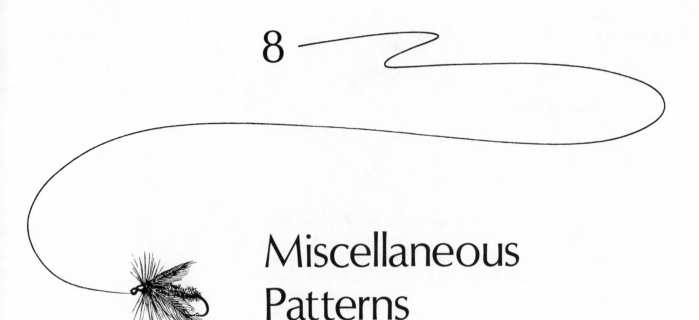

Miscellaneous
Patterns

If you have been able to follow the instructions in the preceding chapters, I think there are very few dry flies you will not be able to tie. Even if a fly is unfamiliar, you should be able, with a little study, thought, and experimentation, to master its intricacies and quickly relate them to the practices you've studied. Still, to complete the picture, we will go over a few more patterns which are a little on the odd side or have certain peculiarities. A brief discussion about certain unique imitations will enhance your knowledge that much more.

CADDIS FLIES

The primary difference between a caddis imitation and nearly every other is the shape. The wing of the caddis does not stand upright or lean slightly. It lies flat, flush with the body, as it does on the natural insect.

Caddis flies, both dry and in the pupa stage, are becoming increasingly popular, perhaps because the insect imitated is a hardier sort than the ephemeral mayfly. It can withstand slightly less pure and oxygenated water. Trout may prefer mayflies to caddis flies, but they will feast on caddis simply because they are there—in enough abundance, I might add, to interest not only the trout but the angler as well.

Tying caddis imitations is relatively simple, though there are a few tricks you should learn to make the procedure more fun. The order for the caddis is body, wing, hackle.

The following is a fairly basic, yet effective, caddis imitation. It is called the Tan Deer Hair Caddis:

TAN DEER HAIR CADDIS
BODY: Olive/brown mink fur or similar dubbing
WING: Fine tan deer body hair
HACKLE: Brown

The hook is a Mustad 94840, size 14. (A 14 is the proper size for this pattern; however, it is more difficult to learn a new pattern on a small hook, so by all means practice this pattern on a 12 or 10 hook.)

Spiral some light brown or tan thread onto the shank of the hook beginning behind the eye and winding to the bend. Spin some olive/brown dubbing onto the thread to form the body.

Unlike the body of the conventional dry fly, the body of the caddis does not build in a taper toward the eye. The caddis body is almost the reverse, though not quite. It is heavier and more rounded near the bend of the hook than it is in the thorax area or near the eye, where the wing and hackle are tied in. For the correct shape and tying procedure, see Figure 1.

The wing is tied on in what is called downwing fashion. When you see a pattern listed as a downwing, chances are that it will be some form of caddis imitation.

The fibers for our pattern are taken from the leg of a whitetail deer. The hair in this area is much lighter in color and, more importantly, finer in texture. It is not the kind of hair that will flare too readily.

Clip a small bunch, about one-third of a wooden matchstick in diameter, of these fine light brown fibers from your piece of hide. Align the tips as evenly as possible.

Lay a bed of thread on the shank just in front of the dubbed fur, where you are going to fasten your deer hair wing. In other words, wind your thread in an open spiral toward the eye, covering the bare shank where

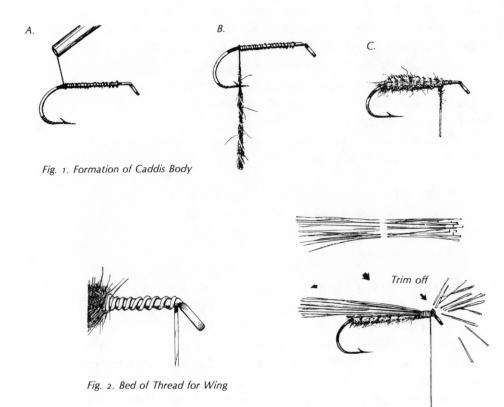

Fig. 1. Formation of Caddis Body

Fig. 2. Bed of Thread for Wing

Fig. 3. Deer Hair Wing Tied In

the wing is to be tied. This little trick was shown to me by Robert Brandt of Mount Tremper, New York, when he saw that the wings of my caddis flies tended to pull out at a slight tug. The bed of thread gives the fine, smooth deer hair something to hold on to (see Figure 2).

Spread a touch of head cement on the top of the thread for additional insurance, and we're ready to go.

Tie in the wing so that the tips of the deer hair extend one-third of the shank length past the bend. Take a few extra turns of thread around the shank in this area. Make sure the hair is secure. Clip the excess butts (see Figure 3).

You will notice that the butts of the wing have been trimmed almost at the eye of the hook. This means you will have to wind your hackle collar over the base of the wing and not the hook shank.

The hackle collar is formed in the usual manner. On a size 14 hook

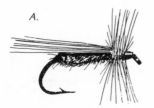

A.

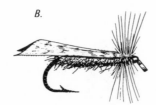

B.

C.

D.

two hackles are usually required. The hackle collar should be tied fairly full. A whip finish and touch of head cement complete the pattern.

Having tied this pattern, you should have very little difficulty in tying any of the dry fly caddis imitations listed by various companies, as long as you have a fly or a pattern to refer to. The variations usually concern only the wing material and the color of the pattern.

In addition to deer hair you can use mink, woodchuck, chipmunk, and squirrel guard hair for the wings, as well as feathers or quills from such birds as duck, grouse, and turkey. The longer hackle fibers from a top-quality rooster neck are used in many downwing patterns. All of these materials are tied in on top of the hook shank.

If you're tying with duck, turkey, or similar quills, you have to follow a different procedure. Entire quill sections are first trimmed or paired and then tied in as a downwing. Then there are the tent-shaped and delta-winged variety. If this seems complicated, let's unscramble it a bit.

There are four types of wings you can tie on a caddis dry fly (see Figures 4A–D):

A. The clump of fiber, such as we have just tied, which includes animal guard hairs or stiff hackle fibers.
B. The trimmed quill, which is a section of mallard feathers, duck pointers, turkey wings, or the like. Here a single section is cut from the feather, trimmed to shape, and tied in as a unit. It can be tied completely flat along the top of the hook shank or curved slightly downward, semi-cupping the body of the fly.
C. The tent shape, which is used on the time-tested Henryville Special. It has two wing quill sections, as on a Black Gnat, which are tied in a tent-shaped fashion, as you would a grasshopper (see pp. 90–3).
D. The delta wing. This is made by tying a pair of rooster or hen hackle tips on top of the hook shank so that they extend from the body at a 45-degree angle.

Fig. 4. Types of Caddis Wing

A. Clump of Fiber for Straight-backed Wings

B. Trimmed Quill

C. Tent Shape

D. Delta Wing

Fig. 6. Completed Henryville Special

Fig. 5. Palmering Body of Henryville Special

PALMERED HACKLE

Every now and then you will find a pattern that calls for you to palmer a hackle or that says the rib consists of a palmered grizzly (or brown or cream or so on) hackle. To palmer simply means to wind a hackle feather, usually in an open spiral, through the body of the fly.

A good example of a pattern calling for a rib of palmered hackle is the Henryville Special, a caddis fly imitation:

HENRYVILLE SPECIAL

    BODY: Olive floss

    RIB: Grizzly hackle, palmered

    WING: Wood duck fibers over which two slate mallard quills are tied tent fashion

    HACKLE: Brown

Since we are familiar with the basic procedures in the tying of a caddis dry fly, only palmering will be explained and illustrated.

To tie a size 14 Henryville Special, select a grizzly hackle feather of the same size you would use for the hackle collar on a standard size 14 dry fly, and trim the lower portion as you would if you were preparing it for a hackle collar. The grizzly hackle is then tied in by the butt at the bend of the hook.

A 6-inch strip of olive floss is tied in just in front of the grizzly hackle. The floss is wound onto the hook shank, forming a fairly thin body. It is secured near the eye with thread.

Grip the grizzly hackle with a pair of hackle pliers, and wind in an open spiral to the thread (see Figure 5).

To complete the fly once it has been palmered, tie in two of the types of caddis wings you have been shown. The first is the single-fibered wing,

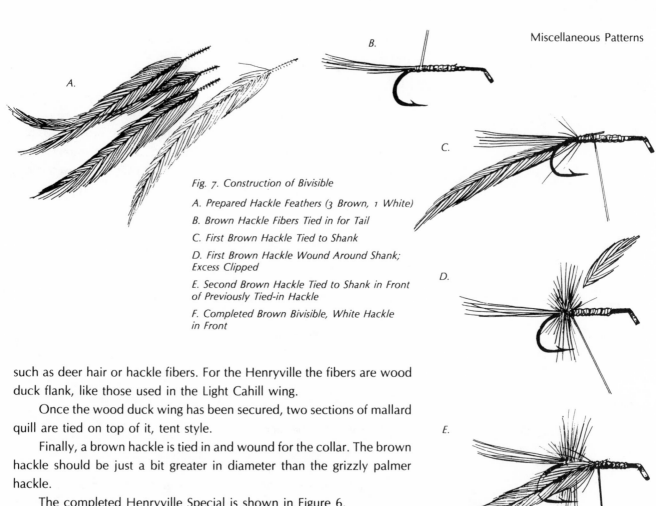

Fig. 7. *Construction of Bivisible*

A. *Prepared Hackle Feathers (3 Brown, 1 White)*

B. *Brown Hackle Fibers Tied in for Tail*

C. *First Brown Hackle Tied to Shank*

D. *First Brown Hackle Wound Around Shank; Excess Clipped*

E. *Second Brown Hackle Tied to Shank in Front of Previously Tied-in Hackle*

F. *Completed Brown Bivisible, White Hackle in Front*

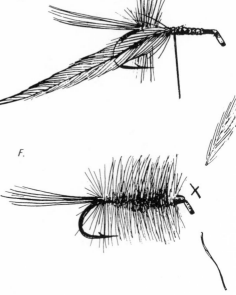

such as deer hair or hackle fibers. For the Henryville the fibers are wood duck flank, like those used in the Light Cahill wing.

Once the wood duck wing has been secured, two sections of mallard quill are tied on top of it, tent style.

Finally, a brown hackle is tied in and wound for the collar. The brown hackle should be just a bit greater in diameter than the grizzly palmer hackle.

The completed Henryville Special is shown in Figure 6.

The bivisibles are another group of flies considered to have palmer-style ties.

The name bivisible comes from the fact that the last hackle wound in is white or cream. Thus while the entire fly is visible to the trout, the two or three turns of white hackle are also visible to the angler—hence, "bivisible." Here the palmering is achieved by filling the hook shank with close, connecting turns of hackle. These flies have no wings, simply a tail and a shank full of hackle.

The construction of a bivisible is simple enough. After the tail has been secured, three or four hackle feathers, depending on hook size, are prepared, tied in, and wound as you would a hackle collar, one after the other, from bend to eye. Excess butts and tips are secured and trimmed. In other words, you are going to get only so many connecting turns of hackle from

107

one feather. You tie down and secure the usable portion of one feather, trim the excess, and tie in a fresh hackle feather where you left off (see Figure 7).

The palmer method of ribbing hackle is used extensively for salmon flies (see Green Highlander).

The most widely used pattern in this group is the Brown Bivisible. However, a bivisible can be made from any shade of hackle as long as two or three turns at the eye of the hook are lighter than the body section. (Actually, I suppose you could reverse the color positions, and who would argue?)

HACKLELESS FLIES

Hackleless flies have come into their own primarily because of the work by Doug Swisher and Carl Richards, described in their book *Selective Trout*. There has been a certain amount of controversy because of the newness, or originality, of this type of fly. Actually, it does not matter, for before the publication of this book, very few anglers were aware that such flies even existed, although they have been around a long, long time. But they were not used to any degree. For their acceptance we owe a debt of gratitude to Swisher and Richards.

There has also been some controversy about their effectiveness. But as Herb Howard once put it to me, briefly and bluntly, while we were discussing the pros and cons of various patterns, "Sometimes they work; sometimes they don't." And that statement can be applied to any pattern or type of fly that exists.

The hackleless fly was never intended for rough water. It originated in Michigan, where there is water everywhere—and anglers to fish it. The forest is dotted with lakes and ponds, linked by rivers and streams—truly, a water wonderland. Yet in all my travels through the Lower Peninsula, I never encountered a stream like the Beaver Kill or the Esopus. The reason is simple. Michigan is not a mountainous state. Its rivers, while rich with life, are gentle; its streams, while flowing, are smooth. Its trout, while no smarter than those in the Appalachian Highland or the Rocky Mountains, have more time to be selective. Thus Michigan is the perfect home for the hackleless fly.

There is also a season and a time for the hackleless fly. Come late summer, with low water and quiet pools, when many of us are looking at trout that are, in turn, inspecting our conventional patterns—and refusing them. This is the time for the hackleless fly.

Flies without hackle are not difficult to tie. If you can tie any standard dry or wet fly, tying a hackleless fly will be child's play. There are, however, a couple of things you should know:

1. Use the finest wire hook you can get that is suitable for the pattern.
2. Use materials that will float, such as those described in Chapter 2. Floatability is more important here than anywhere else, since there is no hackle to add buoyancy.

A hackleless fly has only a tail, a body, and a wing.

The wing is tied in first. It can be made from a number of materials, ranging from the usual wood duck flank or mallard quill to hen hackle or duck shoulder. It can be divided or solid, whether of calf tail, deer hair, or split and clumped duck or turkey fibers. Again I remind you to use waterfowl feathers if at all possible, regardless of pattern.

The body is made from various furs or synthetics purported to be high floating. Once more, your best bet is fur from water animals.

The tail, which is tied in after the wings, is usually made up of a combination of such fibers as deer, elk, and moose tied at an oblique angle in the form of a V. The tail on a hackleless fly acts as an outrigger supporting the fly on the surface. Among my favorites for tailing these flies are the short side fibers from a goose quill.

Why don't we quickly tie one of these patterns to see whether there are any hidden tricks involved. How about a Dark Hendrickson?

DARK HENDRICKSON, HACKLELESS

    WING: Mallard shoulder feathers
    TAIL: Natural gray goose fibers
    BODY: Natural gray beaver

Fig. 8. Mallard Shoulder Feathers Tied in as Wings

If you look at a pair of mallard wings, you'll see there are some very small slate gray feathers at the shoulder of the wing. Pluck two from one of the wings; they don't have to match.

With a Mustad 94833 size 14 hook in your vise, tie in the pair of shoulder feathers using a fine gray thread. The wings are secured to the hook with the same technique used for a quill-winged Black Gnat or Blue Dun (see Figure 8).

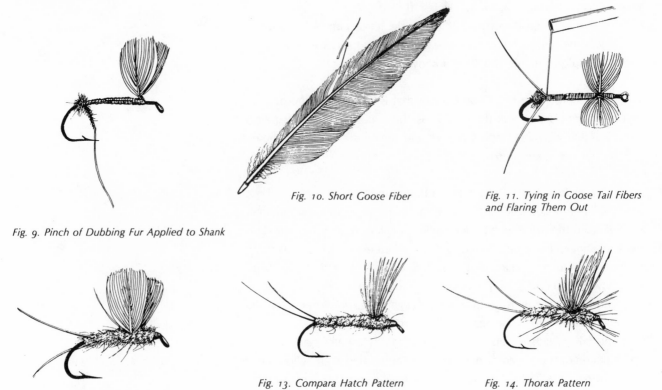

Fig. 9. Pinch of Dubbing Fur Applied to Shank

Fig. 10. Short Goose Fiber

Fig. 11. Tying in Goose Tail Fibers and Flaring Them Out

Fig. 12. Completed Dark Hendrickson, Hackleless

Fig. 13. Compara Hatch Pattern

Fig. 14. Thorax Pattern

The tail is the next material to be tied in, but first a little preparation is in order. We must lay a foundation of sorts from which the tail can flare out. This is done with a small amount of beaver dubbing which will later be used for the body. Spin a very small amount of dubbing onto your thread, and turn it around the hook shank near the bend (see Figure 9).

Pick up a pair of gray goose wing quill feathers. You will note that there are fibers growing from each side of the center stem, long on one side and fairly short on the other. You want the short fibers (see Figure 10). Snip one goose fiber from each of the paired quills. Taking them one fiber at a time, tie them to the shank of the hook against the dubbing you just applied. The dubbing acts as a cushion for your thread to sink into and also as an obstruction to the fibers, preventing them from lying parallel to the hook's shank. The cushion of dubbing, in other words, forces the fibers out at an angle (see Figure 11).

Once the tail has been secured, all you have to do is spin some more beaver dubbing onto your thread and form the rest of the body. The body will extend past the wings, increasing in taper to the thorax and diminishing at the eye of the hook. The completed Hackleless Dark Hendrickson is shown in Figure 12.

In the same category as the hackleless flies are the thorax and compara hatch patterns. The tying procedures for the compara hatch are the same as those for the hackleless flies. In most instances a compara hatch pattern will have a single upright wing, usually made from a clump of deer hair.

The compara hatch flies are the creation of Al Caucci and Bob Nastasi, authors of *Hatches,* which from the day of its publication was quickly accepted as an authority on direct imitation of natural insects, both in emerger and nymph form.

Thorax flies are tied with a hackle. However, after the hackle collar has been tied on a given pattern, the part of the hackle that protrudes from under the hook shank is clipped close to the body. Only the hackles protruding from the side and top of the shank remain. This allows the body and thorax of the fly to lie flush with the surface of the water after being cast—hence "thorax" fly.

The positioning of the wings is also different in a thorax fly. On a thorax pattern the wings are tied in very close to the center of the hook, whereas in a conventional dry fly they are closer to the eye.

The tying order in a thorax fly is wings, hackle, tail, body. The hackle collar, though tied in as the second step, is only wound around the shank after the body has been formed.

There are no hidden tricks in the tying of these patterns. If you can tie the conventional and hackleless patterns, the thorax type will not present a problem.

Figures 13–14 will give you an idea of both the thorax and compara hatch flies.

FAN WINGS AND CUT WINGS

The fan wing is not used much today, though the cut wing seems to be on a slight upswing, perhaps because it gives us a chance to use some of those feathers we rarely tie with. As we all know, fly tiers seldom throw anything away.

The drawback to both types of wings is that they are notorious for twisting a leader during any prolonged casting session. They are also a bit wind-resistant. Nevertheless, they are still being tied, maybe for their beauty alone.

Pretty as they may be, I've heard more than one tier give these wings a good dressing down while trying to fix them to the shank of the hook. Both fan and cut wings seem to fight back. They don't seem to want to flare perkily the way they are supposed to. And yet it need not be so.

Let's try to tie a fan wing properly (the same technique applies for a cut wing). Remember just this one thing, and you'll have no trouble: A fan wing, regardless of what feathers you use, *is always tied on the side of the hook shank,* and a figure 8 is used to secure it.

Pluck a pair of the white feathers from the breast of a wood duck or similar waterfowl. If you don't have this material, a pair of hen hackles, regardless of color, will do, since we are illustrating this procedure just for technique.

Strip all the excess fuzzy fibers from the butt of the feather, leaving only those at the tip which will make up your wing. Do this to both feathers you're using for the wing.

Having laid the usual bed of thread on the shank of your hook (a size 12 is fine), lay *one* of the breast feathers against the far side of the hook shank with the bare butt pointing straight down. Do a figure 8 around the stem of the breast feather (see Figure 15).

Repeat with the other feather, tying it to the near side of the hook shank, again with a figure 8. The fan wing operation becomes much simpler when you tie in one feather at a time.

When both feathers have been tied in using the regular figure 8, make a reverse figure 8 around both of them, manipulating them so that they stand erect and flare evenly (see Figure 16).

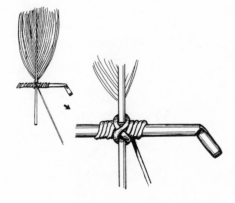

Fig. 15. Tying in One Breast Feather

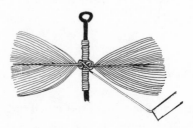

Fig. 16. Securing Both Wings with Reverse Figure 8

Once the wings have been secured, take the butt ends, which have been extending below the hook shank, and bend them back toward the bend. Secure them with turns of thread, spiraling to the rear, and clip the excess butts (see Figure 17).

There you have it. Now you can make all the fan wings you like, whether for fishing or viewing. That part of it will be up to you.

As I stated earlier, cut wings present no other problem in tying technique. However, they do have to be prepared. They are, after all, "cut" wings.

The shaping of cut wings can be done with a pair of scissors. The finished product will be as good as your artistry with scissors. The easier way to do it is to buy a cut wing former, which is a tool with a piece of curved steel embedded in a piece of wood or plastic. The steel should be razor sharp. The cut wing former works on the rocking chair principle. You simply roll this tool over the area you wish to trim. You can make large or very small cut wings from almost any feather. This tool is available through many supply houses.

Having completed the section "Flies That Float," I decided to sit back and relax for a few days, using the time to search my mind and a few catalogs listing fly patterns to see whether there was something I may have missed that you should know about. The catalogs were of no help. Glancing through them, I see now that you can tie all of the dry flies listed just by using the techniques we've covered in the preceding chapters.

Fig. 17. Securing Butt Stems to Shank

III

Subsurface Fly Patterns

9

The Wet Fly—Basic

Wet flies are the oldest patterns, dating back hundreds of years. Wet fly fishing reached its zenith in England, and many of the patterns used in the United States today were introduced by the early settlers and visitors from the British Isles. Until the advent of the dry fly, they were the most popular, and probably the only, patterns fished in American waters.

The trend today is toward nymphs, and the wet fly has, to a degree, been relegated to history, except by those anglers who still take trout with them. Yes, they do take trout. As a modern angler, you may have heard that the going flies in subsurface insect imitation are nymphs, larvae, and pupae. Perhaps you haven't fished a conventional wet fly pattern. You should try it sometime—it may surprise you and convert you.

Tying wet flies is not difficult. In fact, it is not complicated at all. There are, of course, a few little tricks and movements which will make life just that much more pleasant while you are at your tying bench. So let's try our hand on a few of these patterns and see what they're all about.

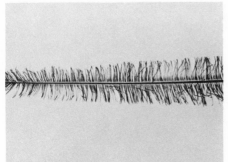

1   2   3

LEADWING COACHMAN

If you're going to fish wet flies, the Leadwing Coachman is one pattern you should not be without. I doubt whether anyone can tell you what species of insect it imitates, but I can tell you that it has broad appeal, resembling as it does various forms of underwater life.

LEADWING COACHMAN
> TAIL: None
> BODY: Peacock herl
> HACKLE: Brown
> WING: Mallard duck quill

Wet flies are tied on hooks of a heavier wire than dry flies for the obvious reason that we want the fly to sink, not float. They are also tied on 1XL and 2XL in addition to standard length. The most common hooks for wet flies are the Mustad 3906, 3906B, 9671, and 3399. There are some others, of course, and for the most part hook choice is a matter of personal preference. For our pattern we'll use the standard Mustad 3906 in size 12, which, incidentally, is a good size to fish with.

Insert your hook into the jaws of the vise, and spiral some fine black thread onto the shank, starting just behind the eye and winding to the bend.

On wet flies, in contrast to dry flies, the wings are tied in last. The normal progression on a wet fly is tail, body, hackle, wings. In this case we do not require a tail. Thus the first material to be tied in will be the peacock herl body.

Select a wide-flued quill from the area about 2 inches below the eyed portion of a peacock tail that has the heaviest herl. Hold the quill by the

Fig. 1. Prepared Quill

*Fig. 2. Peacock Quill Positioned
Against Hook Shank*

Fig. 3. Peacock Herl Tied In

Fig. 4. Peacock Herl Body Formed

4

tip, and run it through your fingers so that the barbules protrude from the stem at right angles (see Figure 1).

Lay the butt end against the shank of the hook next to the thread you have left dangling in your bobbin. The flat shiny side should face the shank (see Figure 2).

Enough of the peacock butt should extend past the tied-in area so that when it is bound down, it will extend almost to the eye of the hook. Bind down the butt by winding thread over it, terminating about one-sixteenth of an inch from the eye of the hook (see Figure 3).

Grasp the tip of the peacock herl, and in connecting turns winding away from you, spiral the herl all the way to the thread. The barbules of the peacock quill should stand erect and not be matted down. This will assure lifelike action (see Figure 4). By the way, peacock herl is a fragile material. To give it strength, many tiers mix a piece of thread with the herl or simply run the thread back and forth over the body. Even though these procedures do strengthen the body, they destroy the action of the herl. So if you are afraid your fly will not last for more than one trout, tie in two peacock herl fibers. Wind the first one forward to the eye. Take your thread, and spiral it to the rear and then forward to the eye again. Grasp your second peacock herl, and wind it over the first. If a trout cuts the outer quill, you only have to snip off the outer peacock herl body. You will still have the reinforced one underneath to fish with. It may not be as good, but it will do the job.

Back to the vise. Your peacock herl body should terminate approximately one-sixteenth of an inch from the eye of the hook, where it has been tied down and trimmed.

Next tie in the hackle. Since this is a wet fly, you will not need a top-quality hackle, which should always be saved for your dry flies. A number-two or wet-grade brown hackle neck will do just fine. Pluck a hackle. The size of the fibers, when tied in, should be long enough to touch

Fig. 5. Forcing Fibers Out

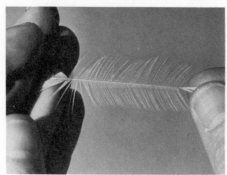

Fig. 6. Holding Hackle for Folding

Fig. 7. Placement of Left Thumb

the point of the hook. You will be able to judge this more efficiently once you have tied your first fly.

Before we can tie the hackle to the hook, it must be prepared. Hackling a wet fly really differs greatly from hackling a dry.

Take the hackle feather by the tip with the thumb and forefinger of your right hand. Place your left thumb and forefinger below your right hand, and grasping the stem, slide your left thumb and forefinger down the length of the hackle feather. This will force the fibers out, away from the stem. They should be at an approximately 90 degree angle (see Figure 5).

Your next step—and if you can accomplish it, you will save many a weary hour in tying—is *folding the hackle.* It will be a bit difficult at first, but I urge you to practice it, daily if possible, until it becomes second nature to you. It's like making your first blood or barrel knot on a leader. Your fingers don't seem to do what you want them to until you've done it enough times.

Hold the hackle feather near the butt between the third and fourth fingers of your left hand and the tip between your right thumb and forefinger (see Figure 6). The shiny side of the hackle should face you.

Extend your left thumb up to your right thumb, and place the pad against the hackle feather (see Figure 7).

During this procedure the entire hackle feather is being held fairly taut. Now put the pad of your left forefinger against the pad of your left thumb (see Figure 8).

You are now in position for the actual folding. Allow your left forefinger to slide off your left thumb, moving *down and to the rear* across the hackle fibers. This motion should bring your left forefinger all the way back to your third and fourth fingers, which are still holding the hackle feather near the butt (see Figure 9).

Fig. 8. Placement of Left Forefinger and Thumb   *Fig. 9. Folding Hackle*   *Fig. 10. Folded Hackle*

Rolling and sliding off the thumb across the hackle folds the fibers on one side of the stem so that they lie close together in an acute angle (see Figure 10). If this motion gives you too much trouble at first, try moistening the pads of your left thumb and forefinger before folding the hackle; this helps. If you can master this folding technique, you'll be able to make the fibers extending from each side of the hackle feather almost touch each other. If you still have trouble folding the hackle properly, don't let it prevent you from completing the pattern. Just tie in the hackle feather at the point where the normal separation would be, and as you make your turns of hackle, stroke them to the rear with your left fingers.

At the separation between the folded hackle and the tip of the feather, place the entire feather against the hook shank, and tie it in. The tip extends past the eye of the hook. This is a complete reversal of the dry fly procedure (see Figure 11).

Make sure you have tied in your folded hackle feather securely by binding the tip area down well. If you don't, it may slip out during the first turn. Clip the excess tip.

Take a pair of hackle pliers, and attach them to the butt end of the hackle feather. Wind the hackle around the shank of the hook about four times in turns going away from you (see Figure 12). As you make your turns moving toward the eye, work them so that each turn of hackle stem lies directly in front of the previous one.

The fibers of the hackle, with the shiny side out, should point to the rear. You may have to stroke them with the fingers of your left hand in order to get them to lie properly. This is not difficult.

When you have made the required turns of hackle, tie the hackle feather down on top of the hook shank with your thread, and clip the excess butt. The tied-in hackle collar appears in Figure 13.

121

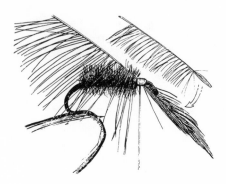

Fig. 11. Tying in Folded Hackle

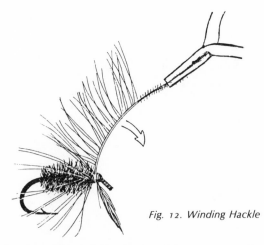

Fig. 12. Winding Hackle

Fig. 13. Completed Hackle Collar

The last major operation is the tying in of the wings. In this case you will need a pair of natural gray duck pointer quills. These are the primary flight feathers from the left and right wing of a mallard. The best quills for the purpose are the third and fourth feathers in from the outside pointer quill. Incidentally, quills from almost any other slate gray duck will do.

Do you recall the instructions in Chapter 3 for selecting a section from each of a matched pair of duck pointer quills? The same technique applies here.

Snip a right and left section of duck pointer quills about one-sixteenth of an inch wide from your matched pair. (The width of the section varies with the size of hook.)

There are two methods for tying in the wings of a wet fly, at least as far as duck quill sections are concerned. One is the common, or fast, method, used by most commercial tiers. In this method the wing sections are paired and tied directly on top of the hook shank. The second method takes a little more time but is actually the proper way to tie in wet fly duck quill wings. It was shown to me by Walt Dette of Roscoe, New York. Walt is a professional tier's tier. He is meticulous not only in the manner in which he ties his flies but also in the material he uses for them. Neither he nor his wonderful wife, Winnie, will accept second best. Here is Walt's method of tying in the duck quill section wings of a Leadwing Coachman.

With a pair of tweezers grip the duck quill section that is to form the far side of the wing on the hook shank. Hold and measure the section against the hook shank. The tip of the quill should flare up where the bend curves down (see Figure 14).

Now that you know where the quill is to go, you can hold the quill between your left thumb and forefinger and release it from the tweezers. Allow the quill to slide slightly down the side of the hook shank so that

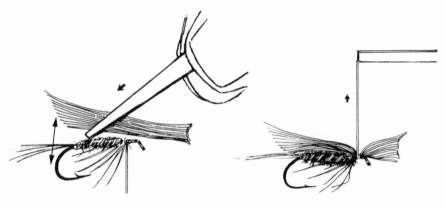

Fig. 14. Aligning Duck Quill Section with Tweezers

Fig. 15. Far Side Duck Quill Section Tied In

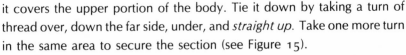

Fig. 16. Aligning and Tying Second Duck Quill Section

it covers the upper portion of the body. Tie it down by taking a turn of thread over, down the far side, under, and *straight up.* Take one more turn in the same area to secure the section (see Figure 15).

Pick up the other duck quill section with your tweezers, and measure it against the first one. Now you'll see how very easy this method is compared with trying to align the quill sections in your fingers before tying them in. Cover the upper portion of the body with the second duck quill while aligning the top edges of both quills. Tie it in (see Figure 16). Note that the concave sides of the quills face each other. Secure the area with thread, and clip the excess butts.

Spin a neatly tapered head to the fly. It should not be large or bulky or have a severe drop-off ledge. A touch of head cement on the head, and you have a completed Leadwing Coachman, as shown in Figure 17.

GOLD-RIBBED HARE'S EAR

What the Light Cahill and the Adams are to the dry fly fisherman, the Gold-ribbed Hare's Ear is to the subsurface angler. It is the most popular subsurface pattern in the United States and is tied as both a wet fly and a nymph.

Fig. 17. Completed Leadwing Coachman

GOLD-RIBBED HARE'S EAR

TAIL: Brown hackle fibers

BODY: Hare's ear and mask dubbing

RIB: Fine flat gold tinsel

WING: Slate mallard duck quill

HACKLE: Plucked guard hairs

123

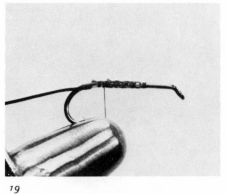

Fig. 18. Holding Tinsel in Position

Fig. 19. Tinsel Tied In

Clamp a Mustad 3906B hook, size 12, in your vise, and spiral some fine black thread onto the shank, terminating at the bend.

Tie in a tail of brown hackle fibers, just as if you were tying a dry fly.

Cut a 3-inch section of fine flat gold tinsel. Lay the tinsel diagonally under the hook between the shank and the thread (see Figure 18).

Tie in the tinsel by winding the thread over it part of the way to the eye and back again (see Figure 19). Take one turn of tinsel around the shank, and bind it down with thread. This will give you a headstart on forming the rib of the pattern. For the time being forget the tinsel, or insert the end of it into your material clip if you have one.

We are now ready to form the body, which in this case is made of a slightly different kind of fur. The face and ears of a hare have two kinds of furs, or hair and fur, if you will. It is a mixture of soft and coarse material. And we want both. Take a pair of scissors, and cut some of the soft mask underfur. Also cut some of the short, coarse guard hairs from the ear. Mix them. A blender will save quite a bit of time on this. If you intend to tie a number of these patterns, prepare a good quantity of this fur blend, and store it in a jar to be used when needed.

Though you are familiar with the conventional method of spinning dubbing fur to thread for making bodies (Light Cahill, Dry, Chapter 3) this particular fur blend may give you a bit of trouble, primarily because of the slippery guard hairs. The fur *can* be spun on in the conventional manner, but why go to all that trouble when we have an easier and much better method?

Take a small amount of the blended fur in the palm of your hand. Try to stretch it out so that it forms a sort of line (see Figure 20). Moisten the fingers of your other hand, and roll them over the fur. It's like shaping the

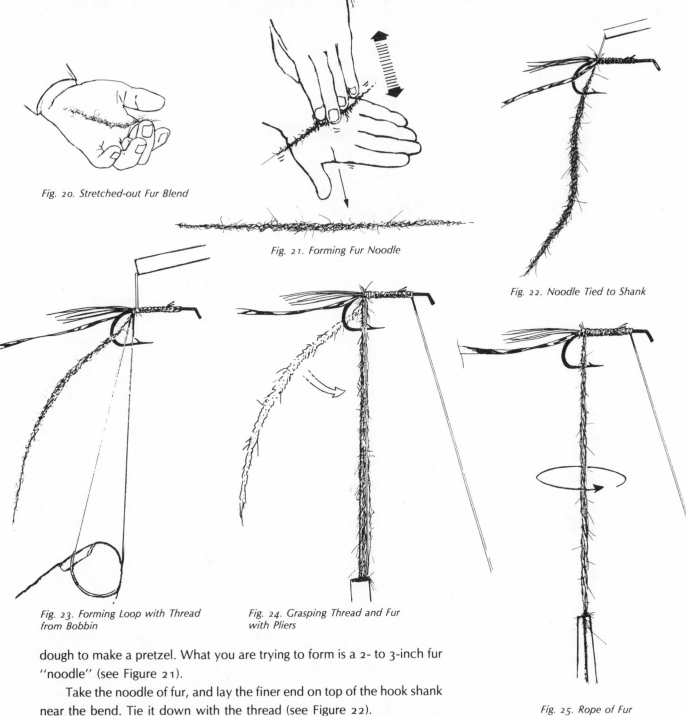

Fig. 20. Stretched-out Fur Blend

Fig. 21. Forming Fur Noodle

Fig. 22. Noodle Tied to Shank

Fig. 23. Forming Loop with Thread from Bobbin

Fig. 24. Grasping Thread and Fur with Pliers

Fig. 25. Rope of Fur

dough to make a pretzel. What you are trying to form is a 2- to 3-inch fur "noodle" (see Figure 21).

Take the noodle of fur, and lay the finer end on top of the hook shank near the bend. Tie it down with the thread (see Figure 22).

Unwind your bobbin so that about 8 inches of thread are exposed. Hold the bobbin in your right hand, and place the index finger of your left hand against the center of the thread between the hook and the bobbin.

125

26

27

Fig. 26. Coarse Hair Added to Fur
Fig. 27. Tinsel Ribbed Through Body

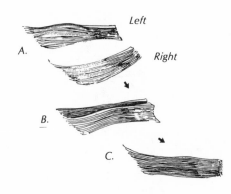

Left

A.

Right

B.

C.

Fig. 28. Alignment of Wing Quill Sections

Keeping tension against the thread with your index finger, bring the thread over it and to the hook shank once more (you are simply forming a loop). Take four or five turns of thread around the shank near the bend, making sure that each turn covers all the previous turns (see Figure 23).

Slip the noodle of fur into the loop of thread, and grasp the fur and both sides of the loop with a pair of hackle pliers near the bottom of the noodle (see Figure 24). Now spin or twist the pliers, trapping the noodle between the thread and thus forming a fur rope (see Figure 25).

Spiral your thread to the wing tie-in area just before the eye. Wind and form your rope fur body to the thread as you would any other material, and taper it.

Pluck a few more guard hairs from the ear of the hare's mask, and add them to the front portion of your body to bulk it up (see Figure 26). Spiral your tinsel through the fur, tie it down with thread, and clip the excess (see Figure 27).

We are now ready for the wings. From a right and left mallard pointer feather, clip a section of quill approximately three-sixteenths of an inch wide.

Align the quill sections by placing the concave sides together. In other words, curve the tips of the quills toward each other, not away from each other (see Figure 28).

Lay the quill sections directly on top of the hook shank so that the tips extend as far as the bend and curve away from it. Tie them in in the usual manner by bringing the thread around the quills and shank and pulling *straight up.* Once the wings have been secured, trim the excess butts.

Even though you are not yet finished, you should whip finish and head lacquer the fly. Now take your dubbing needle, and with the point poke

126

29   30

Fig. 29. *Poking Out Guard Hairs*
Fig. 30. *Completed Gold-ribbed Hare's Ear*

out some of the guard hairs so that they protrude from the body. These will form your rough hackle (see Figure 29).

That completes your Gold-ribbed Hare's Ear, which is shown in Figure 30.

DARK HENDRICKSON

There is very little on the Dark Hendrickson wet fly that you do not know how to tie, except perhaps the wing. And that is not difficult; it's just that we haven't covered it. Very briefly, let's see what it's about:

DARK HENDRICKSON
    TAIL: Wood duck flank fibers
    BODY: Muskrat fur
    HACKLE: Medium dark dun
    WING: Wood duck flank fibers

Place a size 12 Mustad 3906B hook in your vise, and spiral some fine gray thread onto the shank, terminating at the bend.

Snip a section of wood duck fibers approximately one-sixteenth of an inch wide from a flank feather, and tie them in for your tail. They tie as easily as hackle fibers.

Build your tapered body of muskrat fur dubbing, and wind in your hackle collar as you did in the Leadwing Coachman. There. We've now covered all parts of the fly but the wing, which is why we're tying this pattern in the first place.

127

31

32

Fig. 31. Wood Duck Fibers Tied in for Wing
Fig. 32. Completed Dark Hendrickson

The wing we are going to tie here is generally referred to as the rolled type. It is the most commonly used, the easiest to tie, and no less effective, when fished, than any other wing.

From the flank feather of a wood duck, cut a section of fibers almost half an inch wide. Make sure you have the tips evenly aligned before you apply the scissors.

Roll or crush the fibers into one clump.

Lay the section of bunched fibers along and on top of the shank so that the tips reach the bend of the hook. Tie them down as you would any other wing (see Figure 31).

Clip the excess butts of the wood duck fibers, and with your thread spin on a head, finishing it with a whip finish knot. A touch of head lacquer completes your Dark Hendrickson (see Figure 32).

The reason for making a pattern with rolled wings was to add a little more weight to a point I am going to make. It is this: Thus far we have tied only three wet flies; how many more patterns do you think you are now able to tie just by having learned the techniques of these three? Your guess may be way off. It's much more, more than I would care to list, since we don't have the room here. But just to give you an idea, here are other wet fly patterns you can tie without further instruction.

BLACK GNAT
TAIL: Black
BODY: Black chenille
HACKLE: Black
WING: Slate mallard quill

BLUE DUN
TAIL: Medium blue dun hackle fibers
BODY: Muskrat
HACKLE: Blue dun
WING: Mallard quill

LIGHT CAHILL
TAIL: Wood duck flank
BODY: Cream dubbing
HACKLE: Dark cream
WING: Wood duck flank

COWDUNG
TAIL: None
BODY: Olive floss with gold tinsel tag
HACKLE: Brown
WING: Slate mallard quill

PROFESSOR
TAIL: Red duck quill (three fibers)
BODY: Yellow floss
RIB: Fine flat gold tinsel
HACKLE: Dark ginger
WING: Mallard flank

QUILL GORDON
TAIL: Wood duck flank
BODY: Stripped peacock quill
HACKLE: Medium blue dun
WING: Wood duck flank

GINGER QUILL
TAIL: Golden ginger
BODY: Stripped peacock
HACKLE: Golden (buff) ginger
WING: Light slate gray mallard

DARK CAHILL

TAIL: Wood duck flank

BODY: Muskrat

HACKLE: Brown

WING: Wood duck flank

COACHMAN

TAIL: None

BODY: Peacock herl

HACKLE: Brown

WING: White duck quill

FEMALE BEAVER KILL

TAIL: Mallard flank

BODY: Muskrat with egg sac of fine yellow chenille

HACKLE: Brown

WING: Mallard duck quill

GRAY HACKLE

TAIL: Dyed red hackle fibers

BODY: Peacock herl

HACKLE: Grizzly

WING: None

MONTREAL

TAIL: Dyed red duck quill (three fibers)

BODY: Claret floss

RIB: Fine flat gold tinsel

HACKLE: Claret

WING: Turkey wing quill, mottled

10

The Wet Fly—Salmon

When I began fly tying, I considered salmon flies an art form as exotic as the feathers once used in their dressing. I believed I would first have to master all other patterns—the dry fly, the streamer, the wet, the nymph —before I could even attempt a Silver Doctor or Green Highlander. How wrong I was. And so are you if you think tying salmon flies is beyond your reach.

All salmon flies, with a few exceptions, are considered wet flies, even though some of them resemble heavily dressed streamers. Tying them is relatively simple. What makes them seem difficult is that more of the conventional methods are used on each of them, which, in turn, is a result of the variety of materials *once* used in their makeup. This no longer holds true. Effective modern salmon fly patterns are tied much more sparsely, and in most cases hair and fur fibers have replaced the exotic feathers of rare birds.

Traditional or classic patterns such as the Jock Scott and the Silver Wilkinson are still being tied, but mainly for the sake of the art. They are

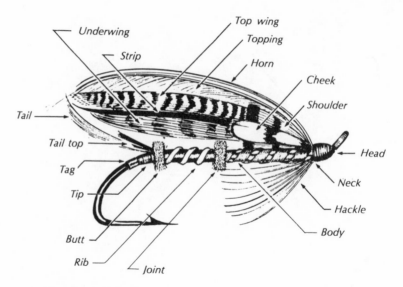

Fig. 1. Fully Dressed Salmon Fly

usually framed or used on brooches. They are rarely fished, at least not by knowledgeable anglers.

Although these patterns still adhere to the original listings, it is now almost impossible to follow them because many of the birds whose feathers were used are protected. The few classic materials left are scattered far and wide in the hands of a few collectors. Substitute feathers, in most cases goose and turkey, can, of course, be used if you wish to tie some of these creations. If you are so inclined, more power to you. Tying salmon flies is a beautiful art.

For our own purposes, however, we are going to cover a few of the contemporary patterns just to learn what is different about them and to uncover a few secrets. I assure you that if you master all the techniques in this book, you will have little trouble tying the classic salmon flies. So for your knowledge Figure 1 lists the entire nomenclature of a fully dressed salmon fly.

GREEN HIGHLANDER—HAIRWING

What makes the Green Highlander a contemporary pattern? The added word "hairwing."

This pattern is a perfect example of the transition from the classic to the modern form of salmon fly for the sole purpose of fishing effectiveness.

Many of the tying operations are identical to those of the classic. Simplification enters the picture primarily in the wing dressing. This particular pattern will cover most of the procedures you'll find necessary in tying all salmon flies, so let's tie one!

GREEN HIGHLANDER—HAIRWING

TAG: Silver tinsel

TIP: Pale yellow floss

TAIL: Golden pheasant crest half covered by a few strands of barred teal or wood duck fiber

BUTT: Black ostrich herl

BODY: Rear third, yellow floss; fore two-thirds, green floss

RIB: Oval silver tinsel over entire body

HACKLE: Green over fore two-thirds of body

THROAT: Yellow hackle collar

WING: A few strands of golden pheasant tippet covered with green and yellow bucktail

CHEEK: Jungle cock

HEAD: Black

Salmon fly hooks are generally japanned black and have a looped-up eye. Hook style, in itself, is almost classic. In the case of standard patterns, like the above, the most common hook in the United States is the Mustad 36890. Place a size 4 in your vise.

Spiral some black thread onto the shank, starting just before the bend and winding to it.

We are going to tie on our materials in the order in which they are listed. Use only enough material to do the job it is intended for. This is very important in tying salmon flies because of the number of materials.

First tie in the tag of flat silver tinsel. All you will need is a section 2 to 3 inches long.

Hold one end of the tinsel diagonally between the hook shank and the thread. With the bobbin bind down the tinsel. Four turns of thread should secure it.

Grasp the tinsel, and wind to the rear, away from you, into the bend and then back to the thread. Secure the tinsel with the thread, and clip the excess. Your tag should be approximately one-eighth inch long (see Figure 2).

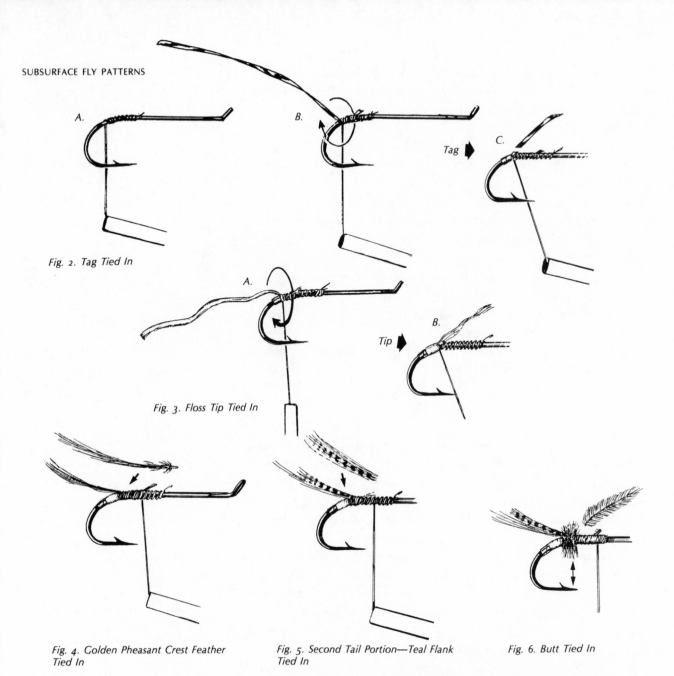

Fig. 2. Tag Tied In

Fig. 3. Floss Tip Tied In

Fig. 4. Golden Pheasant Crest Feather
Tied In

Fig. 5. Second Tail Portion—Teal Flank
Tied In

Fig. 6. Butt Tied In

Cut a single strand of pale yellow floss, and tie that in where you left
off with the tinsel (the area where the excess tinsel was clipped away).

Let your thread dangle from the bobbin for now. Grasp the floss, and
again wind to the rear, covering part of the tinsel tip. Only one-sixteenth
of an inch of the tinsel should be exposed. Wind the floss forward to the
point where you left your thread. Bind down the floss with the thread, and

clip the excess. The floss should extend to a point on the shank almost directly above the point of the hook (see Figure 3).

The tail is the next piece of material to be tied in. It is made from a single crest feather of a golden pheasant. Crest feathers have a natural curve. You want to tie it in so that the feather curves up, away from the down curve of the hook bend.

You will find, as you try to tie in some of these feathers, that they have a tendency to slip or twist because they are so smooth. If they should misbehave, try wetting them with a bit of saliva. Just moisten your thumb and forefinger and dab the saliva on the feathers. Don't put the feathers into your mouth unless you are absolutely certain they are clean. If you are overly concerned about germs, use some water.

Once you have wet the crest feather, place it on top of the hook shank at that point where you left your thread idling after you clipped the excess floss. Again, the tip should curve away from the bend of the hook and should mirror its bend.

Take one turn of thread around the crest feather and the hook shank, and *pull straight up.* Take two additional turns of thread in the same area to secure. Clip the excess butt section (see Figure 4).

The second part of the dual tail consists of a few fibers of teal or wood duck flank. They are measured and tied in on top of the crest but cover only half the distance to the tip of the crest feather. They are tied on in exactly the same area (see Figure 5).

The butt of ostrich herl is now tied in. During this procedure take three turns of black ostrich herl directly over the area where the tail was secured, and wind slightly forward, covering this area (see Figures 6 and 7).

When the tag, tip, tail, and butt are tied in and secured, which in themselves are extremely simple operations, the butt should lie directly over the point of the hook. In other words, you should be able to place a straightedge at a right angle to the hook shank and its edge should line up perfectly with the ostrich herl butt on the shank and the point of the hook below (check Figure 1 for the parts of a salmon fly).

You may also have noticed that as material was tied in, it covered the exposed tie-down area of the preceding operation. This principle will hold true throughout the pattern.

Fig. 7. Tag, Tip, Tail, and Butt Secured

The ribbing for the body must be tied in now, though it will be wound when the body has been completed. For a salmon fly of this size, a medium oval silver tinsel is required. Oval tinsel is made by winding tinsel over a cotton core.

Take a 5-inch strip of tinsel, and remove the metallic covering from one end. Expose a core of cotton about an eighth of an inch long. The tinsel is tied to the shank of the hook by binding down the cotton core, thus preventing unnecessary bulk at the tie-in area. Tie the tinsel section directly in front of the butt (see Figure 8). Occasionally you'll come across some oval tinsel which tends to unravel as you wind it around the body of a fly, thereby exposing the core. To prevent this, simply dip a rag into a bottle of vinyl cement, and brush the tinsel with it prior to use. If I'm tying a number of flies of the same pattern, I will coat a foot or two of the tinsel with the cement. Vinyl dries very fast, and oval tinsel treated with it will be ready for use in approximately five minutes. Some tiers prefer to dip the exposed core into a bottle of cement before tying it to the shank. This prevents slippage and can also keep the tinsel from unraveling during the first turn around the body.

Once the tinsel has been secured to the shank, it should be placed in a material clip, out of the way.

The body of this pattern is two-toned, with the rear third yellow floss and the fore two-thirds green floss. Though not overly bulky or heavily wound, the body of this pattern should have some substance. There are many types of flosses on the market. My own preference for salmon and streamer fly bodies is single-strand acetate floss. It builds fast and smoothly and winds evenly.

I should add here that the types of floss used by fly tiers vary greatly, and which is best for a given fly is pretty much a matter of opinion. When you come right down to it, the type that does the best job for you is the best one for you.

All flosses, whether rayon or silk, are soft-fibered and tend to fray as they are being wound. In order to prevent this, wet the tips of your thumb and fingers as you work with the floss. You'll be surprised how easy it becomes. (As you wet the floss, you will find that it changes color. This is normal. Most materials darken when they are wet. When it is dry, the floss will return to its original shade.)

Cut a section of yellow floss approximately 4–5 inches long, and tie it in a little above, or in front of, where you tied in your tinsel ribbing. Wind it slightly to the rear, covering any exposed bulky portions which may have been created by the tinsel and the ostrich herl butt, and then wind it forward, building a very slight taper. You have to cover only one-third of the hook shank with it. After you do this, clip the excess floss (see Figure 9).

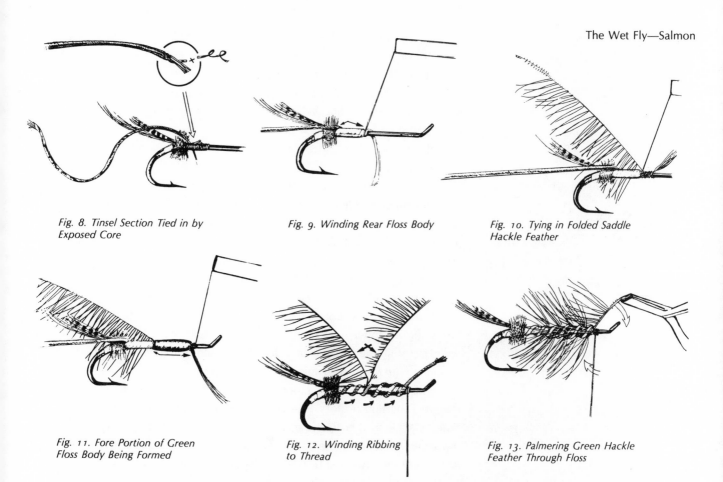

Fig. 8. Tinsel Section Tied in by Exposed Core

Fig. 9. Winding Rear Floss Body

Fig. 10. Tying in Folded Saddle Hackle Feather

Fig. 11. Fore Portion of Green Floss Body Being Formed

Fig. 12. Winding Ribbing to Thread

Fig. 13. Palmering Green Hackle Feather Through Floss

The fore portion of the Green Highlander has a green hackle palmered through it all the way to the throat. This must be tied in before we proceed with the green floss.

For the hackle I prefer an Indian saddle cape which has been dyed a fresh spring grass green. This shade is on the light side, but bright. The reason for an Indian saddle cape is simply that domestic saddles or rooster necks generally do not come in the proper size range. In addition, Indian saddle hackle feathers seem to fold and behave a little better.

In the previous chapter we learned how to fold a hackle and tie it in by the tip, not the butt. Do this now, using a hackle feather on which the barbules are as long as the gap of the hook is wide. It should be tied in at the point where you secured your yellow floss (see Figure 10). The green saddle hackle feather, like the tinsel, will remain idle while we complete the rest of the floss body.

137

Fig. 14. Completed Body, Rib, and Hackle of Green Highlander

The front two-thirds of the body is formed with a shade of floss as close to the color of the saddle hackle as possible (don't worry about a perfect match, however; that's unlikely).

Cut a 5- to 6-inch section of green floss, and tie it in just forward of the saddle hackle feather. Wind it to the rear, connecting with the yellow floss, and then forward in an even, continuous taper all the way to that part of the hook shank where the looped portion of the eye begins (see Figure 11).

At this point the body on this pattern has been formed, but the tinsel rib and palmer hackle are still hanging idly from the fly. Which one shall we wind forward first? If you took the hackle and formed the palmer, you would have difficulty ribbing the tinsel through all those fibers, wouldn't you? This may sound like just plain common sense, and it is, but would you believe that is what I did five minutes ago? Yes, I had to retie that portion of our Green Highlander.

The ribbing is wound to the thread first. It should be in an open spiral, consisting of about five turns. As you approach the protruding hackle feather, just lift the feather out of the way (manipulate it fore and aft), and continue with your even spirals (see Figure 12).

Now we're ready to palmer our green saddle hackle feather through the green portion of floss. The easiest way is to grip the butt end of the saddle hackle feather with a pair of hackle pliers. Wind the hackle to the thread *while stroking the hackle fibers to the rear with your left thumb and forefinger.* This will help make the hackle behave and lie to the rear as it is supposed to for this pattern.

The turns of hackle feather should be between the turns of tinsel ribbing previously wound on. On reaching the thread, tie down the hackle feather, securing it, and clip the excess (see Figures 13 and 14).

In addition to the palmered hackle, the Green Highlander also calls for a throat tied as a hackle collar. It can be made of either a saddle or neck hackle feather which has been dyed a bright light yellow. It, too, is folded, tied in by the tip, and wound on as you would the collar of any ordinary wet fly. Make believe you are tying a Leadwing Coachman at this point. The fibers of the throat collar should be slightly longer than the saddle hackle fibers which were used for palmering (see Figure 15).

We are now ready to tackle the wing, which is not unlike that of a bucktail fly. It consists of three parts: six to ten strands of golden pheasant tippet, ten to 12 fibers of green bucktail, and ten to 12 fibers of yellow bucktail.

The golden pheasant tippet fibers must be taken from a fairly large feather, otherwise they will not be long enough to reach and align with the tip of the tail on the fly. Cut a section of six fibers from one of the golden pheasant tippet feathers.

Measure them along the top of the hook shank so that the tips of the tippets extend to the tip of the tail. Tie them in directly on top of the hook shank just a smidgeon in front of the tie-down point of the throat hackle collar (see Figure 16).

Now comes the green and yellow bucktail. However, if you don't have bucktail or if you would prefer to use calf tail dyed the same shade, by all means do so. If anything, calf tail will behave better since it is not as coarse or hollow. As we've learned, most deer hairs have a tendency to flare, even those from the tail. Therefore, if you do use bucktail, try to find some that is soft and fine. It will make life a little easier for you when tying on a salmon fly wing.

From a bright green dyed bucktail, snip a section of fibers approximately one-third of a matchstick in diameter. Align the tips. Tie them in on top of the hook shank over the previously secured golden pheasant tippet fibers (see Figure 17). Repeat this using the same amount of yellow

Fig. 15. Throat Hackle Collar

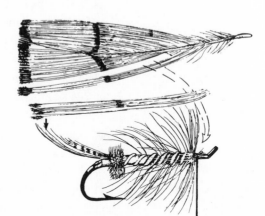

Fig. 16. Tying in Golden Pheasant Tippets for Wing

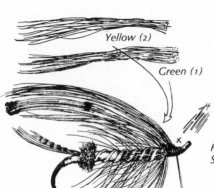

Yellow (2)

Green (1)

Fig. 17. Green and Yellow Bucktail Wings Secured in Two Stages and Staggered

bucktail or calf tail. Tie these fibers on top of the green. The tips of both should be as long as the golden pheasant tippets.

As you clip the excess butts of your bucktail, try to clip the green section a little closer to the eye than the yellow. This will give you a staggered effect and help you attain a natural taper with your thread when you form the head of the fly during the last operation.

All that remains to dress up your fly for the fair are the cheeks of jungle cock eyes. Here you may have a real problem, since the jungle cock is now protected. Nevertheless, there is so much sentiment attached to the jungle cock eye that for some tiers its inclusion is a must.

If you do not have natural jungle cock eyes, by all means use an imitation. There are a few supply houses that carry a very good one. Or you can use a lacquered quail or starling body feather. If you have the real thing, this is how you would tie it on as a cheek for this pattern. Select two medium-sized jungle cock eyed feathers. Note that they seem to have three spots of yellow—the large eye, a smaller one, and, last, a touch of yellow. At the point where the small oblong streak of yellow begins, stroke back the fibers of the jungle cock nail, separating them from the main eyed portion (it's just like separating a dry fly hackle feather before trimming). This is going to be the tie-in point on the feather.

With your dubbing needle put a small drop of head lacquer on the underside of the jungle cock feather where you separated the fiber. It will help keep the slippery nail feather in place. Place one of the nail feathers against the wing and tie-in area at the same upward angle as the wing. Tie it in (see Figure 18). Make sure the hackle is well secured with thread and will not slip out of position (hackles have a tendency to do this).

Repeat the procedure on the far side of the hook shank with the other jungle cock feather, aligning it so that it matches the first one. That's all there is to tying in the cheek.

Once all the materials on the Highlander are secured, you have to build a neatly tapered head with your thread. If you have been careful and cut the excess butts of the tied-in wing materials at a slant (that is, staggered

Fig. 18. Jungle Cock Cheeks Being Tied In

the cutting), it will be fairly easy to taper the head. If you have not been careful, some lumps may tell on you, even after the final lacquering.

To taper a trim cone-shaped head, you only have to place the turns of thread carefully so there will be a smooth flow of thread from the wing and throat area to the eye. After the whip finish a few coats of black varnish should achieve the desired effect—a smooth and glossy head. Your completed Green Highlander should resemble Figure 19.

Fig. 19. Completed Green Highlander Hairwing

"MARRIED" WINGS

You have just learned to tie one of the most popular contemporary salmon hairwing flies, derived from a classic pattern. This pattern alone will give you the inside "how to" on most of the contemporary salmon patterns.

Still you may say to me, "I want to tie a brooch," or "I want a fly for framing; how do you fully dress a classic pattern?"

Okay. If you look over a list of classic salmon fly patterns, you will see that all of them are different, yet there are a few things they all have in common. Only one procedure is top priority as far as technique is concerned—"marrying" wings. If you insist on tying traditional flies, you must know this technique.

Married wings are simply this: Two or more sections of like or unlike feather fibers from such wing quills as goose, turkey, or duck are joined (hinged) to form a single two-toned or multishaded wing. In a nutshell this covers it all. But how do you do it? Perhaps it can best be explained this way. Imagine every feather fiber with a row of sawtoothed edges on either side. You can't see them, but they are there.

Or ask yourself this. What keeps the fibers on a duck or goose quill joined? Why do you have to pry them apart with the point of a pair of scissors? They are not wet, and they aren't impregnated with glue or resin. No, nature has locked these fibers with these sawtoothed edges.

Take a single duck or goose feather. Pull the fibers apart. Now take the feather as a unit, and stroke the fibers from the base to the tip. They fall back into place together. That's what marrying wings is all about—making the sections of quill mesh their edges.

Married units are made by snipping equal sections from matched left and right wing quill feathers. In other words, if you wanted to make the wing for the classic Green Highlander, it would consist of yellow swan,

141

green swan, and mottled brown turkey. Two sections of each would be made, one for the right side of your fly and one for the left.

Note that the classic Highlander calls for swan, a feather you cannot purchase because of wildlife restrictions. Goose wing quills, dyed the same shade, will do just fine.

If you've read this far, you are probably interested in attempting a classic pattern. Therefore, we'll marry one wing section so you can see how really simple this old salmon-tying secret is.

Cut a section of fiber almost an eighth of an inch wide from three right and three left wing quill feathers of yellow goose, green goose, and brown turkey. Lay the green section on top of the yellow one, fiber to fiber, but do not let its tip reach the tip of the yellow one.

With the fingertips and thumb of your free hand, stroke the upper fiber gently toward the tip to align it; in other words, slide the top section along the bottom one until the tips appear to be one. The sawtoothed edges of the fibers seem to mesh better when they are forced forward rather than backward. Sometimes a little sliding back and forth will get the fibers to lock, but the final push should be forward.

Once the green and yellow goose sections have been joined, the turkey section is laid on top of them, and the procedure is repeated until you have what looks like one feather ranging from yellow to green to mottled brown.

You have now completed half of the wing for the classic Green Highlander. Repeat the procedure for the other wing. When both units have been assembled, they are tied in, forming the wing section of the pattern. Neither cement nor glue is used to marry a wing. Check Figure 20 for details.

Salmon fly wings are tied on in a semi-tent. They are usually used as a veil to cover an underwing of sorts.

"Veil" is a term that means just what it says—cover a part of the pattern that has already been tied in. "Sheath" is another term you will run into. It is similar to veil but refers to a previously tied-in material.

Both veils and sheaths form part of what is listed as the wing of the pattern. They are never listed by themselves in the pattern description.

Two more salmon fly patterns are included in this chapter, one because of its unusual construction and the other because it is tied on a double

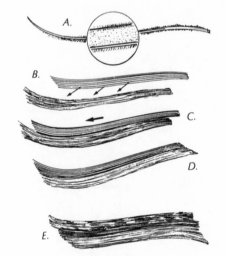

Fig. 20. Marrying Wings

hook. Both patterns are among the most popular and successful flies used in the rivers today.

BUTTERFLY

At first glance the Butterfly, an extremely popular salmon pattern, does not appear difficult to tie. I'm afraid, however, that it will fool you. Since this is a wet fly, you'd think the wings would be tied in last, which would normally be the case. Not so. They are tied in first. No problem, right? Wrong again—that is, if you try to tie them in completely. Actually they are tied in and later tied down. Does that confuse you a little? I hope so, because I don't relish being the only tier who has been confronted by this dilemma. Why don't we tie one and solve the Butterfly riddle?

BUTTERFLY
   WING: White goat hair, sparse
   TAIL: Red hackle fibers
   BODY: Peacock herl
   HACKLE: Brown

We shall need a Mustad model 36890 hook in size 12 and some fine black thread.

Spiral your thread onto the shank of the hook beginning just behind the eye and forming a bed of thread about an eighth of an inch long.

From a piece of white goatskin cut a rather sparse clump of about 20 fibers, which, when tied in, will stand higher than the shank is long. If you do not have any goat hair, use calf tail or bucktail, preferably in a fine graded variety if you can locate some.

Goat hair is a very soft fiber to tie with, yet it retains its stiffness. A good piece of goat hair should taper well. It should not be brittle or have broken tips. You'll know when you have the proper piece of goat hair. It's beautiful to work with and looks very neat and straight. You'll actually feel the difference as your fingers handle it.

Tie in your clump of goat hair exactly as you would a clump of calf tail for a White Wulff dry fly. Make a figure 8 and reverse 8 to divide the clump into two equal parts. Clip the excess butts (see Figure 21).

Bring your thread to the bend of the hook.

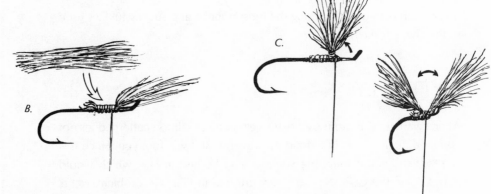

Fig. 21. Wings Tied In

From a dyed red rooster or saddle cape, select a feather with fairly long fibers. Clip a dozen or so, and tie them in as your tail. The tail on this pattern should be approximately one-quarter of an inch long.

Select three long and full peacock herl quills from an eyed tail that has a bronze, as opposed to the usual olive green, cast. Tie all three in at the bend of the hook simultaneously.

Wind your thread forward to a point directly behind the wings. Grasp two of the peacock quills, and wind them in connecting spirals to the thread. Bind the two down with the thread. When they have been secured, wind the thread in an open spiral to the bend and back again to a point directly behind the wings. (This is the same method that was used in reinforcing the body of the Leadwing Coachman. The only difference is that here we are working with three quills instead of two.)

Grasp the third and last peacock quill, and wind it along the wing where the thread is waiting to secure it. This last quill, covering the two previously reinforced quills, will give us the movement and action we need. Clip the excess ends (see Figure 22).

Up to this point the tying operations have been fairly conventional. But now we have to make the wing, which was tied in earlier, slant backward to look like a living butterfly. The natural tendency of the wing is to lean forward toward the eye of the hook because of the manner in which it was tied in. We don't want to destroy that tendency since it will make the fly undulate when it is fished.

Therefore take the thread in the bobbin, which was left just behind the wing, in your right hand. With the thumb and forefinger of your left hand, grab the far wing section. In a clockwise motion encircle the base of the fibers you are holding *three times while pulling and slanting the*

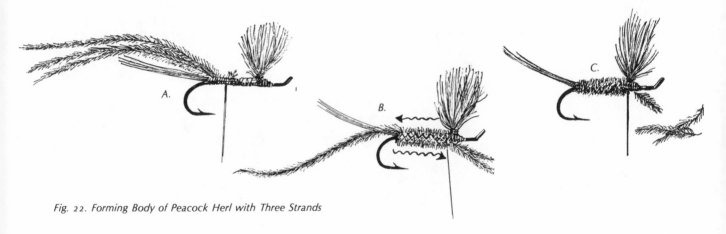

Fig. 22. Forming Body of Peacock Herl with Three Strands

fibers backward toward the bend of the hook. As you make the turns, you will find that your left thumb and forefinger are in the way. You have to release the section of fibers each time the thread passes and then grasp them once more, always pulling backward. You will see, as each turn is made, that the fibers are being locked into position (see Figure 23).

When you have completed the turns on the far section, bring the thread toward you, through the division of the wing, and, *in a counter-clockwise motion,* encircle the base of the wing section near you with three turns of thread. Again, pull and slant the wing section toward the rear as you make the turns (see Figure 24).

When you have completed the turns on the near section, bring your thread *through the division of the wing* for one more turn down, under, and around the hook shank, and bring it in front of the wing (see Figures 25 and 26).

The wings will still have a tendency to lean forward. Place a drop of vinyl cement into the division of the wing fibers. It will help keep them in place.

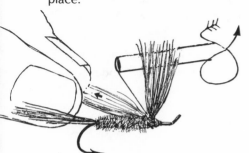

Fig. 23. Winding Thread Around
Far Wing Section

Fig. 24. Slanting and Tying Down Near Wing

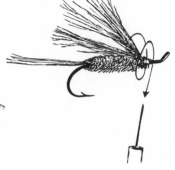

Fig. 25. Securing Wing

145

Fig. 26. Butterfly Wing Tied Back
Fig. 27. Completed Butterfly

The final step in this pattern is the hackle collar. If you try to tie it in as you would an ordinary wet fly, you are going to have trouble. *Tie the brown hackle collar in as you would for a conventional dry fly.* That is, trim the butts of one brown hackle. Tie it in diagonally *in front of the wing.* Take two turns of hackle in back of the wing and two turns in front of it.

As you wind your hackle, stroke the fibers backward so that they lie and behave in the proper wet fly fashion. Don't worry if they stand a little more erect than is usual for a subsurface pattern. This will enhance the performance of this fly.

Complete the pattern by winding a neat head. Whip finish and lacquer. A completed Butterfly is shown in Figure 27.

BLUE CHARM (LOW-WATER DOUBLE)

The Blue Charm differs from other salmon flies for two reasons. First, the pattern is tied on a double hook, which is used very often in salmon fishing, and second, it is tied in a style used for low-water conditions, which in this case means that you tie your materials on the fore portion of the hook only and keep them short and sparse.

If you have never tied a low-water fly, it will throw all your proportions out of whack, at least during your first attempts. You'll find that what you thought was short enough is still too long.

BLUE CHARM   (Low-water double)
   TAG: Flat silver tinsel
   TAIL: Golden pheasant crest
   BODY: Black floss

Fig. 28. Tip and Tail Secured

Fig. 29. Body and Rib Completed

RIB: Fine oval silver tinsel

THROAT: Light blue hackle

WING: Bronze mallard, teal flank, golden pheasant crest

HEAD: Black

The English double hook in size 6 will do nicely for our project. Thread, of course, is fine black.

When you place your hook in the vise, you'll find that you have to tilt the angle of the barrel and rotate the stem a bit in order to align the hook in the jaws properly. You fix the near hook of the double in the vise.

The thread is spiraled onto the hook shank, ending at the center.

A small strip of flat silver tinsel is cut and tied in as the tag in the usual manner.

A tail of golden pheasant crest is tied in, curving up. The tip of the feather should not quite reach the bends of the hook (see Figure 28).

The silver oval tinsel is tied in at this point and left hanging.

Black body floss is tied in just above the oval tinsel, wound to the rear for a smooth connection, and then wound forward to the eye. The taper and bulk of floss are held to a minimum.

The rib is now spiraled through the floss and secured (see Figure 29).

The throat, a fairly short one, is tied in next. The easiest way to tie it in and save a lot of exasperation is simply to turn the hook upside down in the vise and proceed to tie it in. Here all that is required is about a dozen dyed light blue rooster hackle fibers which are tied to the shank as you would a calf tail or bucktail wing. The tips should extend to the rear approximately one-quarter of the length of the hook shank.

If the throat will not stand out properly for you, take one or two turns of thread *under* the fibers as you bind it down while winding over. These

147

turns will force the fibers up (down once the hook has been returned to its normal position; see Figure 30).

The hook is now returned to its natural position in the vise.

The wing consists of three parts—bronze mallard, teal flank, and golden pheasant crest. If you have trouble getting either the bronze mallard or the teal flank, then wood duck or dyed imitation wood duck and mallard flank will do just fine.

Bronze mallard comes from a drake. The feathers are found on the back of the bird near the wing (shoulder) area, and there are usually only six of them on a prime bird. The color is a rich rusty bronze with a barred effect.

Take one of these feathers, and after aligning the tips, cut a quarter-inch section from the feather. Roll the fibers into one solid clump, and place it along the top of the hook shank so that the tip extends three-quarters of the way to the hook bend. Tie the fibers in.

Now snip a much smaller section of teal fibers, and tie them in directly over the bronze mallard clump. Finally select another golden crest feather, and tie that in as a topping. It should curve in a downward slant over the previously tied in mallard and teal fibers. After the head has been neatly tapered with thread, apply a coat of glossy black lacquer.

A completed Blue Charm (low-water double) appears in Figure 31.

Having learned these salmon wet flies, here is a list of some of the more popular flies you should now be able to tie:

BLACK BOMBER

    TAG: Silver tinsel

    TIP: Yellow floss

    TAIL: Golden pheasant crest

    BODY: Black wool

    RIB: Oval silver tinsel

    HACKLE: Black neck or saddle hackle

    WING: Black bear hair

    CHEEKS: Jungle cock

    TOPPING: Golden pheasant crest

    HEAD: Black

Fig. 30. Tying in Throat and Forcing Fibers Down

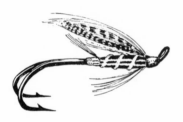

Fig. 31. Completed Blue Charm

THE RAT

TAG: Flat gold tinsel

BODY: Peacock herl

WING: Mixed black and white calf tail

HACKLE: Badger

HEAD: Black

RUSTY RAT

TAG: Flat gold tinsel

TAIL: Four or five peacock sword fibers

BODY: Rear third, orange floss; fore two-thirds, one-half orange floss
followed by peacock herl. In the division of the two orange
floss sections, an extra strand forms a second tail tied down
so that it extends half the length of the peacock sword tail
fibers

WING: Gray fox guard hairs

HACKLE: Badger or furnace

HEAD: Black

SQUIRREL TAIL

TAG: Silver tinsel

TAIL: Golden pheasant crest

BODY: Black seal fur

RIB: Fine oval silver tinsel

HACKLE: Brown neck or saddle hackle

WING: Fox squirrel tail

HEAD: Black

COSSEBOOM

TAG: Silver tinsel

TAIL: Olive floss, short

BODY: Medium olive floss

RIB: Oval silver tinsel

WING: Gray squirrel tail

HACKLE: Light yellow hackle collar

CHEEKS: Jungle cock

HEAD: Red

RED BUTT

TAG: Gold tinsel

TIP: Fluorescent red floss

BODY: Black floss

RIB: Oval silver tinsel

HACKLE: Black

WING: Black bear

HEAD: Black

ORANGE BLOSSOM

TAG: Silver tinsel

TIP: Orange floss

TAIL: Golden pheasant crest half covered with red hackle fibers

BUTT: Black ostrich herl

BODY: Embossed silver tinsel palmered with yellow hackle

RIB: Oval silver tinsel

WING: Light brown natural bucktail

HACKLE: Bright orange hackle feathers wound as a collar

HEAD: Black

ORIOLE

TAIL: Golden pheasant red body feather fibers

BODY: Black wool

RIB: Fine oval silver tinsel with two turns taken under tail to form a tag

THROAT: Brown hackle wound as collar and pulled down

WING: Golden pheasant brown/red body feathers; over and surrounding these are four (two on each side) mallard flank sections dyed green drake

HEAD: Black

SILVER RAT

TAG: Flat gold tinsel

TAIL: Golden pheasant crest

BODY: Flat silver tinsel

RIB: Oval gold tinsel

WING: Gray fox guard hairs, sparse

HACKLE: Grizzly hackle wound as collar

CHEEKS: Jungle cock tied short or substitute (optional)

HEAD: Red

11

Nymphs

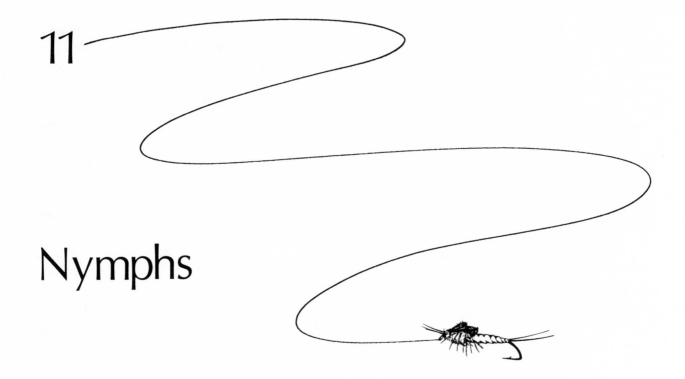

If someone were to ask me what I thought the most important ingredient in a nymph imitation was, I would answer, "Life."

I suppose I've said the same thing about dry and wet flies, and I will probably say it again in the appropriate places for bucktails and streamers. Yet important as a lifelike appearance is for all types of flies, it is almost crucial for nymphs.

Nymph fishing is like worm fishing—an art. Don't laugh. It's true. If you don't believe me, seek out an acknowledged bait-fishing expert. Try to beat him at his own game, and see how you fare. Proper nymph fishing is not easy. It takes many seasons to develop the subtleties involved, for I'm not talking about the "chucking and chance it" method, where the line is cast across stream and a few trout are hooked on the sweep or down-current eddy. I'm talking about an upstream cast, a completely drag-free float, and the setting of the hook the moment a trout has inhaled it, before he spits it out. If you take trout consistently using this method, you are a nymph fisherman.

Why do I go to all this trouble about nymphing methods when we're concerned here with tying them? Because I'm trying to drive a point home. If you do become, or are, an accomplished nymph fisherman, why defeat your own purpose by using a pattern that has been improperly tied—in other words, one that does not have life? Remember, there is a difference between looking like the real thing or being like the natural (alive). If exact imitations worked, someone could make a fortune mass-producing nymphs simply by using a plastic mold. After all, anything can be duplicated this way. I might add that this has been tried. It does not work.

Yes, we are going to learn how to tie nymphs. After you have learned the techniques, you may wish to experiment with your own imitations, which is as it should be. This is why I want to impress you again with one thought: Create and improvise to your heart's desire, but make your fly look alive.

The bodies and tails of many modern nymph patterns are similar in appearance and tying procedure to the wet fly. Where they differ completely and constantly is in the thorax, or wing, area. A good nymph pattern for basic design and effectiveness when fished is the March Brown Nymph. It's a good one to get your feet wet on.

My own favorite version of this pattern is the one used by Art Flick of Westkill, New York:

MARCH BROWN NYMPH
> TAIL: Three fibers from ringneck pheasant center tail
> BODY: Amber seal mixed with fawn fox fur
> RIB: Single strand of brown embroidery cotton
> WING CASE: Section from ringneck pheasant short tail
> LEGS: Partridge hackle

For these patterns long-shanked hooks like the Mustad 9671–2XL, 9672–3XL, or 79580–4XL are used, size depending on the type of nymph. For some of the stoneflies a 6XL such as the Mustad 9575 is occasionally recommended. The perfect model for our purpose is the 9671. Place a size 12 in your vise.

Spiral some fine brown or gray thread onto the shank of the hook, beginning just before, and winding to, the bend.

The tail of the March Brown Nymph is made from three fibers from the center tail of a ringneck pheasant. You'll notice as you pry these fibers apart that they do, indeed, have markings very similar to the natural nymph we are imitating (see Figure 1).

Lay one of the fibers directly on top of the hook shank with the curve of the fiber pointing down and the tip extending beyond the bend. Tie it down with one or two turns of thread. The tail itself should be approximately as long as the hook shank.

Take the next fiber, and place it against the side of the hook shank nearer you. Tie it in with the curve of the fiber coming toward you. It should be as long as the first fiber tied in.

Repeat the procedure with the last fiber, on the far side of the shank, this time with the curve flaring away from you. Use as few turns of thread as necessary. Your triple-fibered tail should look like Figure 2.

Fig. 1. Three Fibers Separated Prior to Cutting

If for any reason you have a problem getting a spread, or flared, separation of the pheasant fibers, use the little trick, described in Chapter 8 for thorax and compara hatch flies, of tying in a minute amount of body fur first. This allows the fibers to crunch down in the soft material and thus flare out and separate naturally.

Once the butts of the fibers have been secured, clip the excess. Your thread should still be near the bend of the hook.

Take a 6-inch piece of brown embroidery cotton, and tie it in as you would any rib of tinsel. If you cannot locate any embroidery thread, just take a fairly heavy thread, such as a size A, and use that for your rib. This choice is not critical. For now place the embroidery thread into your material clip, and forget it.

The body and thorax of this nymph imitation call for a blend of fawn-colored fox fur and amber seal. The color fawn is just that. Picture a young deer with its soft red/tan fur, and you'll see the shade.

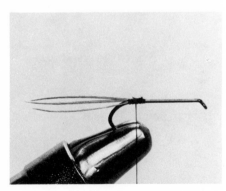

Fig. 2. Triple Tail Tied In

The second half of the blend, amber seal fur, is a rich yellow/orange. Picture an amber light. If, however, you cannot get seal fur—seals are a protected species—you can, in this instance, substitute the same shade of dyed polypropylene yarn, preferably precut. Lacking that, you will have to cut and chop your own yarn, which is a bit of extra work.

You are now ready to mix the fur. And, as long as you are mixing, why not mix a substantial amount so that you will have enough for a number of flies? The March Brown is a popular nymph, and you're just being economical by increasing the quantity of the blend.

To arrive at the right shade, blend equal amounts of fox and amber seal (or poly yarn) fur cuttings. If you own a blender, the chore will be quick and efficient. If you don't, you'll have to throw the clippings into a jar of water and shake. The mass can then be squeezed damp dry and placed on newspaper until fully dry. A little fluffing and puffing now and then helps.

To form the body of your nymph, the noodle method of dubbing is recommended. If you have forgotten this procedure, go back and check it in Chapter 9.

Once your noodle has been formed, wind your thread approximately two-thirds of the hook shank toward the eye. Wind your fur noodle to the thread, and secure it with the thread.

Take the brown embroidery thread from the material clip, and wind it forward in an open spiral, forming the rib and segmenting the body. Clip the excess.

The wing case is *tied in* next but *formed* later. It consists of a section of fibers taken from one of the shorter tail feathers of the ringneck pheasant. This feather is more mottled than the center tail feathers, and it is the mottling which gives the wing case the proper coloration. Snip a section about three-sixteenths of an inch wide from it. With the glossy side of the feather up, lay the section on top of the hook shank with the tip extending toward the eye just past the point where the thread is hanging from the bobbin. Tie it in at the tip (see Figure 3). Forget about the wing case for now. It will lean back completely out of the way.

The next procedure is the tying in of the partridge hackle feather, which will eventually become the legs of our nymph. When the term partridge hackle is used, it generally refers to a body feather of the English and Scottish grouse. This seems a little unfair to the so-called American partridge, which is actually a ruffed grouse, an entirely different bird. The feathers of the English and Scottish birds have a more distinct barring and are preferred to the American species. Unfortunately, since grouse, or partridge, is considered a wild bird, it cannot be imported. Therefore, you may have some difficulty in finding this feather. There are a few supply houses that have a handful of them and if you can get them, by all means do so. If you can't, substitution is in order. In this case it does not present too much of a problem. Besides other wild birds with similar markings, many domestic and imported hen necks have, at their base, barred and mottled body feathers. There are many variations, and all are suitable for various nymphs.

The coloration of the partridge feather used for the March Brown

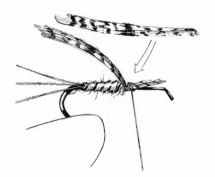

Fig. 3. Section of Short Pheasant Tail Tied in for Wing Case

Nymph is not unlike that of the wood duck flank feather. The shade and barring are just slightly darker.

Before we can tie in our partridge hackle, it must be prepared. You do this by holding the feather by the tip and stroking the main portion of fibers backward, thus forming a separation between the tip and the rest of the feather (see Figure 4).

With the dull side, or underside, of the partridge hackle facing up, lay it on top of the hook shank with the tip of the feather pointing toward the eye of the hook and the place where you separated the feather fiber directly over the thread, which is dangling from your bobbin. Tie it down in this position (see Figure 5). For now forget about the partridge feather, which is relaxing with the wing case pheasant section.

It is time to build the thorax.

Take some blended dubbing, and make another noodle. Wind it around the remainder of the exposed hook shank. As you build the thorax with the fur noodle, allow some of the turns to hug the wing case and leg feather. This will form a slight hump when they are pulled forward later.

Build the thorax so that it is approximately twice the thickness of the body (see Figure 6). After the thorax has been formed, leave the thread hanging just behind the eye of the hook.

With your right thumb and forefinger, grasp the partridge hackle feather, and pull it forward, straight out over the eye of the hook. While the feather is fairly taut, take the bobbin with your left hand, and make two or three turns of thread over it and between the fibers, fastening it to the shank (see Figure 7). Clip the excess butt.

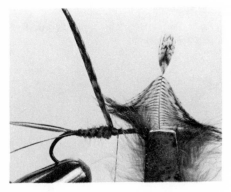

Fig. 4. Prepared Partridge Hackle

Fig. 5. Securing Partridge Feather

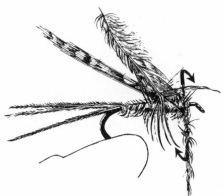

Fig. 6. Building Thorax Area

Fig. 7. Pulling Partridge Hackle Forward and Tying It Down

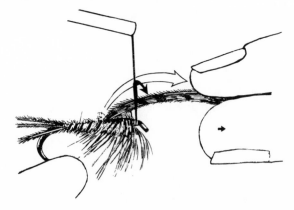

Fig. 8. Pulling Wing Case Feather Forward and Tying It Down

Now grasp the wing case, and pull it forward in the same manner. Hold it taut with your right hand, and tie it down with the bobbin in your left hand (see Figures 8 and 9).

Pulling the wing case forward over the previously secured partridge feather will force the partridge fibers down to form "legs." Clip the excess wing case fibers.

Taper a small head with your thread, winding up to, then just over, the eye joint and ending with a whip finish knot. Lacquer the top of the wing case with vinyl cement.

Using the March Brown Nymph as our model has given us a chance to incorporate most of the procedures used in a conventional nymph, as well as some of the more difficult maneuvers. There are many nymphs that will be easier to tie. One example is the Dark Hendrickson Nymph:

Fig. 9. Wing Case Tied Down

DARK HENDRICKSON NYMPH
    TAIL: Wood duck flank fibers
    BODY: Muskrat
    RIB: Fine silver wire
    THORAX: Muskrat
    WING CASE: Dark brown duck or goose quill
    LEGS: Wood duck flank fibers

For this pattern the tail is tied on in the conventional wet fly method. The body and thorax are simply straight dubbed muskrat. The wing case is the same as the March Brown. The legs are tied in the conventional "beard" style of a wet fly—that is, under the hook shank. Figure 10 gives us an idea of what a completed Dark Hendrickson should look like.

Instead of a wing case, some nymphs have what is called a wing pad. This is simplicity itself. A good example of a nymph with a wing pad is the Light Cahill:

Fig. 10. Completed Dark Hendrickson Nymph

LIGHT CAHILL NYMPH

TAIL: Wood duck flank fibers

BODY: Cream fur tapered through thorax

LEGS: Wood duck flank fibers

WING PAD: Mallard flank or breast feather cut short

You should know how to tie all the parts of this pattern, but if the word wing "pad" leaves you pondering, here is how you make one.

Pluck a well-marked mallard breast or flank feather. Separate the tip from the rest of the fibers. With a pair of scissors cut the tip of the feather at a right angle so that the edge is straight. After being squared off, some wing pads have a slight V-shaped indentation cut into them. Check Figure 11. A completed Light Cahill Nymph should look like the one in Figure 12.

Fig. 11. Making a Wing Pad

What is the most popular nymph fished in the United States? You won't be far from wrong if you answer, "The easiest one to tie."

One of the easiest and truly most popular flies is the Muskrat Nymph. Here are two pattern descriptions for it, one easier than the other.

MUSKRAT NYMPH (1)

TAIL: Blue dun hackle fibers

BODY AND THORAX: Muskrat fur built to a gradual taper

HACKLE: Dark dun hackle fibers

MUSKRAT NYMPH (2)

TAIL: None

BODY AND THORAX: Gradual taper of muskrat dubbing

HEAD: Black ostrich (or peacock herl)

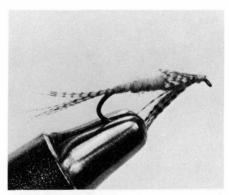

Fig. 12. Completed Light Cahill Nymph

With the procedures and the techniques learned from the nymphs we have just tied and your knowledge of wet flies, it is possible to tie these nymph patterns without further instruction:

OTTER NYMPH

TAIL: Wood duck flank fibers

BODY: Brown otter fur tapered through thorax

WING CASE: Wood duck flank

LEGS: Plucked-out otter fur guard hairs

ATHERTON MEDIUM

TAIL: Three ringneck pheasant fibers
BODY: Hare's ear fur
RIB: Fine oval gold tinsel
WING CASE: Dyed bright blue duck wing quill
LEGS: Partridge hackle

HARE'S EAR NYMPH

TAIL: Brown hackle fibers
BODY: Dubbing from hare's mask and ears
RIB: Fine oval gold tinsel
WING CASE: Section of gray duck or goose quill
LEGS: Plucked hairs from dubbing

BREADCRUST NYMPH

TAIL: None
BODY: Orange wool over which orange seal fur is spun
RIB: Stripped quill from Rhode Island Red rooster (or equivalent)
HACKLE: Brown

ZUG BUG

TAIL: Three peacock sword fibers tied short
BODY: Peacock herl tied full and thick
RIB: Fine silver oval tinsel
WING PAD: Mallard flank
HACKLE: Brown

ISONYCHIA NYMPH

TAIL: Three peacock fibers tied short
BODY: Blend of claret seal and black rabbit
WING CASE: None
HACKLE: Brown partridge tied as collar

BLUE QUILL NYMPH

TAIL: Blue dun hackle or hen fibers
BODY: Stripped peacock quill
THORAX: Muskrat dubbing
HACKLE: Blue dun hen feather wound as collar

TELLICO NYMPH

TAIL: Red hackle fibers

BODY: Yellow chenille

RIB: Peacock herl

WING CASE: Ringneck pheasant tail fibers tied as a shell covering entire body

HACKLE: Bronze ringneck neck feathers wound as collar

MONTANA NYMPH

TAIL: Three crow tail fibers or black hackle

BODY: Doubled extra fine black chenille tied in side by side

THORAX: Large yellow chenille ribbed with black hackle

WING CASE: Black chenille (same chenille as used for body; it was not clipped as excess and is now pulled forward and tied down)

There are numerous other patterns that could be added to this list. These, however, are among the most effective and popular fished today.

WEIGHTING NYMPHS

Almost all the nymphs discussed here can be weighted with lead wire so they will swim deeper. There are three basic methods of weighting; their use depends on the type of nymph and the effect desired.

First is the simple expedient of wrapping coils of lead wire around the shank of the hook. It is rarely used since most of the nymphs we imitate have a flat or flat/oval shape. We shall go over the two remaining and important methods of weighting nymphs here.

For the flat-shape method of weighting nymphs, cut two appropriately sized pieces of lead wire, one for each side of the hook shank. They should measure almost the distance from the bend or the head, or eye, of the hook. Each piece of wire should be cut at a slant, or diagonal, so that both ends of the wire taper naturally to the hook shank (see Figure 13). The wires are tied onto the side of the shank *one at a time* by back and forth windings of thread.

Once the pieces of lead wire are fairly secure, a liberal amount of head lacquer is applied to the windings, and more turns of thread are taken over the area. If the wire does not taper smoothly to the shank, even it out with a few additional turns of thread fore and aft. The overall effect should be one of flatness and smoothness. In addition, the lead wire should be fastened in such a way that it does not slip when other materials are tied over it.

The flat/oval-shape method of weighting combines the side by side procedure and the overwind technique. It works this way.

A fairly long piece of wire, depending on the size of the hook, is cut

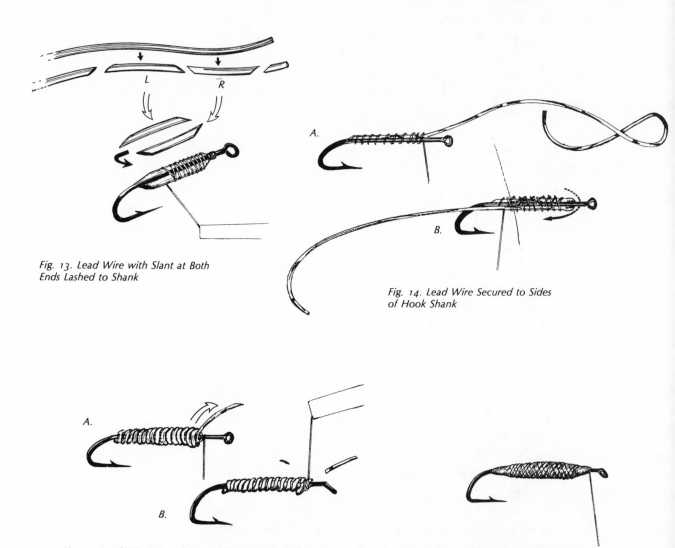

Fig. 13. Lead Wire with Slant at Both Ends Lashed to Shank

Fig. 14. Lead Wire Secured to Sides of Hook Shank

Fig. 15. Lead Wire Wound Around Shank to Thread

Fig. 16. Flat/Oval Weighted Body

from the spool. One end is placed along the far side of the hook shank and bound down by the tying thread (see Figure 14A). When you reach the thorax area, double the wire back along the near side of the shank. Wind the thread over both parts of the wire and the shank (see Figure 14B).

We now have the flat shape with a slight bulge under the thorax, the best place for it. The wire is not cut. The thread is brought forward to just in front of the wire at the thorax area, and the wire is wound around the shank in connecting spirals to the thread (see Figure 15A). The excess wire is clipped off just behind the thread (see Figure 15B), and a liberal amount of head cement is applied to the wire coils. The thread is now brought back through the coils of wire to the bend. Allow some strands of thread to slip between the coils for extra security. When you reach the rear portion of wire, take enough turns of thread behind the wire to build a taper between the wire and the shank.

Bring the thread forward again, and build another taper (see Figure 16). This is about all you need to know about weighting nymphs.

STONEFLY

Most tiers I know seem to have their own version of the stonefly imitation. I don't think I've ever seen any two tied alike. The stonefly requires a few materials and techniques that differ from those for the conventional nymph. Most of what I have learned in this field has been from one of the real experts, Ted Niemeyer of New Caanan, Connecticut, who is constantly probing, innovating, and creating new imitations, one more realistic than the other.

Compared with mayfly nymphs or caddis larvae, stoneflies are large. They are extremely effective for large trout. We are going to tie one here, using some of the advanced techniques but keeping the fly relatively simple and alive.

The living stonefly appears to have a hard shell; if you picked one up, however, you would find that it is not truly hard, but of a yielding firmness. Its abdomen looks softer and has a lively motion. In addition, it has legs, gills, and feelers, all of which have movement in the stream. The motion is what we are going to try to imitate and suggest in the following pattern, which can, incidentally, be changed in size and color. Only the tying operations will remain constant.

Though this pattern is a modification of some of Ted's ideas, I have named the fly after him since it would not have existed without his labor and love. It is called Ted's Quill Stone:

TED'S QUILL STONE

TAIL: Two peccary fibers

UNDERBODY: Two strips of lead sided to hook shank over which yellow polypropylene yarn is tapered

ABDOMEN: Section of mallard quill strip

GILLS: Fine light gray ostrich herl

LEGS: Partridge

WING CASE: Dark brown turkey doubled

THORAX: Cream seal fur or coarse poly dubbing

FEELERS: Natural gray goose fibers or peccary

HEAD: Collar of dark gray ostrich herl

Fig. 17. Peccary Tail Fibers Tied In

Fig. 18. Lead Wires Secured

Stoneflies are usually tied on size 4–8 hooks. Here we are going to use a Mustad 9575, size 8. Thread will be fine yellow.

Fix the hook in your vise, and spiral some thread onto the shank, terminating at the bend.

From a piece of peccary (javelina) hide select two fibers, and tie them in as your tail. The texture of peccary is stiff yet pliable. Once it is tied in, you will be able to bend it out without breaking it. When you have it secured, place a drop of vinyl cement at the tie-down point (see Figure 17).

Tie in two strips of fine lead wire, one on each side of the hook shank. Secure them by the flat-shape method (see Figure 18).

We are now ready to tie in the body of the nymph, which, in this case, is the stripped quill from the center stem of a mallard pointer. Before you tie it in, prepare it by immersing the feather in a jar of water and letting it soak for at least an hour. By soaking the feather, you soften the fiber. When it is stripped, you then have a fuller-bodied quill. If you don't soak it, you get only a thin film of strip. Both types have their uses, but for the stonefly we want a strong one.

It is easy to immerse and strip a number of quills. Those that are not immediately required can be stored for future use.

Select mallard pointer feathers with fairly light quills that have darker edges. A feather like this will produce a segmented effect.

Once the quill has been immersed and softened, it is laid flat on your tying bench. With either a very sharp pen knife or a razor blade, cut a small nick into the quill stem near the tip (see Figure 19).

The loose piece of quill stem is then lifted with a pair of tweezers and pulled from the feather all the way to the base (see Figure 20). The stripped quill is now tied to the shank of the hook just in back of the lead wire (see Figure 21).

Bring your thread forward to the thorax area.

Cut an 8-inch section of yellow polypropylene yarn. (Yellow floss can be used to build the underbody, but is a little too hard. We want to keep the body soft under the quill.) Tie the yarn in at the thorax area (see Figure 22).

In overlapping turns wind the poly yarn toward the rear, forming a firm, neatly tapered body. Poly yarn is somewhat like floss in that it can be spread thinly or heavily, thus creating whatever thickness is needed. The final turn of poly yarn should be at the thorax area, where it is secured by the thread (see Figure 23).

Fig. 19. Nicking Center Stem with Knife

Bring the thread back once more so that it hangs about one-third of the way down the hook shank from the bend. Now we have to tie in the ostrich herl gills, which will be secured a bit later.

Snip two light gray ostrich herl flues from a mini-ostrich plume. Mini-plumes are just that—smaller feathers with finer fibers. Tie one herl on the far side of the underbody and one on the near (see Figure 24).

The mini-ostrich herl is tied in by the tip. If you want a bit more gill action, by all means tie in two herls on each side or simply double them.

Bring the thread forward to the thorax area once more. Place a liberal amount of vinyl head cement on the poly yarn underbody. Take the tied-in stripped duck quill, and in connecting turns wind it to the thread. Bind it down securely (see Figure 25A).

The quill body should be wound slightly more than halfway down the shank toward the eye. If you have trouble securing the quill with the thread, make a small V-shaped nick in the quill with a pair of scissors at the point where the thread will cross it when it is being tied down (see Figure 25B).

Apply a very small amount of vinyl cement to the sides of the body.

Pull the ostrich herl forward along the sides of the hook shank (where you applied the cement), and tie them down (see Figure 26).

The feelers of goose fibers, taken from the short side of a natural dark gray goose quill, are tied in next. The tips extend past the eye for approximately a quarter of an inch (see Figure 27).

The wing case is now tied in. It is taken from a fairly dark and mottled turkey tail feather. The wing case section should be at least one-quarter of

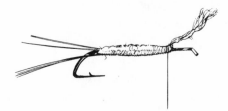

Fig. 20. Stripping Quill

Fig. 21. Quill Strip Tied In

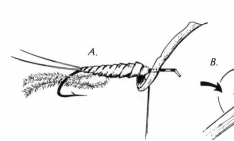

Fig. 22. Poly Yarn Tied In

Fig. 23. Poly Yarn Underbody Formed

Fig. 24. Gill of Mini-ostrich Herl Tied In

Fig. 25. Winding Duck Quill Strip to Thorax (A); Nicking Quill (B)

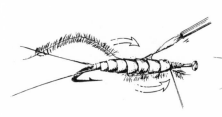

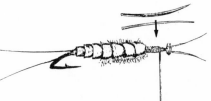

Fig. 26. Ostrich Herl Brought Forward

Fig. 27. Tying in Goose Quill Feelers

Fig. 28. Wing Case Tied In

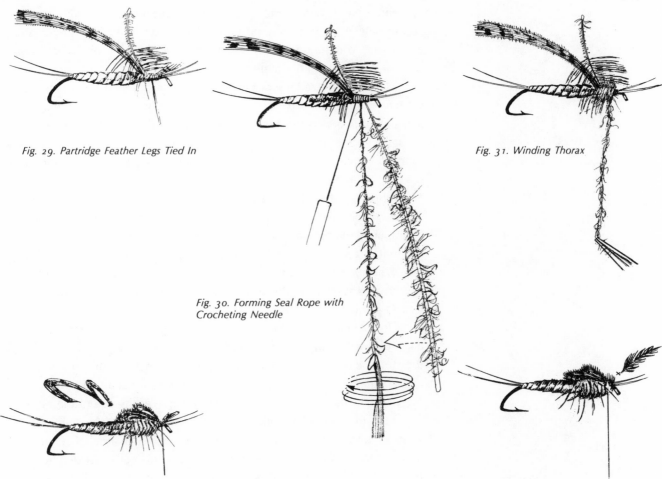

Fig. 29. Partridge Feather Legs Tied In

Fig. 31. Winding Thorax

Fig. 30. Forming Seal Rope with Crocheting Needle

Fig. 32. Doubling Wing Case

Fig. 33. Winding Head of Ostrich Herl

an inch wide (see Figure 28). I advise that the turkey wing case feather just tied in be coated with some vinyl cement or plastic spray. This will keep the fibers from splitting when it is time to fold over the wing case.

Right on top of the wing case, tie down a dark brown mottled partridge or grouse feather upside down, just as you did on the March Brown. The partridge feather will form the legs (see Figure 29). Both the partridge feather and the turkey quill are left hanging for now.

The next step is tying in the thorax of cream-colored seal fur. If this is unavailable, a similar shade of coarse poly dubbing will do. There are

165

also a number of fur blends on the market which will do fine for this operation. All of them come in cream. Seal fur and, to a certain extent, coarse poly are very difficult to dub, or spin, onto thread. It is even an annoyance to roll a noodle with it in the palm of your hand. Therefore, we will illustrate another method.

Make the double loop of thread on the shank of your hook as if you were tying a noodle. Separate the two strands of thread with your fingers, and apply a coat of head cement to each strand of thread. Place your seal fur between and on top of the two strands of thread, allowing it to adhere to the cement. Take a crocheting needle, and insert it into the bottom of the loop of thread.

Allow the thread to close, trapping the seal fur between the two strands. If necessary, align the seal fur. Spin the crocheting needle between your thumb and forefinger—in one direction only. Keep twisting until the fur itself begins spinning. You will form a tight rope with the fur inside.

When you have made the rope, take a pair of hackle pliers, and grip the thread just below it. Begin winding your thorax with the fur rope (see Figures 30 and 31).

Do not build the thorax all the way to the eye; leave room for the eyes and head. When the thorax is finished, the partridge legs can be pulled forward and tied down in the conventional manner; clip the excess.

The turkey quill wing case is also pulled forward and tied down, *but the excess is not clipped.* It is left protruding over the eye of the hook.

Take the protruding turkey section between your right thumb and forefinger, and with your left hand place the center of a dubbing needle against it from underneath. With the dubbing needle pull the section to the rear, folding it so that it covers half the lower wing case you just formed. All you are doing is doubling the turkey section back on itself.

Once the doubled portion has been formed, slide the needle from the fold. Hold the folded section in place with your right thumb and forefinger, and secure it with thread. Clip the excess (see Figure 32).

All that remains is to tie in a head collar of dark gray ostrich herl. This is as simple as it sounds. Snip a piece of dark gray mini-ostrich, and tie it in where you left off with your thread. Wrap three or four turns of the ostrich around the shank just in front of the eye, secure the ostrich herl, and clip the excess (see Figure 33).

Whip finish, and apply a touch of cement to the thread. Your completed nymph should look like Figure 34.

The stonefly is one of the most difficult patterns to tie, perhaps be-

Fig. 34. Completed Ted's Stonefly

cause there are a number of new or different techniques involved or perhaps because there are so many steps. As you attempt to tie these patterns, don't try to do them all at once. Take one operation at a time. Stop for a break now and again; walk away from the fly for a bit. Then just sit there, and study it for a while. Many ideas will come to you if you take your time.

The stonefly we have just tied is fairly basic. Even this type can become more involved. It can be made to look more realistic, but when you carry this too far, I believe you lose some of the naturalness of the action. You may have noticed that though we have a rather hard body (by comparison with other types), we made sure that the rest of the pattern was soft and alive. The gills, thorax, and legs create much action, and to a certain extent so do the feelers and tails.

The principles we've employed here can be used on all other stonefly imitations, as I mentioned earlier. Only the size, color, and shape have to be adjusted.

Incidentally, the technique of stripping a quill from a duck pointer feather for the body can be applied to just about any feather from any bird. I am repeating myself, but I feel it is rather important, since it is in this area that you will find, through exploration and experimentation, many uses not only for stoneflies but also for all other types of nymphs, as well as dry and wet patterns.

LARVAE AND PUPAE

There is very little to learn about the larvae of various insects. They are tied to look like what they are—an elongated, segmented, fuzzy (or not so fuzzy) worm. Larva imitations can be created by the simple expedient of spinning, or dubbing, fur or wool onto the shank of a hook, segmenting it with thread or a clipped hackle (in the case of fuzziness), and tying in a head of peacock or ostrich herl.

CADDIS PUPA There is one type of pupa that does require a little more attention—the caddis. It is not difficult, just a little tricky. When I began tying these imitations, I had trouble getting the short mallard wing to lie just right, and it was not until Phillip Pirone of Beacon, New York, showed me how it was done that I was able to master this procedure. Let's tie a caddis to see what it's all about:

GRAY CADDIS PUPA

BODY: Muskrat fur
RIB: Brown Maxima leader material 10–12-pound test
LEGS: Gray mallard flank
WINGS: Mallard quill
HEAD: Dark gray mini-ostrich herl

A good hook for this pattern is the Mustad 3906B, which has a 1XL shank and a sproat bend. The thread is a fine black.

Spiral some thread onto the shank of your hook, ending the winding well into the bend.

Snip a piece of Maxima leader material or any other brownish monofilament testing approximately 10 or 12 pounds, and tie it in for a rib to be used later.

Give your thread a couple of extra strokes through the wax, and spin a goodly amount of muskrat dubbing onto it. As you build your body, taper it so that the heaviest portion is closer to the bend than the eye of the hook. The taper of caddis pupae is almost the reverse of a dry fly. Build the muskrat *all the way to the eye of the hook.* This is important, as you will see when it is time to tie in your wings.

Bring the thread back again, and let it hang about a quarter of the distance from the eye.

In an open spiral wind your monofilament rib to the thread, and tie it down. Clip the excess mono (see Figure 35).

We are now ready for those wings. From a left and right mallard quill, snip a section an eighth of an inch wide. Turn the cut sections of wing quill so that the dull sides face outward. They are going to be tied in with the tips pointing down.

Place one quill at a time on each side of the shank, and tie it in so that the tip covers about two-thirds of the shank (see Figure 36). Note that the wing seems to run along the side of the shank and curve down slightly.

If you placed the proper amount of muskrat dubbing under the tie-in area of the wing, the wing should lie fairly flat and hug the body. If you tried to tie it to the bare shank, it would have tended to flare out and misbehave. If the wing still flares a little after you have built an underbody of muskrat, remove it, and add some more bulk with your thread. In other words, harden the tie-down area. You will notice the difference immediately.

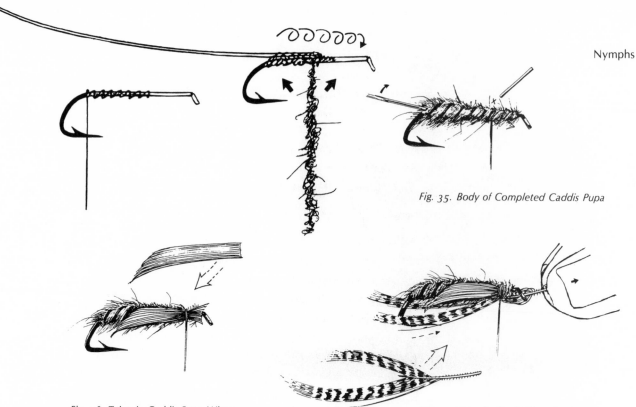

Fig. 35. Body of Completed Caddis Pupa

Fig. 36. Tying in Caddis Pupa Wings

Fig. 37. Tying in Flank Fibers for Legs

The legs of the caddis pupa can be tied on in one of two ways. In the first method you tie in a very small mallard breast feather or partridge hackle by the tip and wind it two turns as a wet fly collar. You may not find an appropriate feather small enough if you use a small hook. Or you can follow the techniques used by such salmon fly tiers as Charles De Feo of New York City, which is simplicity itself.

Select a mallard flank feather, and cut the tip at the stem. Removing the tip produces a V at the top of the feather. Invert the V, and slide it down onto the hook shank so that the side tips point down, where the legs will be. Tie it down with two turns of thread.

Take the feather by the butt, and begin to pull it out from the turns of thread until the tips of the fibers are exactly as long as you want them to be—almost to the bottom bend of the hook (see Figure 37).

The head of the fly is formed by wrapping two or three turns of ostrich herl around the shank in that area.

Whip finish, apply cement, and the Gray Caddis Pupa is completed (see Figure 38).

Fig. 38. Completed Gray Caddis Pupa

Other Caddis pupas you may wish to tie are:

BROWN CADDIS PUPA

BODY: Dark brown dubbing
RIB: 12-pound monofilament
LEGS: Wood duck or partridge
WING: Mallard quill
HEAD: Dark gray mini-ostrich

TAN CADDIS PUPA

BODY: Tan Australian opossum
RIB: 12-pound monofilament
LEGS: Wood duck or partridge
WING: Mallard quill
HEAD: Brown mini-ostrich herl

CREAM CADDIS PUPA

BODY: Cream dubbing fur
RIB: 12-pound monofilament
LEGS: Wood duck or partridge
WING: Mallard quill
HEAD: Light gray mini-ostrich herl

GREEN/OLIVE CADDIS PUPA

BODY: Green/olive dubbing
RIB: 12-pound monofilament
LEGS: Wood duck or partridge
WING: Mallard quill
HEAD: Dark gray mini-ostrich herl

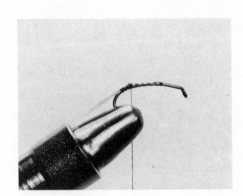

Fig. 39. Tail Tied in on Hook Bent to Shape

SHRIMP AND SCUD

Though they are not true nymphs, such subsurface creatures as shrimp, scud, and other small crustaceans are included in the general classification. Shrimp and scud are not difficult to tie. In fact, most of the procedures we've learned thus far can be applied to them. Since, however, there are a few slight variations, we will attempt one here just to fill out the picture:

CREAM/TAN SCUD

TAIL: Dark cream hackle tip

BODY: Light tan opossum fur

COVERT (SHELL):   Goose quill

RIB: Fine monofilament (6 pound)

LEGS: Dark cream hackle

EYES: Burnt monofilament

Here again a Mustad 3906B is a good hook. A size 12 will do nicely. The tying thread can be either yellow or cream.

Place the hook in your vise. Clamp it very tightly.

Take a pair of pliers, and crimp a slight bend into the shank of the hook. This will give you the natural curvature of the scud.

Spiral your thread onto the shank of the hook starting at the center and winding to the bend.

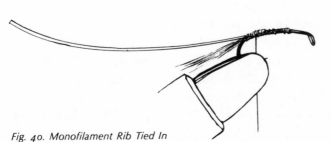

Fig. 40. Monofilament Rib Tied In

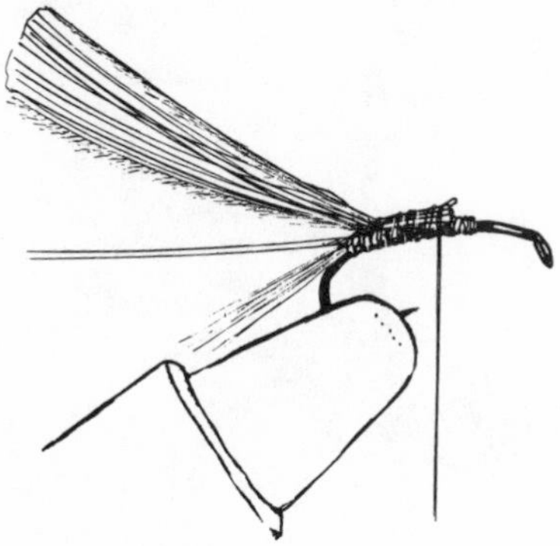

Fig. 41. Goose Quill Section Tied In

Fig. 43. Hackle Palmered and Trimmed

Fig. 44. Goose Section Pulled Forward over Eye and Segmented with Mono

Fig. 42. Hackle Feather Tied in for Legs

Pluck an entire hackle feather from a dark cream rooster neck, and tie it so that the tip extends past the bend.

Now wind down and into the curve of the bend, binding the tip of the feather in a downward slant with the thread. The thread will also close up the fibers a bit (see Figure 39).

Cut a 5-inch section of 6-pound test monofilament, and tie it in for the rib. Forget it for now (see Figure 40).

From a light gray goose feather cut a section of fibers approximately one-quarter inch wide. Tie it in by the tip on top of the rib, and let it hang for a while also (see Figure 41).

From a dark cream neck or saddle cape select another hackle feather that is no wider than the hook gap. It should be prepared the same way as a hackle feather for a conventional wet fly. Tie it in where you left off with the goose section (see Figure 42). After this feather is secured, it is also left alone for the moment.

From a piece of Australian opossum, pluck some of the creamy yellow belly fur, and spin it onto your thread. Form a body that almost extends to the eye of the hook and that gets just a little heavier at the thorax area.

Go back to the dark cream hackle feather, and in an open palmer spiral, wind it to the thread. Tie it down, secure it, and clip the excess.

Trim all the fibers that protrude above the hook shank (see Figure 43).

As you would with a nymph wing case, grasp the goose quill section, and pull it straight out over the eye of the hook. Bind it down with thread, and clip the excess. Again in an open spiral, wind the monofilament rib forward to the thread, forming a natural segmented body as you do so (see Figure 44).

The only operation left is the forming of the eyes. This requires a little preparation.

Cut a 2-inch section of 20-pound test monofilament, and pick it up in the center with a pair of tweezers. Light a candle. Hold one end at a time to the outer edge of the flame. Do not put the ends into the flame itself. The heat will begin to melt the monofilament and form a small black ball. The two balls will become your eyes (see Figure 45).

Lay the mono eyes on top of the hook shank just behind the eye, and secure them with crisscross turns of thread. Whip finish and lacquer. Your completed Scud should look like the one in Figure 46.

These instructions for tying a scud can be applied to all shrimp imitations. Only size and color will vary.

Fig. 45. Monofilament Eyes

Fig. 46. Completed Scud

IV

Bucktails and Streamers

12

Bucktails

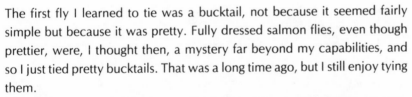

The first fly I learned to tie was a bucktail, not because it seemed fairly simple but because it was pretty. Fully dressed salmon flies, even though prettier, were, I thought then, a mystery far beyond my capabilities, and so I just tied pretty bucktails. That was a long time ago, but I still enjoy tying them.

Bucktails *are* the easiest patterns to tie in the sense that all they require is a tinsel body and a few hair fibers lashed to the shank of the hook. This is, of course, a bit of oversimplification since there is always a better way of tying them and there are a few tricks that help create a well-dressed pattern. So why didn't we begin by learning to tie this type of pattern instead of the dry fly? The answer is simple. Even though 90 percent of a trout's diet consists of subsurface creatures, 90 percent of all fly fishermen prefer to take them on dry flies or on other floating patterns. A trout striking is a thrilling sight. We enjoy seeing the trout take the fly before feeling its struggles vibrating through our lines. Hence, most anglers are eager to learn the art of tying dry flies.

Bucktails and streamers were left to the third and last section of this book because, unfortunately, they are the least favored by fly fishermen, who prefer, in order of popularity, dries, nymphs (wet), and then bucktails and streamers. But when you ask, "What takes the largest fish?" the answer invariably is, "Bucktails and streamers."

Why, then, if bucktails and streamers generally take the largest fish, are they the least preferred by fly fishermen? Is it because of the work involved? Consider the constant casting, stripping, and retrieving. Or perhaps it is the fact that not as many trout, bass, or even panfish are taken with this type of pattern, though the few that are, are usually of good size. But I suppose pondering the eccentricities of fly fishermen is futile. We are a strange and unique lot, but I doubt whether anyone enjoys life as much or does more to preserve our natural heritage.

Probably the most important requisites for any bucktail or streamer are attraction, action, and imitation, in that order. In other words, you must first get the fish's attention (attraction). Second, make your offering appear alive, arouse the trout's instincts (action), and third, once the trout has taken an interest, maintain it by using colors the trout will identify with a natural (imitation).

Of the three requisites I would say action is the most important, but you will need attraction to help the fish locate your fly in the first place. Occasionally you will find a selective trout that wants the proper shade or shape in your pattern (imitation), so it behooves you not to overlook this aspect. And as you know, selective trout usually live to an age and size we classify as trophy.

Let me state this once more. In tying bucktails or streamers put *attraction, action, and imitation* into every pattern you tie. For myself this lesson has been pounded home during many seasons on the stream. Remember it well, and I assure you that you will have many moments to brag about.

The word "bucktail" generally applies to patterns on which the wing is tied with various hair fibers, such as bucktail, calf tail, bear hair, and woodchuck. Streamers, on the other hand, are made with wings of feathers, such as neck and saddle hackle, and shoulders and cheeks of such body feathers as silver pheasant and jungle cock. For instance, the Black-nosed Dace and Mickey Finn would be classified as bucktails while the Gray Ghost and Nine Three are considered streamers. There is no distinction in use between bucktails or streamers. Both are fished in the same manner, with the same idea, which is to imitate a darting baitfish.

Many times you will hear an angler refer to a bucktail as a streamer, and vice versa, for the terms are used loosely. For our purposes we'll classify this way: bucktails are made with hair fibers, and streamers with feathers.

BLACK-NOSED DACE

I've selected the Black-nosed Dace as our sample bucktail for two reasons. First, it is among the ten most popular bucktail and streamer patterns used today, and second, it incorporates many of the techniques you will need for tying other patterns.

We'll follow the same procedure here that we have used throughout this book. We are going to take the first pattern of this section and tie it very slowly and methodically so that all the steps are clearly understood. This will enable you to tie most patterns listed with very little difficulty.

BLACK-NOSED DACE
    TAIL: Short tuft of red wool
    BODY: Flat silver tinsel ribbed with oval silver tinsel
    WING: White polar bear under black bear hair under natural brown bucktail
    HEAD: Black lacquer

The hook for this pattern and most bucktails and streamers is the Mustad 9575, which is a 6XL shanked hook with a looped-down eye. The looped eye of this particular hook will allow you to form a neatly tapered head during the tying operation and, in addition, will not cut your leader when the fly is being fished.

Place a size 8 hook in your vise, and spiral some fine black thread onto the shank beginning just before the bend and ending when you reach it.

Cut a 5-inch strip of medium oval silver tinsel, and expose the cotton core by removing the tinsel covering at one end. Dip the tip of exposed cotton into a bottle of head cement.

Tie the strip of tinsel to the shank of the hook near the bend by binding down the cotton core (see Figure 1).

Snip a single strand of red wool about 3 inches long. Wool is generally multistranded, sometimes with four, and sometimes with only two, strands in a piece. Whatever the case may be, just pry the strands apart, and pull out one.

Tie the yarn on top of the hook shank so that a very short tuft extends past the bend of the hook (see Figure 2).

Take the wool in your right hand, and pull it tautly along the top of the hook shank and out over the eye. With your left hand take your bobbin, and bind down the wool on top of the shank by spiraling thread over it toward the eye (see Figure 3). Clip the excess wool.

When you have a choice of materials to secure along the shank, always keep materials lighter than the shank on top and heavier than the shank (such as lead) on the bottom. This allows the fly to ride properly when it is being fished. In this instance we extended the wool all the way to the head of the fly to ensure overall smoothness. Had we cut the excess off near the bend, we would have created a slight bulge in the body.

The oval silver tinsel has been left, for now, hanging at the bend. Our thread is dangling in its bobbin near the eye.

Cut a 10-inch section of medium flat silver tinsel. Lay one end of it diagonally under the hook between the shank and the thread. Count out four turns of thread around the tinsel just to hold it in place. Do not cut the excess (see Figure 4).

In close but not overlapping spirals, wind the tinsel to the bend of the hook and then forward to the eye once more. As you approach the eye and just before you are about to make the last turn of tinsel over the thread which first secured your tinsel, *stop*. Keep the main portion of tinsel taut between your left thumb and forefinger, and with the bobbin in your right hand, remove the four turns of thread you took over the original end of the tinsel. As you unwind the thread, count the turns again—one two, three four.

As the last turn is removed, take one turn around the area with the tinsel you are holding in your left hand, and bind it down with the original four turns of thread. What you are actually doing is *binding the tinsel down with itself* (see Figure 5).

Once the tinsel has been secured with the thread, grip both excess tips of tinsel with a pair of hackle pliers. Work them back and forth until they break off; do not cut them with scissors. Allowing them to break off —and they will do it right next to the thread—creates a little metal burr on the end of each tip. These prevent the tinsel from slipping through the thread.

You will be surprised at the smooth connection this method produces.

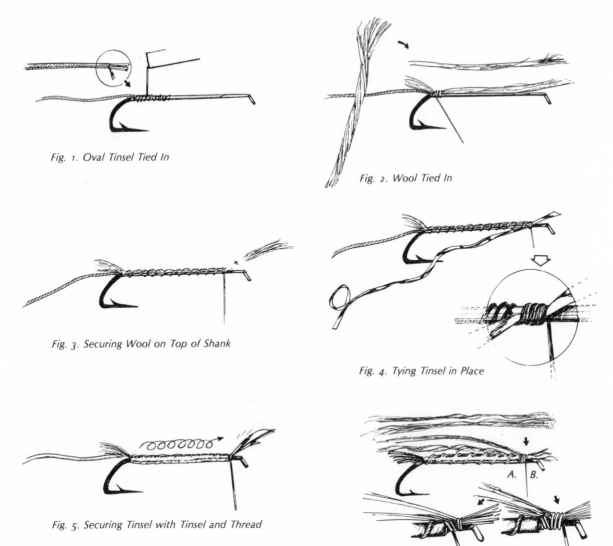

Fig. 1. Oval Tinsel Tied In

Fig. 2. Wool Tied In

Fig. 3. Securing Wool on Top of Shank

Fig. 4. Tying Tinsel in Place

Fig. 5. Securing Tinsel with Tinsel and Thread

A. B.

Fig. 6. Tying Down and Wedging Hair Fibers

There will be no trace of the bulge that usually occurs in this operation. This method should be used wherever possible. It is applicable mostly on plain tinsel bodies which do not call for a floss or wool body prior to the rib. The only time to avoid this technique is when you are tying with the newer synthetic Mylars, which are very thin and have a certain amount of stretch.

It is now time to go back to the piece of oval tinsel you left hanging. In an open spiral wind it forward, forming an oval rib. Tie it down, and secure it with your thread upon reaching the point where the thread was left idling.

The wing of the Black-nosed Dace consists of three different materials—polar bear, black bear, and brown bucktail. The only one that may be difficult to get is polar bear, which has restrictions placed on it by certain states. These restrictions may well be justified because of the indiscriminate slaughter of these beautiful animals. However, fly tiers do not contribute to the sale of this hair in the least, since all we can afford are the scraps or cuttings; nevertheless, the law makes no exceptions.

If you have any difficulty in getting polar bear hair, by all means use a substitute. Calf tail is excellent. While it does not have the luster or translucency of polar bear, it is white and crinkly and works well in water.

The first part of the wing to be tied in is the white polar bear. Examine the hide. If the hair is very long, I suggest you use the shorter guard hairs, as long as they are long enough. There will be more of them, they will be straighter though crinkly, and you'll be able to align them easily. If the piece of hide you own has short guard hairs, use those.

Align the tips as best you can, and clip a section of hair about one quarter the thickness of a wooden matchstick. You don't want it too full since you have two other materials in the wing makeup.

Take the clump of hairs you have removed from the hide, and further align the tips. If there is too much underfur in the clump, remove most of it. It is always a good idea to leave some underfur in any wing to allow the hairs to remain slightly open, thus giving the fibers a breathing action.

Lay the clump of polar bear on top of the hook shank so that the tips extend one-quarter of an inch past the bend of the hook. Place a drop of head cement on the part of the hook shank where you plan to secure the polar bear. Secure the fibers with enough turns of thread to keep it in place. (Always remember to pull *straight up* with the thread when cinching the fibers to the shank.)

Most hair fibers, if they are bound down with just turns of thread, can easily be pulled out. This is especially true of polar bear, which is very smooth and slippery. In order to prevent the fibers from being pulled out, you must wedge them with your thread. Do this by taking four or five turns of thread under and in back of the tied-down wing and four or five turns in front of it and under the butts (see Figure 6).

Once the hair fibers have been wedged, clip the excess butts at an angle very close to the eye of the hook (see Figure 7). This will be important later. Place a drop of head cement on top of the secured area.

Fig. 7. Cutting Excess Polar
Bear Fibers

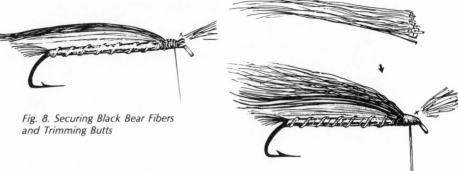

Fig. 8. Securing Black Bear Fibers
and Trimming Butts

Fig. 9. Tying in Brown Bucktail
Fibers

Our next material for the wing is a clump of black bear hair. Again align the ends. The size of the clump should be the same as that of the polar bear just tied in. The tips of the black bear should align with the tips of the polar bear.

Tie the black bear on top of the polar bear, and secure it. Since black bear is not quite as smooth and slippery as polar bear, you will need only one or two wedging turns of thread.

Once you have secured the hairs, clip the excess butts; this time, however, clip just a little farther back from the eye of the hook (see Figure 8).

To complete the wing on our Black-nosed Dace, clip an appropriate section of natural brown fibers from the back of the tail of a whitetail deer. Put a drop of head cement on top of the area where you tied down the black bear.

Place the brown bucktail on top of the black bear, and align the tips with the black bear and polar bear. Secure the bucktail to the shànk on top of the black bear. Trim the excess butts, this time still farther back from the eye.

At this point you should note that we have been creating a staggered effect by clipping the excess butts a little farther behind the eye with each clump of fibers we've tied in. This makes the formation of a tapered head just that much simpler (see Figure 9).

Once the entire wing has been secured, all that remains is to taper the head with turns of thread. The head itself should not be overlarge, but rather a natural taper leading to the eye of the hook.

Taper and whip finish the head, and coat it with black lacquer. Usually the first coat will be absorbed into the thread, so apply the second coat after the first has fully dried. A completed Black-nosed Dace is shown in Figure 10.

Fig. 10. Completed Black-nosed Dace

181

LLAMA

I am going to describe the tying of only one other fly in this chapter. It will be the only *new* fly in this entire volume. And yet it is not new, having been tied over 30 years ago by a Menominee Indian named Mile Tourtilloutt, who died recently. The name of the pattern he has left us is the Llama —an unusual name. It came from an old English pattern book which described a similarly constructed fly.

The pattern has been successfully fished by a number of anglers in many parts of the world. I introduced it in *Fly Fisherman Magazine* because its tying procedures best illustrate one or two little tricks I think you should learn and because it's one of the most successful patterns I have ever fished with.

LLAMA

TAIL: Grizzly hackle

TAG: Flat gold tinsel

BODY: Red floss

RIB: Flat gold tinsel

WING: Woodchuck guard hair

COLLAR: Grizzly hackle

HEAD: Black with black dotted white pupil

The Llama is one of the few patterns in which the hook is sized to the hair length because of the natural marking of the woodchuck guard hairs. The average size for this pattern is 8. The Mustad 9575 is perfect.

Fix the hook in your vise, and spiral some fine black thread onto the shank ending at the bend.

Cut a section of fibers from a grizzly hackle neck, and tie them in as your tail in the conventional manner.

From a spool of medium flat gold tinsel, snip a section of tinsel approximately 7 inches long. Secure it to the hook shank a quarter of an inch in front of the bend. Wind the tinsel to the rear toward the tail, and bind the windings down with thread. The tinsel is wound on in this manner to educate it for moving in the proper direction. Later you will have no difficulty with it when you need it for the tag and rib (see Figure 11). Let your thread hang from the bobbin at the bend.

Before we proceed with the floss body, I recommend that you wrap some very fine lead wire to the center of the hook shank—enough to cover a half inch of the shank center. This will add just enough weight to sink the fly. When I first fished this pattern, I had difficulty getting it to submerge because the woodchuck guard hairs, for some reason, seem to float better than deer hair. The amount of lead wire will determine how deep this pattern swims. During spring high water I will use a medium-sized lead wire covering the same distance on the hook shank.

Once the center of the hook shank has been wrapped with fine lead wire, we are ready to tie in the floss body. For streamer flies with floss bodies, I like to use a bobbin for most of the operation. Floss has a tendency to fray if it is handled too much, and in a bobbin your fingers will never touch it. Tie in your floss at the center of the hook shank (see Figure 12).

Many anglers tie in their floss near the bend, resulting in an uneven taper. By tying your floss in at the center of the shank, which is the highest point of the taper, you avoid unnecessary bulge at both ends. You can then approach the bend and eye areas with a very fine turn of floss and quickly back off, thus making for a neat taper. Once I have tied in my floss, I wind my thread forward to the eye, half hitch it a couple of times, and cut it from the hook temporarily. Now you have room to work the floss dangling from the bobbin.

The floss body is formed by wrapping it around the shank. You'll find that use of a bobbin creates a tendency for the floss to twist into a solid mass. If this occurs, just twist the bobbin in the opposite direction, and the floss will once more wind flatly. The body shape you are aiming for is a cigar, the slim, tapered variety.

Incidentally, you can use any floss you wish, but as far as bodies for bucktails are concerned, I've found that the single-strand heavy flosses are the best. I used acetate floss on the sample pattern. It spreads and lies very nicely. Four-strand floss has a habit of straying and misbehaving.

Try to build most of your body with the bobbin. For the final touches, however, strip off about an 8-inch section of floss, and wind the last of it by hand.

You can fill in many of the uneven areas of the floss body by "bouncing" the floss. To bounce, release the tension on the floss between the hook shank and your thumb and forefinger, and then quickly apply it again (see Figure 13). This is done in a staccato series with your thumb and forefinger, something like rapidly tapping a tabletop with your fingers or like a woodpecker's beak pecking at a dead tree. The bouncing spreads the floss and fills in the gaps (see Figure 14).

Fig. 11. Tail Tied in (A); Tinsel Tied in (B)

Fig. 12. Lead Wire (A) and Floss (B) from Bobbin Tied In

Fig. 13. Bouncing Floss

Fig. 14. Securing Floss to Form Body

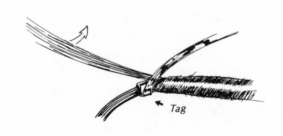

Fig. 15. Forming Tinsel Tag

Fig. 16. Looping Base of Wing with Thread

Fig. 17. Trimming Butts at a Slant

Fig. 18. Tying in Hackle Collar

As you wind the last 8 inches of floss with your fingers, moisten it with saliva or water now and again. This will keep it from fraying (licking the tips of your fingers will do it nicely).

When your floss body is complete, hold the end of the leftover floss tautly between your left thumb and forefinger near the eye of the hook. Pick up your bobbin, and also grip the thread with your left thumb and forefinger while you spiral the thread back onto the hook shank at the eye with your right hand.

When the thread has once more been secured to the hook shank, tie down the floss with it. This will feel a little awkward at first, but it is readily accomplished. Clip all excess floss, and thread ends.

The tag and rib of flat gold tinsel are next.

To form the tag, simply lift the tail of grizzly hackle, and take one turn of tinsel over the hook shank under it. The turns should be made in the same direction as the floss, going away from you as the tinsel crosses over the top of the shank (see Figure 15).

From the tag continue immediately with the tinsel over the grizzly tail, and in an open spiral wind the tinsel to the thread. Tie it down, secure it, and clip the excess. Put a drop of head cement on the windings.

The wing, which is made from the guard hairs of a woodchuck (groundhog), is next. The guard hairs are the outside hairs of the animal, as opposed to the softer underfur. Observe that from the skin out woodchuck hair runs black, tan, black, white tips. We want to get all these colors into the Llama wing.

Align the tips of a section of woodchuck fibers before cutting them from the skin. You'll find that you can easily keep the tips even if they have been cut from the hide properly.

Some woodchucks have abundant guard hairs; others are sparsely coated. If there seems to be too much underfur, do remove some. But remember we do want to have some substance in the fiber base so the wing will perform properly when fished. Since woodchuck guard hairs are fairly fine, the clump should be half to three-quarters of a wooden matchstick thick.

Place the clump of woodchuck fibers on top of the hook shank so that the tips extend as far back as the tip of the tail, or approximately a quarter of an inch past the bend of the hook. Tie and secure them to the shank with several turns of thread.

Take two or three turns of thread under the wing, both behind and in front, to form the wedge. Lock the fibers in well. In addition to the wedge now *take one loop of thread around the base of the woodchuck wing without going around the shank.* As you do, lift the wing off the shank at an angle (see Figure 16).

The loop of thread at the base of the wing forces it up against its will. When the fly is fished, this tends to flatten the wing as it is being pulled on the strip of a retrieve and to make it bounce free again on the pause, thus creating an undulating action. This will arouse a bit more interest from whatever fish you are after. When you try your Llama in a stream or pond, notice how it breathes and pulsates. (It's a good idea to observe all subsurface patterns you tie. Hold the fly on a short leader, and let it submerge in front of you when you stand in a stream or a lake. Twitch it, and see what happens. Do the feather or hair fibers move or undulate? Does the fly have action? It takes very little time to do this research, but it pays big dividends.)

Once the loop has been formed at the base and the fibers sit up at an angle, you can trim the excess butts at the eye. When you trim them, cut them off at an angle. This is a single-winged fly so we won't be able to use the stagger effect (see Figure 17).

Do you remember how to tie in a conventional wet fly hackle collar? That is your next step.

Select a grizzly hackle feather on which the fibers are approximately one-quarter inch long. Fold it (if you've practiced), and tie it in by the tip at the rear of the tie-down area of the wing. Tie it in *just in front* of the looped area, not on top of the looped thread area, or you will force the wing down again.

Wind the hackle around the shank toward the eye three or four times. Secure, and clip the excess (see Figure 18).

You may ask why we need a hackle collar on such a sleek fly. The answer is simple: action.

With your thread form a neatly tapered head, just as you did with the Black-nosed Dace. Whip finish, and cut the thread.

You want a glossy finish, so apply two or three coats of lacquer to the head of the fly. Allow the head to dry completely.

We are now ready to paint an eye on our pattern. There are arguments pro and con the eye. I like to think it helps attract fish. In the final analysis, however, only the trout can tell you that. But the pattern calls for an eye, so let's make one.

Dip a toothpick into a bottle of white lacquer. Try to form a small droplet at the tip of the toothpick.

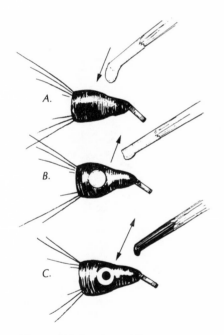

Fig. 19. Painting Eyes of Llama

Hold the Llama in your left hand, and rest it on your left knee. Hold the toothpick between the thumb and forefinger of your right hand, and rest it on your right knee. Bring your knees together. Bring the base of your palms together, keeping your fingers apart for now.

At this point all the parts of your hand and arm that may shake or quiver are locked into fair immobility. Only your fingers have free movement. Using this method you will be able to pinpoint the eye on the streamer.

Now touch the toothpick with the white lacquer to one side of the glossy black head, and then back off right away. The application should leave a very neat round white eye. Repeat the procedure on the other side of the head.

Let the eye dry completely.

Lock your arms and hands again, and use the fine point of a dubbing needle to make a black lacquer pupil. Touch the tip of the needle to the center of each eye. Let the pupils dry. That's it (see Figures 19 and 20).

The Llama is also tied in many other colors. The only thing that does not change is the woodchuck wing. Here are some of the other combinations anglers have had success with:

Fig. 20. Completed Llama

Fluorescent red body/gold rib
Yellow body/silver rib
Black body/silver rib
White body/silver rib

This pattern, incidentally, has not only been used with success on trout but has proved effective for Atlantic salmon, black bass, and pike. It is tied in sizes 4 through 10.

Now that you know the Llama and Black-nosed Dace, here are a few other patterns in the bucktail family that you should have little, if any, difficulty in tying.

MICKEY FINN

BODY: Flat silver tinsel with oval silver tinsel rib

WING: Equal amounts of yellow, red, and yellow bucktail or calf tail in that order

HEAD: Lacquered black

187

SQUIRREL TAIL

BODY: Flat silver tinsel ribbed with oval silver tinsel

WING: White calf tail over which gray squirrel tail fibers are tied

HEAD: Black with black dotted yellow eye

LITTLE BROOK TROUT

TAIL: Short section of green calf tail over same length of red floss

BODY: Cream wool ribbed with flat fine silver tinsel

THROAT: Orange bucktail

WING: White bucktail, orange bucktail, green bucktail, barred badger guard hairs (calf tail may be substituted for bucktail throughout)

HEAD: Lacquered black

LITTLE BROWN TROUT

TAIL: Ringneck pheasant breast feather

BODY: White wool ribbed with fine flat gold tinsel

WING: Yellow bucktail, reddish orange bucktail, dark squirrel tail, dark brown squirrel tail

CHEEKS: Jungle cock (optional)

HEAD: Lacquered black

LITTLE RAINBOW TROUT

TAIL: Green bucktail

BODY: Pink angora rabbit ribbed with fine flat silver tinsel

THROAT: Pink bucktail or calf tail

WING: White bucktail, pink bucktail, green bucktail, barred badger hair (calf tail may be used throughout for bucktail)

CHEEKS: Jungle cock (optional)

HEAD: Lacquered black

LIGHT EDSON TIGER

TAIL: Barred black and white wood duck flank section

TIP: Flat gold tinsel

BODY: Peacock herl

WING: Yellow bucktail or calf tail, red hackle fibers covering half of the yellow bucktail

SHOULDER: Jungle cock

HEAD: Lacquered black

DARK EDSON TIGER

    TAIL: Yellow hackle fibers

    BODY: Medium yellow chenille

    THROAT: Red hackle fibers

    WING: Brown bucktail or calf tail

    CHEEK: Jungle cock

    HEAD: Lacquered black

SKYKOMISH SUNRISE   (steelhead fly)

    TAIL: Mixed yellow and red hackle fibers

    BODY: Red chenille ribbed with flat silver tinsel

    WING: Sparse white polar bear or calf tail tied to extend past tail

    COLLAR: Mixed red and yellow hackle

    HEAD: Black lacquer

SKUNK   (steelhead fly)

    TAIL: Red hackle fibers

    BODY: Black chenille ribbed with flat silver tinsel

    WING: White polar bear or calf tail

    COLLAR: Black hackle

    HEAD: Lacquered black

Many of the above patterns were originated specifically for trout or for salmon, and they are listed in appropriate sizes. This does not mean they cannot be used for many other types of fish or tied in larger or smaller sizes. All streamers and bucktails can be tied in sizes up to 2/0 or down to 16 provided you keep the overall proportion of the fly in proper ratio (and have the material to fit the hook).

13

Streamers

Some flies are tied to catch fish, some to catch fishermen. In most cases streamer patterns catch the imagination of both. Happily so. Streamers are seen more often than any other fly in hatbands, on brooches, and in picture frames as displayed art. They win the admiration of the angler as he watches the pulsing multicolored imitation dart toward him at the end of his retrieve, and they excite the imagination of trout, bass, and salmon.

Of all the patterns in this category, one stands above the rest in fame and popularity. It is almost as famous as the Royal Coachman/dry or the Gold-ribbed Hare's Ear/wet. It is the Gray Ghost, the creation of Carrie Stevens. It has taken more trout and a goodly number of other species than any other streamer simply because it has been fished more.

The Gray Ghost is tied in a full range of sizes, from a small 14 to a husky 3/0. It has been effectively used for panfish, bass, trout, pike, salmon, and certain saltwater fish. Quite a record.

GRAY GHOST

The pattern description for the Gray Ghost is:

GRAY GHOST

    BODY: Orange floss

    RIB: Medium flat silver tinsel

    THROAT: White bucktail covered by golden pheasant crest feather

    WING: Golden pheasant crest feather, followed by four bronze dun saddle hackles over which are tied five or six strands of peacock herl

    SHOULDER: Silver pheasant body feather

    CHEEK: Jungle cock or substitute

    HEAD: Lacquered black

The hook for the most popular sizes is the Mustad 9575. We'll use a size 6.

Spiral some fine black thread onto the shank beginning just before the bend and winding to it.

Since this pattern does not have a tail, the tinsel will be tied in first. Cut a 6-inch section of medium flat silver tinsel, and lay one end of it diagonally under the hook between the thread and the shank. Tie it down. Take one turn of tinsel over the shank, winding to the rear, and secure it with two more turns of thread. Again, the extra turn of tinsel to the rear will keep it in proper position for ribbing the body after the floss has been tied in (see Figure 1).

The orange floss body is next. In Chapter 12 we learned to tie a proper floss body on the Llama. Form this body in exactly the same way (see Figure 2).

When you've completed the body, go back, and in an open spiral, form the rib of the fly with the tinsel. Again, standard procedure (see Figure 3).

Apply a touch of head cement to the windings that secure the floss and tinsel.

The throat of the fly is next. It consists of white bucktail or calf tail and a golden pheasant crest feather tied under the shank of the hook. The simplest way to tie in the throat is to turn the hook upside down in the vise. Leave the bobbin attached.

Select a clump of five or six bucktail or calf tail fibers, and tie them

Fig. 1. Tying in Tinsel Rib

Fig. 2. Tying in Orange Floss for Body

Fig. 3. Forming Silver Tinsel Rib

Fig. 4. Tying in Bucktail Fibers for Throat

Fig. 5. Golden Crest Tied in for Complete Throat

Fig. 6. Preparing and Pinching Golden Pheasant Crest Feather Before Tying In

Fig. 7. Tying in Golden Pheasant Crest

Fig. 8. Preparing Saddle Hackle Feathers for Wing

Fig. 9. Tying in Hackle Feathers

Fig. 10. Securing and Lifting Wing

Fig. 11. Close-up of Fig. 10

in. They should extend to the point of the hook (see Figure 4). Clip the excess butts.

Now select one of the shorter golden pheasant crest feathers (save the longer ones for later), and tie it in on top of the white bucktail. The curve of the feather should cup the bucktail fibers (see Figure 5). Clip excess butt.

Put a drop of head cement on the windings, and right the hook.

Let's pause right here. Did you notice anything different? If you are familiar with other descriptions of this pattern, you should have. Usually this pattern is tied with a peacock herl topping on the bottom, covering the throat we have just tied in. This dressing is attributed to the pattern's originator, Carrie Stevens. Why not, then, stick with the original dressing? Because we want our Gray Ghost to ride right side up when it is retrieved. Remember the basic rule: Wherever possible, lighter materials on top of the hook shank, heavier on the bottom. Here we have kept the peacock herl in the pattern but have moved it from under the hook shank to over it. It will later form the final part of the wing.

Dave Whitlock tells me the Gray Ghost was created to imitate a smelt, a baitfish used in Maine and other northeastern states. Today, however, most anglers are unaware of this and use the Gray Ghost as an all-purpose baitfish imitation. Most of the baitfish I have seen seem to have a darker topside. In other words, if there is a color variation in a baitfish, it usually runs from light at the bottom to dark at the top. So in addition to behaving properly when fished, the Gray Ghost will do very well with its peacock herl on top since it will also look like most other baitfish.

Back to the vise. Our many-materialed wing is next.

The first part of the wing consists of a fairly long golden pheasant crest feather. Pluck one from the base of the skin. Note that the fibers have a natural curve. The idea is to get this long, very smooth curved feather to lie naturally along the top of the hook shank—which it never wants to do. It will talk back to you, no matter how much you chew it out in your

Fig. 12. Tying in Topping of Peacock Herl

Fig. 13. Gray Ghost with Wings Complete

frustration. Before you tear it (and your own hair) out, *pinch it between your thumbnail and index finger at the point where it is to be fastened to the shank* (see Figure 6). Pinching lets the feather retain its natural curve but at the same time gives you a flat base to lash it to the shank with. If the feather still misbehaves, tug it a few times from side to side. It *will* conform.

The length of the crest feather should be almost twice the length of the shank. Tie it in, and trim the excess butts (see Figure 7).

You need four bronze dun hackles for the second part of the wing makeup. You can use either neck or saddle hackles. I prefer the feathers from a saddle patch. They seem to curve and behave the way I want them to a little better than neck hackle feathers, at least for such streamers as the Gray Ghost.

As you pluck these feathers, note that they seem to droop to either the left or the right. Okay, you will need a pair of matching hackles, two that droop left and two that droop right. Look for the droop, or floppiness, from the shiny side of the feather.

Measure the hackle feathers along the shank so that when they are tied in, the tips will reach the tip of the golden pheasant crest feather. At the point where the hackle feathers are to be tied in, trim the excess fibers from the stem butts as you would on a conventional dry fly (see Figure 8).

Take the two left drooping feathers, and lay them one on top of the other, shiny side facing you. Place the butt ends on top of the hook shank at the tie-in area. They should be *slightly off-center,* closer to your side of the shank. Take two turns of thread over the feathers, and apply just enough tension to hold them in place (see Figure 9).

Repeat this operation with the two right drooping saddle hackles, placing them slightly off-center on the far side of the shank. Again, the shiny sides of *all* feathers face out. All four feathers should be the same length, the length of the crest. Note that the feathers droop down toward the bend.

Secure the feathers to the shank. You may have to manipulate them a bit to make them behave, but they won't give you much trouble. Once they are fairly secure, lift all four hackle feathers and the golden pheasant crest feather from the shank, and take two turns of thread under the wing. This will prop the feathers up a bit, ensuring lifelike action when they are fished (See Figures 10 and 11).

Clip the excess butts, and apply a touch of head cement.

The last part of the wing is the topping of peacock herl. Here is your chance to use some of that long fine stuff you rarely get a call for when tying your dries and wets. Snip six or seven peacock quills from an eyed tail.

With the tips of the herl pointing down, tie them in on top of the hackles. They should also be as long as the golden pheasant crest and saddle hackle feathers (see Figures 12 and 13).

The shoulder of the Gray Ghost is formed with a silver pheasant body feather. These are white feathers with faint black barring. You should have no difficulty tying them in.

The length of the body feather is determined by the length of the hook shank. Separate the fibers from the feather until only a section long enough to cover half the shank remains. Prepare two such feathers, and tie in one on each side of the shank at the tie-in area (see Figures 14 and 15).

The cheeks are next. Here again the jungle cock eyed feather is called for. If this is unavailable, by all means use one of the substitutes recommended earlier. The jungle cock eye should be half the length of the shoulder feather.

Separate the fibers for the tie-in area as you did for the silver pheasant feather.

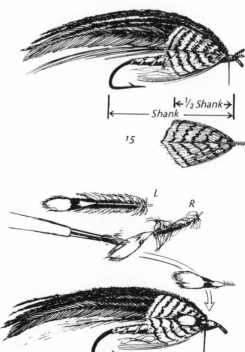

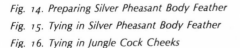

Fig. 14. Preparing Silver Pheasant Body Feather
Fig. 15. Tying in Silver Pheasant Body Feather
Fig. 16. Tying in Jungle Cock Cheeks

Put a little head cement on the inside of the jungle cock eye, and press it against the shoulder feather. Secure it with thread. Repeat this on the other side of the fly (see Figure 16).

Taper your head neatly, and whip finish. Your completed Gray Ghost should look like Figure 17.

Fig. 17. Completed Gray Ghost

OTHER GHOSTS

From the success of the Gray Ghost, it followed quite naturally that other patterns with the same second name would be developed, very similar to the Wulff series of dry flies or the Butt salmon flies.

Here are the pattern descriptions of two other famous Ghosts:

BLACK GHOST

    TAIL: Yellow hackle

    BODY: Black floss

    RIB: Medium flat silver tinsel

    THROAT: Yellow hackle

    WING: Four white saddle hackles

    CHEEK: Jungle cock eye or substitute

    HEAD: Lacquered black

GREEN GHOST

    BODY: Orange floss

    RIB: Medium flat silver tinsel

    THROAT: White bucktail

    WING: Four green saddle hackles over which are tied six strands of peacock herl

    SHOULDER: Silver pheasant body feathers

    CHEEK: Jungle cock eye or substitute

    HEAD: Lacquered black

MARABOU STREAMERS AND MYLAR BODIES

Just recently I had a chance to glance over a list of the ten most popular bucktail and streamer patterns. Three of the top ten positions were held by streamer flies with wings of marabou. Obviously these patterns took more than their share of fish. But why? Because of the nature of marabou. I cannot think of a material that pulses, undulates, seduces, or breathes more than a clump of marabou fibers. This is *action* in its most inviting form.

A fairly current "discovery" is a synthetic tinsel-like material called Mylar, which comes in a variety of forms, the most popular of which is called Mylar piping. Mylar piping is a braided metallic yarn used for trimming hats and clothing. It was discovered by fly tiers sometime in 1966 or 1967 and has increased in popularity ever since. Because of the braiding the finish on a piece of silver or gold Mylar looks just like a glittering mass of fish scales. What could better fill the bill for appeal in a streamer?

It was inevitable that marabou and Mylar (action and attraction) would make an unbeatable pair. And so they do.

Mylar-bodied marabou streamers are not difficult to tie, only different. Two of the most popular patterns are the yellow and the white. Here is the pattern description for the Yellow Mylar Marabou:

YELLOW MYLAR MARABOU
    TAIL: Red hackle fibers
    BODY: Silver Mylar piping
    WING: Yellow marabou over which are tied four strands of peacock
            herl
    HEAD: Lacquered black

The hook is a Mustad 9575, size 8. The thread, however, changes. This time we shall need some fine red thread, the same color as the tail.

Fix the hook in your vise, and spiral your red thread onto the shank, terminating at the bend.

Snip a section of fibers from a red hackle feather, and tie them in as the tail. The tail should extend approximately one-quarter inch past the bend.

Though it is not absolutely necessary, we are going to tie an under-body on this pattern. It can be made from various wools or flosses or stretchy sponge plastic material. I've used Curon for our sample pattern.

The underbody gives bulk and shape to the body of the fly, that's all. The color of the underbody material is of no consequence since it will only be covered with Mylar piping in the next operation.

Tie in the underbody material just in front of the bend of the hook. Leave the thread dangling at the bend.

As you would with a floss, wind the material back and forth across the shank to form the shape of the fly. In this instance I'm making the conventional cigar shape used on most streamers. When the underbody has been formed, secure it with the thread at the bend of the hook (see Figure 18). Apply a touch of head cement to the windings at the bend.

Cut a 1-inch section of medium silver Mylar piping, and with a pair of tweezers remove the cotton core inside it.

Slip the now hollow Mylar piping onto the shank of the hook by pushing it past the eye to the bend.

Coat the end of the Mylar piping—the part at the bend of the hook —with vinyl cement. It will remain flexible but will prevent unraveling of the braided Mylar. Tie it down at the bend with your thread.

Clip any excess pieces of Mylar that protrude past the tying thread at the bend. Continue wrapping the thread until you have covered the ends of the Mylar and there is a neatly tapered flow from tail to thread to Mylar body (see Figure 19).

You'll note that the red thread creates a continuous flow of color right up to the silver body. For any fly with a tail, always try to use a thread at the bend which is the same color as the tail. If a tail is not called for, use a red thread. Most baitfish have red in them somewhere.

Once the tail and body have been secured at the bend, whip finish the thread, and cut it away. Apply a touch of head cement to the windings.

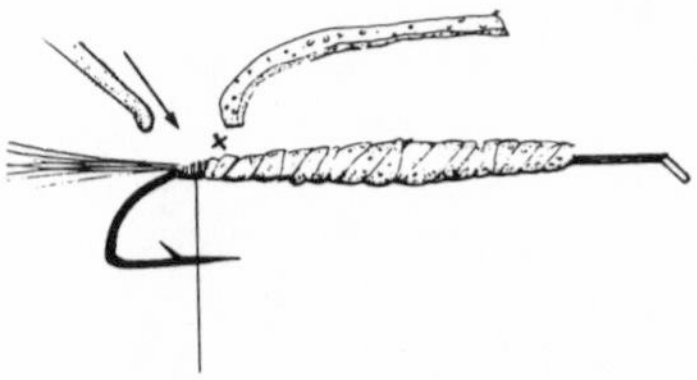

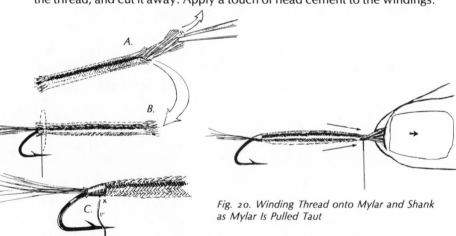

Fig. 18. Forming Underbody

A.

B.

C.

Fig. 19. Securing Mylar at Bend

Fig. 20. Winding Thread onto Mylar and Shank as Mylar Is Pulled Taut

Change over to a fine black thread.

The Mylar tubing has now been secured at the bend of the hook. The other end of the Mylar, which now covers and protrudes beyond the eye of the hook, must also be secured and trimmed.

Because the Mylar tubing is covering the part of the shank near the eye where your thread is to go, you will not be able to see it. You can, however, feel the eye through the Mylar. Find exactly where it is, and spiral your thread around both the Mylar and the shank just behind the eye.

As you wind your thread around the Mylar and the shank, grip the end of the Mylar which protrudes out beyond the eye, and pull it taut. Continue taking turns of thread as you pull (see Figure 20).

Once the area has been secured so that the Mylar will not slip backward, clip the excess Mylar in front of the thread (cut away the entire excess tubing in front of the thread windings).

After you have trimmed the excess Mylar, some stubs remain. Cover these with thread, and apply a touch of head cement to the windings (see Figure 21).

The marabou wing is next.

Marabou comes in both long and short. And there is a difference between them. The long, or regular, marabou generally runs from 4 to 6 inches. If you have this type, you'll *have* to use fibers which come off the main stem. If you have short marabou, sometimes called blood feathers, you'll be able to use the entire feather (see Figure 22). I prefer short

Fig. 21. Mylar Marabou Body Formed

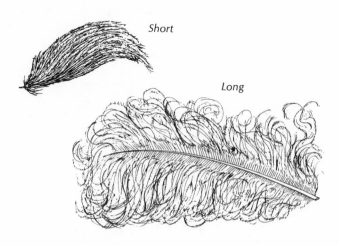

Short

Long

Fig. 22. Two Types of Marabou Feather

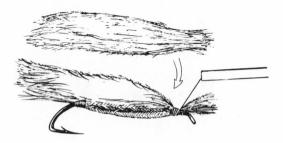

Fig. 23. Marabou Plume Tied in as Wing

Fig. 24. Completed Yellow Mylar Marabou

marabou. You don't have to cut from the stem and fuss with the fibers to align them. In addition, the shorts are actually longer than the long as far as their use in fly tying.

Pick (or cut a section of) a marabou plume on which the tips are fairly evenly tapered. The base of the plume should be about a matchstick in diameter.

Put a touch of head cement on your windings.

Lay the plume or section of fibers on top of the hook shank so the tips extend as far back as the tail. Tie it in (see Figure 23).

Cut four strands of peacock herl, and tie them in on top of the marabou.

Taper a head with your thread, whip finish, and apply a coat of black lacquer.

A completed Yellow Mylar Marabou appears in Figure 24.

MYLAR BUCKTAIL

Mylar piping, incidentally, is also used to form part of the wing on streamer or bucktail flies. It works best, however, on flies with hair fibers or marabou in their makeup. It does not seem to fit on such streamers as the Gray or Black Ghost, the wings of which are primarily neck or saddle hackles. What am I talking about? From what kind of Mylar can you make a hairlike wing? It is the very same Mylar piping with which we have just made the body on the Yellow Mylar Marabou, only this time it is destranded.

To illustrate, let's tie a very simple fly which we shall call the Mylar Bucktail. Colors on this pattern can vary to suit any imitation you wish to make. Here is a basic pattern description:

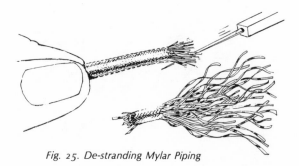

Fig. 25. De-stranding Mylar Piping

Fig. 26. De-stranded Mylar Wing Tied In

TAIL: Red hackle fibers

BODY: Green floss

RIB: Flat gold tinsel

WING: Destranded silver Mylar over which is tied white calf tail

The hook is a Mustad 9575 in size 8, and the thread is black.

The tail, body, and rib should present no problems. By now you should be accustomed to tying them. Therefore, complete the fly to the wing stage.

Cut a 1-inch section of fine or medium Mylar tubing, and remove the cotton core with a pair of tweezers.

With a dubbing needle poke and stroke the end of the Mylar until the strands come apart. Keep separating them until all you have left intact is a quarter inch (see Figure 25).

Fig. 27. Completed Mylar Bucktail

Place a drop of head cement on top of the windings where you have tied off your rib. Lay the destranded section of Mylar piping on top of the hook shank, and tie it in as you would a clump of calf tail. The ends should extend as far back as the tail (see Figure 26).

Put a drop of head cement on the windings.

Tie in the upper wing of white calf tail on top of the Mylar piping in the conventional manner. Clip all excesses, taper a head, and whip finish. A coat of black lacquer completes the fly (see Figure 27).

OTHER PATTERNS

Mastering the procedures in this chapter and Chapter 12 should enable you to tie most of the streamer flies described today. This list has only a few of the patterns you should, without further instruction, be able to tie for your own use and enjoyment:

SUPERVISOR

TAIL: Red wool

BODY: Flat silver tinsel

THROAT: White hackle fibers

WING: A few strands of white bucktail over which are tied four blue saddle hackles topped with five or six strands of peacock herl

SHOULDER: Light green saddle hackles tied two-thirds the length of the wing

CHEEKS: Jungle cock or substitute

HEAD: Lacquered black

DARK SPRUCE STREAMER

TAIL: Three or four peacock sword fibers

BODY: Rear half, red floss; fore half, peacock herl

WING: Dark furnace saddle hackles

HACKLE: Furnace wound as collar

HEAD: Lacquered black

NINE THREE

TAIL: None

BODY: Flat silver tinsel

WING: A few strands of white bucktail over which are tied two green saddle hackles covered by two black saddle hackles and topped with five or six strands of peacock herl

CHEEKS: Jungle cock or substitute

HEAD: Lacquered black

SILVER DARTER

TAIL: Section of silver pheasant wing or mallard flank

BODY: White floss

RIB: Flat silver tinsel

THROAT: Three peacock sword fibers

WING: Two white badger saddle hackles

SHOULDER: Jungle cock or substitute extending along the badger hackle for a quarter of its length

HEAD: Lacquered black

MAGOG SMELT

TAIL: Section of teal flank fibers

BODY: Flat silver tinsel

THROAT: Red hackle fibers

WING: White, yellow, and lavender bucktail or calf tail in that order, topped by five or six strands of peacock herl

CHEEKS: Teal flank

HEAD: Lacquered black

THOR   (steelhead fly, tied in sizes 2–8)
> TAIL: Orange hackle
> BODY: Red chenille
> WING: Polar bear or substitute
> HACKLE: Brown hackle collar
> HEAD: Black

POLAR SHRIMP   (steelhead fly, tied in sizes 2–8)
> TAIL: Bright red hackles
> BODY: Fluorescent salmon red chenille
> WING: Natural polar bear
> HACKLE: Hot orange hackle collar
> HEAD: White

UMPQUA SPECIAL   (steelhead fly, tied in sizes 2–8)
> TAIL: White polar bear or substitute
> BODY: Rear third, pale yellow wool; fore two-thirds, red chenille
> RIB: Flat gold tinsel
> WING: A few strands of dyed red polar bear over which is tied a substantial wing of white polar bear or a substitute
> HACKLE: Brown hackle collar
> HEAD: Red

DESCHUTES FAVORITE   (steelhead fly, tied in sizes 2–8)
> TAIL: Red hackle fibers
> BODY: Fluorescent salmon red chenille
> RIB: Flat silver tinsel
> WING: White polar bear or substitute
> HACKLE: Bright red hackle collar
> HEAD: Black

GOLDEN DEMON   (steelhead fly, tied in sizes 2–6)
> TAIL: Golden pheasant crest fibers
> BODY: Gold Mylar tubing
> WING: Red fox squirrel tail
> HACKLE: Hot orange hackle fibers
> HEAD: Black

FALL FAVORITE   (steelhead fly, tied in sizes 2–8)

TAIL: None

BODY: Silver Mylar tubing

WING: Orange polar bear or substitute

HACKLE: Claret hackle wound as collar

HEAD: Black

BRAD'S BRAT   (steelhead fly, tied in sizes 2–8)

TAIL: White polar bear over orange polar bear or substitute

BODY: Rear third, orange wool; fore two-thirds, red wool

RIB: Flat embossed gold tinsel

WING: White polar bear over which is tied orange polar bear or substitute

HACKLE: Brown hackle wound as collar

HEAD: Black

Although steelhead flies are sometimes tied on other hooks, most western anglers prefer to tie them on an Eagle Claw 1197B.

14

Saltwater and Other Specialized Streamers

Most of the patterns you will tie for your fishing will conform to the accepted and fairly standard procedures you have learned. And there is really no need to deviate from these procedures since the patterns have proved themselves for their purpose. They are either impressionistic or realistic imitations, and if you tie them bearing in mind the basic ingredients attraction, action, and imitation, they will take their share of trout and other fish.

Occasionally, however, you are faced with unusual circumstances or unusual waters, which may call for new techniques. A fly that comes to mind for this kind of situation is the tandem streamer.

GRAY GHOST TANDEM

The dressing for the Gray Ghost Tandem is the same as that for the single hook form. In this instance, however, we are going to have two bodies instead of one. And because of the technique involved in connecting the

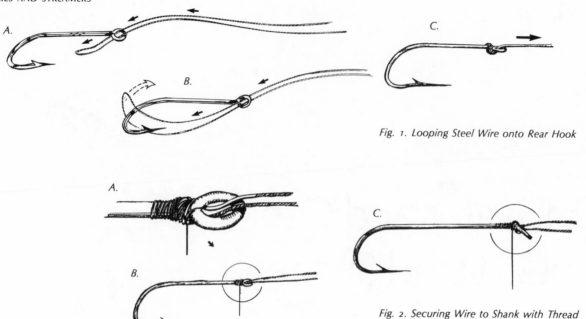

Fig. 1. *Looping Steel Wire onto Rear Hook*

Fig. 2. *Securing Wire to Shank with Thread*

two hooks, we are going to use a different style of hook. A Mustad 38941 will do nicely for our purposes.

Tandem streamers are fished primarily in deep water, usually lakes. They can be cast, but trolling with them seems to produce more results. Since tandems are basically designed to imitate a large baitfish, a size 4 hook is in order.

Before the hook is inserted into the vise, you have to loop a section of stainless steel wire through the eye and over the shank of the rear hook. This will become the rear hook of the fly.

Cut a 10-inch section of 20-pound test stainless steel stranded wire. Bend the wire in half with a pair of flat-nosed pliers—in other words, form a loop.

Insert the looped portion of the wire into and down through the eye of the hook. Slip the loop over the point and bend and onto the shank; pull it forward (see Figure 1).

Now you can place the hook into your vise. Pull the wire loop as snugly as you can against the eye of the hook.

Spiral your thread onto the shank of the hook behind the eye and over the wire. Take enough turns to secure it well. Apply a touch of head cement to the windings (see Figure 2).

Spiral your thread back to the bend.

Form a body of orange floss, and rib it with flat silver tinsel exactly the way you did when you first tied this pattern in Chapter 13. When you complete the body, whip finish a small head, and cut the thread. At this point your tandem Gray Ghost should look like Figure 3.

Notice that the two strands of wire coming through the eye of the rear hook are very close and neatly aligned. We want to keep them that way.

Remove the rear hook from the vise, and insert another hook of the same type and size into the vise.

Spiral your thread onto the shank of the hook beginning at the eye and winding to the bend. Keep the turns of thread close, and cover the shank well. Apply a coating of head cement to the threaded shank.

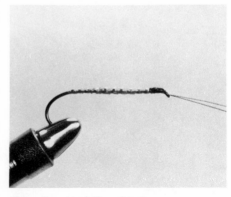

Fig. 3. Rear Hook Completed

Lay the two pieces of wire coming from the rear hook on top of the hook shank now in the vise. Leave about a half inch between the eye of the rear hook and the bend of the one in the vise. With your thread bind down the wire on top of the hook shank by winding almost to the eye. When you have almost reached the eye with your thread, stop and push the ends of the wire through the top of the eye. Take both ends of the wire protruding from the eye of the hook, and bend it backward alongside and slightly under the shank (see Figure 4).

Wind your thread to the rear, covering the wire that has just been folded back. Keep the turns close and tight.

With a wire cutter clip any excess starting one-eighth of an inch from the bend. You'll need a little clearance to form the body properly (see Figure 5). Apply a liberal coat of head cement to the shank.

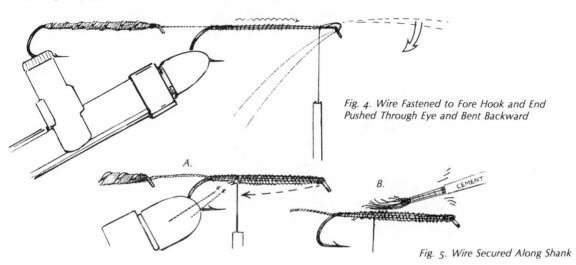

Fig. 4. Wire Fastened to Fore Hook and End Pushed Through Eye and Bent Backward

A.

B.

Fig. 5. Wire Secured Along Shank

Slipping the strands of steel wire through the eye of the fore hook will ensure a firm link between the two hooks.

Complete the body of the front fly by winding orange floss and silver tinsel onto the shank.

You are now ready to tie in the throat, wings, shoulder, and cheek. The same materials will be used. However, since you are tying in tandem, these materials must be long enough to cover both hooks.

The throat, which is made of white bucktail and golden pheasant crest, should be tied in under the fore hook so that the tips of both materials extend to the rear hook.

The wing, of golden pheasant crest and four bronze dun saddle hackles, should, with the peacock topping, extend approximately half an inch past the bend of the rear hook.

The shoulder of silver pheasant and the cheek of jungle cock should be tied just slightly larger.

The head is tapered with thread, and a coat of black lacquer is applied to it. The completed Gray Ghost Tandem is shown in Figure 6.

Fig. 6. Completed Gray Ghost Tandem Streamer

MYLAR TANDEMS

The tandem streamer fly has been around quite a while; Mylar piping is still relatively new. But what a marriage! Truly, tandems and Mylar were made for each other, especially for the lake and saltwater fly rodder.

The nature of Mylar not only gives this type of fly the necessary attraction but also is about as imitative of a baitfish as you could want to get. The stranded steel wire that connects the two hooks gives the streamer a suppleness which is lacking when you use a single hook. Additional movement and imitation are, of course, created by the wing, whether of feathers or hair.

Knowing how to tie a Mylar body, which is covered in Chapter 13, and just having learned how to tie a tandem streamer, you would think that it would be fairly simple to tie a Mylar tandem streamer. Unfortunately, this is not the case. There is a bit of a trick involved in making the combination. Let's tie one, and see what it's all about. Here is a pattern called the Mylar Eel that is effective in both fresh and salt water:

MYLAR EEL
TAIL: Black hackle tips

BODY: Mylar piping covering both hooks and wire connector

WING: Yellow and grizzly saddle hackles topped with six to seven strands of peacock herl

If you are tying this pattern for salt water, a good hook would be the Mustad 3407 in sizes 1/0 and 2/0. For freshwater lake fishing any size 2 standard wet fly hook will do fine. Some you can use are the Mustad 3906, 7948A, and 7957B. For our example I've used the saltwater model 3407 in size 2/0.

The thread is black. For this pattern you can go to a heavier diameter, such as a 2/0, if you wish, though fine thread will do the job just as well.

Cut a section of stainless steel wire approximately 9 inches long. Fold it in half, and loop it through the eye of the rear hook exactly as you did on the Gray Ghost Tandem.

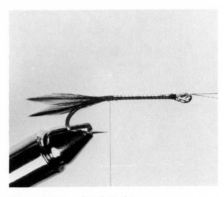

Fig. 7. Wire and Tail Tied In

Spiral your thread onto the shank behind the eye, and secure the wire. Don't forget a touch of head cement.

Bring your thread to the rear toward the bend.

From a black rooster or saddle cape, pluck two medium feathers. Tie one on each side of the hook shank so that the tips of each extend half an inch past the bend. Clip the excess. Thus far, this is all standard procedure. At this point your fly should look like the one in Figure 7.

Cut a 5-inch section of silver Mylar piping. It should be the large size, approximately three-sixteenths of an inch in diameter. Remove the cotton core. Slip the Mylar tubing over the ends of the wire and onto the hook, and secure it with the thread at the bend. Blend the thread into the tail of the fly with an even taper, whip finish, and cut the thread from the rear body (see Figure 8). Remove the rear hook from the vise.

Take another hook, and slip its point into the remaining open end of Mylar tubing. Push it back into the tubing for about one inch, and then force it through the bottom of the Mylar wall. As you do this the Mylar will bunch. As soon as the point of the hook emerges from the bottom of the tubing, the Mylar can be easily pulled back to normal shape once more (see Figure 9).

The hook should be forced through the piping so that only the eye is exposed. Place the hook in the vise.

Take the wire strands, and one at a time, push them through the eye of the hook from the top, as you did on the Gray Ghost Tandem.

Spiral your thread onto the shank behind the eye.

With your left hand pull back on the Mylar tubing, exposing the shank,

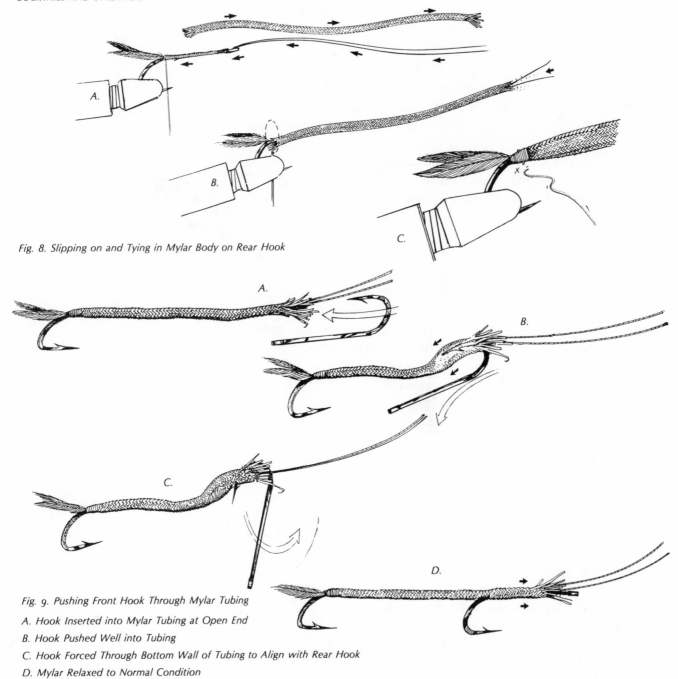

Fig. 8. Slipping on and Tying in Mylar Body on Rear Hook

Fig. 9. Pushing Front Hook Through Mylar Tubing

A. Hook Inserted into Mylar Tubing at Open End

B. Hook Pushed Well into Tubing

C. Hook Forced Through Bottom Wall of Tubing to Align with Rear Hook

D. Mylar Relaxed to Normal Condition

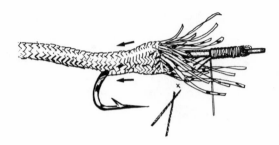

Fig. 10. Wire Bent Backward and Wound with Thread to Eye

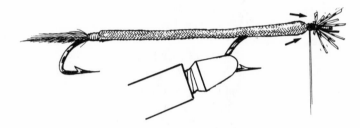

Fig. 11. Mylar Secured near Eye

and wind the thread as far to the rear as you can without covering any of the tubing.

Take the ends of the tandem wire protruding from the eye of the hook, and bend them backward. Hold them tautly with your left hand, and bring the thread forward to the eye once more. Keep the windings of thread close. Apply a touch of head cement to them, and clip any excess wire butts (see Figure 10).

The Mylar tubing, which had been held back, can now be brought forward to the thread and bound down with it (see Figure 11).

The rest of the pattern is conventional. However, you will need some fairly long saddle hackles to reach the tip of the tail with the wing.

First tie in one yellow saddle hackle for each side of the wing, and then cover it with a grizzly saddle of equal length. Top the saddles with six or seven strands of peacock herl.

Taper a neat head, whip finish, and apply a coat of black lacquer. Your completed Mylar Eel should look like Figure 12.

Fig. 12. Completed Mylar Eel

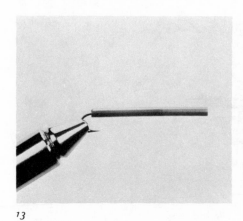

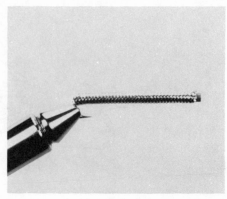

13   14

TUBE FLIES

Mylar has also made possible the easy and realistic construction of tube flies, which have long been used by the English for lake fishing. As the name implies, a tube fly is made from a tube, usually of plastic, though metals are also used.

The first tube fly I ever made was tied on a dried-out ball-point pen cartridge. Just take apart a pen, remove the plastic tube, and cut the tube near the crimp, which holds the ball point. Now you're in business.

The advantage of this type of fly is that when you strike a fish, the tubing, on which the feathers or fibers are tied, usually slides out of the way, while the hook remains imbedded in the fish's jaw.

This following pattern uses a tube:

SILVER TUBE FLY
>   BODY: Braided Mylar tubing
>   WING: White marabou
>   HEAD: Red

Since the plastic tubing cannot be held securely in your vise, it will need a support. For this use a ringed eye hook; a size 6 or 8 will generally do the trick. However, if the inside diameter of your tube is larger or smaller than the hook, simply pick a size that will hold the tubing.

Insert the proper ringed eye hook into your vise.

Cut a 1 1/2-inch section of plastic tubing (the tubing can be cut to *any* length, depending on the size of the imitation you are creating).

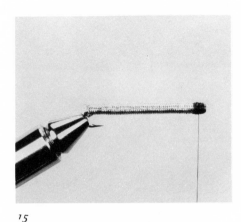

Fig. 13. Tube Slipped onto Bare Hook
Fig. 14. Mylar Slipped on Tube
Fig. 15. Mylar Bound to Tube with Thread

15

Slip the tubing onto the hook. It should fit snugly but not be forced (see Figure 13).

Cut a section of Mylar piping that extends just past the tube.

Leave approximately one-eighth of an inch of plastic tube exposed at the front end for tying on the thread (see Figure 14).

Using your bobbin, spiral some size 2/0 red thread onto the front end of the plastic tubing, and wind to the rear so you will also cover the front part of the Mylar piping. Apply a touch of head cement to the windings (see Figure 15).

Proceed in the conventional manner, and tie in your white marabou wing.

Build a taper with your thread, whip finish, and head lacquer the head. The tube fly is completed.

To use the tube fly for fishing, slip your leader through the tube and attach it to a bare hook (see Figure 16).

You can now see the possibilities and advantages of this fly. You could actually carry an assortment in your shirt pocket and never feel the point of a hook.

OTHER CATEGORIES

There are, of course, other categories of streamer flies being tied for various purposes—saltwater and steelhead flies, to cite two examples. The techniques involved in tying them are, for the most part, identical to those

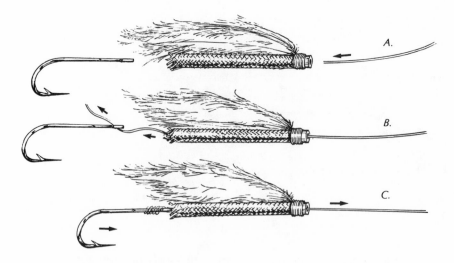

Fig. 16. Passing the Leader Through Tube

learned in the previous chapters. Hook styles and sizes will change, and pattern colors surely will differ, but the basics remain the same.

There are also those flies which, though listed under the general category of streamers and bucktails, do not look like streamers and bucktails. Such flies as the Sculpin or the Muddlers and Spuddlers are in a class by themselves. They can be used in several ways. Sometimes they are used as subsurface creatures, other times as grasshoppers or frogs. Tying is simple. The part of the Muddler, Sculpin, or Spuddler that requires working with clipped deer or antelope heads is adequately covered in the chapter on terrestrials. Once you are familiar with spinning and trimming deer body hair, it is easy to adjust to other shapes in other patterns.

There will always be new developments in fly tying. That is good. Fly tying *is* an art and, like any art form, should be creative. After you have mastered some of the fundamentals, you'll find yourself contributing to the creation of new patterns for trout, salmon, bass, stripers, tarpon, or whatever fish you intend to cast for. (There are very few fish that will not take the right fly.) The extent of your creations will be limited only by your own imagination.

However good you become, always remember that the idea of tying flies is simply to tie your own fly (no matter how good or bad) and take a fish with it.

SALTWATER PATTERNS

With very few exceptions, tying saltwater flies is child's play compared to tying the much smaller and intricate freshwater ones. If you have been tying flies for trout, salmon, bass, and bluegills, you will suddenly find that you have more than enough room in which to work since the hook sizes for saltwater patterns generally average between 2 and 2/0. The smallest is size 6, and the largest 5/0.

Here are some of the more popular saltwater patterns used today.

RED AND YELLOW TARPON

> HOOK: Mustad 34007 in sizes 3/0 to 5/0
>
> THREAD: Red
>
> TAIL: Two yellow saddle hackles tied in at the bend of the hook covered by two red saddle hackles, all of which are 4–5 inches long; the dull side of the feather faces out
>
> HACKLE: Red and yellow saddle hackles tied in as a mixed colored hackle collar half the length of the hook shank beginning at the bend; the fore portion of the shank to the eye is covered with red tying thread and lacquered with clear varnish

Many anglers splay the tail on their Red and Yellow Tarpon by winding matching shades of chenille, wool, or floss around the bend of the shank so that the feathers will flare when stripped through the water.

The long hackles are tied in beginning at the bend of the shank, instead of in wing fashion like a conventional streamer, to keep them from twisting under the shank.

Tarpon flies are also commonly tied in orange, fluorescent orange, and red and orange. Some anglers prefer these shades in dyed grizzly hackle, thus creating a striped effect.

HONEY BLONDE   (used for stripers and bluefish)

> HOOK: Mustad 34007 or 3407 in sizes 1/0 to 3/0
>
> TAIL: Yellow bucktail
>
> BODY: Flat silver tinsel
>
> WING: Yellow bucktail
>
> HEAD: Red

The Honey Blonde was originated by the late Joe Brooks. The butt of the tail should be secured along the shank of the hook from the bend to a point a quarter of an inch in front of the eye. This makes for a smooth tinsel body. The tail itself should extend twice the length of the hook shank past the bend.

The wing is tied in behind the eye and propped up with the thread so that it sits at a 45 degree angle to the shank and thus undulates when stripped through the water. The tips of the wing should extend almost to the tips of the tail.

This is the rest of what is known as the Blonde series.

ARGENTINE BLONDE

HOOK: Mustad 34007 or 3407
TAIL: White bucktail
BODY: Silver tinsel
WING: Medium blue bucktail
HEAD: Black

PLATINUM BLONDE

HOOK: Mustad 34007 or 3407
TAIL: White bucktail
BODY: Silver tinsel
WING: White bucktail
HEAD: Black

STRAWBERRY BLONDE

HOOK: Mustad 34007 or 3407
TAIL: Bright orange bucktail
BODY: Flat gold tinsel
WING: Bright red bucktail
HEAD: Black

LEFTY'S DECEIVER   (striper, bluefish, and other species)

HOOK: Mustad 34007 or 3407 in sizes 1/0 to 3/0
TAIL: Four white saddle hackles tied long
BODY: Flat silver tinsel or Mylar tinsel
WING: White bucktail in two sections, one on top and one under shank of hook; two strips of silver Mylar tinsel along each side of shank
HEAD: Red

This pattern was created by Lefty Kreh and has become the most popular contemporary saltwater pattern.

This pattern was designed to provide a fly that would cast well, with very little air resistance, and sink rapidly after alighting on the surface—all the while maintaining attraction, action, and imitation. It does all this superbly.

The hackles themselves, which are tied in at the bend, are very long, approximately 4–4 1/2 inches when using a 3/0 hook. Two are tied on each side of the shank bend.

The wing, which is tied in in two separate operations, extends slightly past the bend. Thus a section of white bucktail is tied under the hook shank, as in the throat of a salmon fly, with the tips protruding past the bend, and another section is tied on top of the shank. Both sections are the same length. The four strips of Mylar tinsel are then tied in, two on each side of the hook shank extending slightly past the bucktail tips. Because it is stored on a spool or a card, Mylar tinsel has a slight curve. Take advantage of this curve, for when the tinsel is tied in, it will make the Mylar flare out and away from the hook shank.

PINK SHRIMP   (bonefish and permit)
    HOOK: Eagle Claw 254 in sizes 2–6
    TAIL: Pink bucktail
    SHELL: Pink bucktail
    FEELERS: Pink hackle palmered through body
    BODY: Silver oval tinsel
    HEAD: Painted yellow with black pupil

A red thread is used for this fly. The pattern is often tied with some fine lead wire covering the shank to facilitate rapid sinking.

The tail of pink bucktail is tied in first. The tips should extend past the bend by half an inch. The long butt section is temporarily secured with thread so that it extends in the same direction as the tail, out of the way.

The pink hackle fiber is tied in next, followed by the oval silver tinsel. The tinsel is wound in connecting spirals to form the body, after which the pink hackle is palmered through it.

Once the body and feelers have been secured, the bucktail butt section is swung forward along and over the top of the hook shank, as in a nymph case, and tied down near the eye of the hook. The head of the fly is then lacquered red, and a black-dotted yellow eye is painted on the head.

GRASS SHRIMP   (weakfish and striped bass)

HOOK: Mustad 34007 in sizes 1, 2, and 4

THREAD: Gray Monocord

TAIL: Olive saddle hackle tip tied down into bend

BODY: Dark olive wool, over which is dubbed gray seal's fur

SHELL: Strip of polyethylene

RIB: Palmered olive gray saddle hackle, heavy near eye and clipped on top of shank

SEGMENTATION: Rib of 6-pound test monofilament wound over shell in open spiral

EYES: Burnt stubs of 30-pound test monofilament

This pattern was originated by Robert Sater of Lloyd Harbor, New York. It was designed for weakfish but has proved equally effective on striped bass.

Before the tying operation is begun, the hook is bent slightly to imitate the natural curve of the shrimp.

An olive saddle hackle tip is tied well down into the bend to form the tail. Clip the excess butt.

A 6-inch strip of 6-pound test monofilament is tied in at the bend and left temporarily hanging.

A 4-inch section tapering from one-eighth to one-quarter of an inch wide is cut from a common polyethylene bag. It is tied in at the bend by the narrow end and is also left hanging.

A 5-inch section of dark olive wool is tied in next, also at the bend. *The wool is not wound around the shank.* It is lashed along the top of the shank to the eye, then doubled back on itself and lashed down once more. The thread and the wool end at the bend.

A seal's fur rope is then made (see noodle method of dubbing, pp. 124–6), and the body of the fly is formed. The seal's fur dubbing should be heavier near the head of the fly than at the bend.

The olive gray saddle hackle is now wound through the seal's fur to the eye and secured by the thread. The hackle fibers protruding along the top of the shank are trimmed off.

The polyethylene strip is brought forward, as you would a wing case on a nymph, and secured by the thread at the eye of the hook.

The 6-pound test monofilament is then wound in an open spiral to the eye and secured by the thread, thus forming a segmented body.

The eyes of the shrimp are formed by taking a 1-inch piece of 30-pound test monofilament and burning the ends with the flame from a candle. The burning melts the monofilament and produces brown stubs—eyes. The eyes are then laid on top of the hook shank directly in back of the eye of the hook and secured by crisscross (figure 8) wrappings of thread. A touch of head lacquer secures the windings of the completed Grass Shrimp.

SAND'S BONEFISH FLY   (bonefish)

HOOK: Mustad 34007 or 3407 in size 1/0
WING: White bucktail
SHOULDER: Two yellow saddles covered by two grizzly saddles tied as long as wing
HEAD: Black

Hagen Sand created this fly. It is very conventional, with nothing unusual in its makeup. Both the wing and shoulder should extend past the bend of the hook approximately 2 inches, a distance equal to the length of the hook shank.

The shoulder hackle feathers should ridge slightly above the line of the hook shank.

FRANKEE-BELLE BONEFISH FLY   (bonefish)

HOOK: Mustad 34007 or 3407 tied in sizes 1/0, 1, and 2
TAIL: None
BODY: White chenille
WING: Tied on underside of hook shank; natural brown bucktail extending one-half inch past bend and shoulder by two grizzly saddle hackles
HEAD: White

The manner in which this fly is tied allows it to be fished upside down. In other words, the point of the hook will ride higher than the shank. The bucktail fibers, which extend past the bend, also partly cover the point, thus making a slightly weedless fly.

Once the chenille has been tied in and wrapped to form the body, the fly is turned upside down in the vise, and the bucktail wing and grizzly saddle shoulder are secured to the hook. White thread is then wound to the eye of the hook, forming a small white head. The bucktail and the grizzly saddle hackle protrude from the hook between the front of the chenille body and the white thread wrappings.

MATUKA FLIES

Matuka is a fly style that originated in New Zealand. It is used both in fresh and salt water for all patterns and all fish.

The Matuka style was devised to prevent the wing from curling or twisting under the shank of the hook while retaining an imitation of a baitfish. It is especially useful on large flies, such as the saltwater variety.

A conventional streamer fly can be tied Matuka style simply by winding the tinsel rib over both the body *and* the wing. For example, the body of the Black Ghost is usually made of black floss ribbed with silver tinsel. The wing is white saddle hackle feathers tied in near the head and allowed to extend freely along the top of the hook shank an inch past the bend. But if you were tying this pattern Matuka style, you would wind the rib of tinsel over the black floss *and the white saddle hackles.* In winding the tinsel over the saddle hackles, you will, of course, be lashing it to the top of the hook shank. The part of the saddle hackle wing that extends past the bend will still move freely.

As the tinsel is wrapped over the saddle hackle, the fibers of the hackle are stroked forward so that the tinsel lashes down only the stem of the hackle, leaving the fibers exposed, like spines on a baitfish.

With this tying technique use an oval tinsel, even though a particular pattern may call for flat.

Appendixes

Appendixes

Appendix A

Definition of Terms

Though many specialized terms are explained as they are used throughout the text, a brief glossary defining fly-tying terms will be useful.

BODY MATERIAL: Any fur, feather, or synthetic material which can be used to form the body of a fly.

BUTT: In general fly tying the butt, or butt section, refers to the base, or bottom, of a feather or section of fiber. It is the opposite of the tip. "Clip the excess butts" on a hackle feather means cut away the protruding part of the feather after it has been tied in.

In salmon flies the butt may also mean the part of the fly that is tied in after the tag, tip, and tail at a point on the shank directly over the point of the hook. In this case the butt is usually made of ostrich herl.

CLIPPED BODY: The term "clipped body" usually refers to a body made from spun fibers of deer, elk, moose, or caribou hair and trimmed, or clipped, to shape. Any coarse hair that will flare around the shank of a hook can be used to form a clipped body.

CLUMP: A group of fibers—feather or hair—which have been bunched together to form the wings or tail of a fly. A clump form does not have a left or right; it is a solid mass.

COLLAR: As a noun a collar is the part of the fly usually made of feather or fur fiber, which encircles the hook shank near the head of the fly, as in hackle collar. It can be vertical, as in a dry fly, or elliptical, as in a wet fly, nymph, or streamer. To collar a fly (verb) means to wind a hackle feather to form a collar.

DIVIDED WING: Any feather, fur, or synthetic fibers which have been tied to the shank of the hook and divided into two equal parts to form the wing of the fly. Divided wings are the opposite of single wings.

DUB, DUBBING: To dub is to transfer fur, feather, or synthetic fiber onto the hook shank by making the substance adhere to the thread. Thus, the thread becomes the vehicle for transferring.

Dubbing is any material which can be spun onto the thread to form the body of the fly—for instance, muskrat dubbing, beaver dubbing, wool dubbing, polypropylene dubbing.

DUN: A grayish color, as in blue dun, bronze dun, dyed dun, and so forth.

Dun also means the stage of growth in an aquatic insect immediately after the shedding of the nymphal case and emergence as a full-grown insect. At this time the insect, whatever the species, is usually a darker shade than it is in its spinner form (see Spinner).

EXCESS: The waste part of any fly-tying material, the leftover portion, such as the excess hackle butts, or stems. "Clip the excess" means cut away the portion which will not be used in the fly.

EXTENDED BODY: Any fly or pattern on which the formed body extends beyond the bend of the hook.

FIBER: Fiber as such is used to describe the individual filament of a feather, fur, or synthetic; for example, a bucktail wing may be made of ten individual fibers or the tail of a mayfly pattern may have half a dozen cock hackle fibers.

FLUE: Usually means the barb of a feather, as in the flue of a peacock quill or an ostrich herl flue. "Pick a peacock quill with a wide flue" means to select a quill on which the flue or fibers are fairly long.

HACKLE: Pertains to the feathers of a rooster neck in most instances, although it can also be used in referring to other birds, especially when the feather is to be used to hackle a fly.

When the word "hackle" pertains to the fly itself, it describes that part of the fly which is tied behind the eye, as in a hackle collar or hackle throat.

MARRIED WINGS: Married wings or marrying feathers simply mean strips or sections of alike or different feathers that lock to form a single unit, or composite wing. It is used mostly in tying fully dressed salmon flies.

PAIR, PAIRED: A pair of matched wing quills is made from a section of feather fibers from both a right and left wing quill; the sections are paired.

PALMER: The technique of tying a feather rib through the body of the fly. For instance, if a pattern calls for a body of green floss palmered with grizzly hackle, the hackle is wound in a open spiral over the formed green floss body.

PARACHUTE STYLE: Any fly on which the hackle is wound on a horizontal plane above or below the shank of the hook.

PROPORTION: We all know the meaning of the word "proportion," but when it pertains to flies and fly tying, it is a bit more difficult to explain. The proper proportion of a fly—the relation of length, height, and thickness to wings, tail, body, and so forth—is also one of the most difficult techniques to master. A well-proportioned fly is in most cases the product of experience. In other words, the more you tie, the better your proportions will be.

When a pattern description reads "half a dozen fibers for the tail," "four turns of hackle for the collar," or "body tapered to one-sixteenth of an inch in thickness," the instructions are for the given size of a pattern. If the size of the pattern is changed, all the measurements change accordingly.

The chart on dry fly proportions (see p. 38) is only a generalization. Not only the size, but also the type, of hook will affect the length, width, and height. Proportion is perhaps best summed up very simply by considering the fly in respect to the living insect, by the balance of the fly itself, and, if possible, by how pleasing the fly is to the eye of both the fish and the angler.

QUILL: A word with many meanings (*see* pp. 56–7).

RIB: An open spiral of tinsel, thread, hackle, or any other material that segments the body of a fly. To rib a fly simply means to tie in whatever material the pattern calls for and wind it from the tail to the eye, or wing, in an open spiral.

SECURE: To fasten, usually with thread, any material so that it is firmly in place.

SEGMENT: To separate or suggest separation in the body of a fly. For instance, light and dark strips of quill such as those used for the Quill Gordon body create the illusion of two tones. A dark thread wound over a light floss body also creates the impression of a segmented body such as would be found in a natural insect.

SPINNER: A natural insect, usually a mayfly, which has reached the peak of maturity. The wings are usually clear, instead of dark (dun). At this stage mating takes place. Once mating has passed, the flies fall to the water with their wings in a relaxed, outstretched position, leading to the term "spent spinner." Flies tied to represent this stage have spinner wings or their wings are tied spent fashion—that is, extended horizontally to the shank of the hook.

TAILING: Any material—feather, fur, or synthetic—which can be used to make the tail of a fly. For example, calf tail makes excellent tailing on the dry fly pattern Royal Wulff.

TAPER: To form the body or the head of the fly by gradually and evenly increasing or decreasing its dimensions during the procedure.

There are two important body tapers. One is used on dry, wet, and nymph patterns. In most of these cases the taper is widest near the wings, or thorax, of the pattern and diminishes gradually as it approaches the tail, or bend of the hook.

The other body taper, used mainly in streamer or salmon patterns, is shaped very much like a cigar. When the fly is formed and the body material, such as floss, tied in at the bend, it is wound forward to the eye in ever increasing thickness.

"Taper the head" simply means that the thread should be wound in diminishing thickness as it approaches the eye. It is thickest where the last of the materials was tied in, usually the wing, and tapers to a very fine diameter at the edge of the eye of the hook.

THORAX STYLE: A method of hackling a fly in which the hackle collar is either wound in a crisscross X fashion or the hackle collar, after having been tied in, is trimmed at the bottom of the hook shank, leaving a V-shaped gap below. The purpose of the thorax style is to allow the fly to sit closer to the water surface. The thorax style presents a better silhouette to the fish.

TIP: This term can be just a little confusing. It can refer to the tip of a hackle feather, which is the part that grows out of the rooster or bird first.

Tip can also refer to the fine ends of hair fibers, such as the tips of bucktail or calf tail. "Tie in your wing of calf tail so that the tips extend beyond the bend of the hook" means that the finer ends of the hair should lie over or past the bend. To tie in a hackle by the tip means just that—to tie it in by the finer end. However, on something like tinsel either end is the tip, since tinsel is uniform in width.

Tip is also used to describe a part of a fly. It refers to tinsel which is tied in at the bend of the hook and, looking at the hook from bend to eye, precedes all other materials that will be tied in for the pattern. It is used quite often in the tying of salmon flies, in which case it would precede the tag. In other words, if you were tying a salmon pattern you would have, in order, tip, tag, tail, butt, and so on.

TYING SILK: This is just another word for thread. Many years ago silk was (and for many tiers still is) the only kind of thread to tie with. Thus if the pattern specified red tying silk, it meant that red silk thread should be used. Because silk is gradually disappearing from the market, nylon is used by most fly tiers, but the expression tying silk remains.

UNDERBODY: Any material which is not visible and is used to build up the body of the fly. Thus an underbody on a Mylar streamer would give shape to the body of the fly even though it is not seen. Similarly a quill-bodied dry fly is much too thin to simulate the body of a natural insect, so an underbody of floss or some other material may be added to give substance and shape to the fly.

UNDERWING: Exactly what the name implies. It is a term generally used in streamer or salmon patterns. Thus a fly may have an underwing of yellow calf tail over which a more prominent wing of green saddle hackles may be tied.

WEB, WEBBY: That part of a rooster neck or saddle hackle which contains the softer meshed weblike fibers. All neck and saddle hackles have this web. A hackle is considered of good quality if the web does not run along the hackle stem for too great a distance as it approaches the tip. Too webby means that the hackle is generally soft and lacks resiliency because of the abundance of web.

WINGING (WINGING MATERIAL): If I say, ''I am 'winging' the fly,'' it means that I am in the process of forming the wing of a particular pattern. Winging material is any feather, fur, or synthetic fiber that can be used to make the wings of a fly.

ZENITH: The peak you reach when you successfully take a fish on the fly you have tied.

ZILCH: When you don't take a fish.

Appendix B

Sources of Supply

Many fly tiers face the problem of where to buy high-quality materials. While it is preferable to go to a local fly-fishing or sporting goods outlet so you can inspect and personally choose the materials you need, there are some areas that have no stores or have stores that do not stock a complete and comprehensive line. For this reason I have listed the names and addresses of a number of mail-order houses which, in most cases, carry the items you'll require.

One brief word about mail-order houses. They will all try to do their best for you; however, they cannot read your mind or see with your eyes. Whenever you order any item that is specialized or comes in various colors, be as specific as possible. If you have a complaint or a suggestion, let them know about it. Call any error or discrepancy to their attention. If you don't, they'll never know, and you will both have lost on the transaction. If you do let them know, you'll establish a good relationship, and both of you will gain.

The following houses deal in mail orders:

Dan Bailey's Fly Shop
209 West Park Street
Livingston, Montana 59047

Baird's Snow Country
Box 22
Clementsvale, Nova Scotia
Canada BO5 1G0

Beckie's Fishing Creek Outfitters
RD 1, Box 310-1
Benton, Pennsylvania 17814

L.L. Bean, Inc.
2091 Main Street
Freeport, Maine 04033

Blue Ribbon Flies
P.O. Box 1037
West Yellowstone, Montana 59758

Buchner Fly Designs
P.O. Box 1022
Jackson, Wyoming 83001

Cabella's
812 13th Avenue
Sidney, Nebraska 69160

Classic And Custom Fly Shop
477 Pleasant Street
Holyoke, Massachusetts 01040

Dale Clemens Custom Tackle
444 Schantz Spring Road
Allentown, Pennsylvania 18104

Clouser's Fly Shop
101 Ulrich Street
Middletown, Pennsylvania 17057

Cold Spring Anglers
13 N. Letort Drive
Carlisle, Pennsylvania 17013

Wallace W. Doak & Sons, Ltd.
P.O. Box 95
Doaktown, New Brunswick
Canada EOC 1G0

Eddie's Flies And Tackle
303 Broadway
Bangor, Maine 04401

The Fishing Post
114 North Main Street
Greensburg, Pennsylvania 15601

The Fly Shop
4140 Churn Creek Road
Redding, California 96002

Henry's Fork Anglers
P.O. Box 487
St. Anthony, Idaho 83445

E. Hille
815 Railway Street
Williamsport, Pennsylvania 17701

Hunter's Angling Supplies
Central Square
New Boston, New Hampshire 03070

Bob Jacklin's Fly Shop
P.O. Box 310
West Yellowstone, Montana 59758

Jack's Tackle
RD 1, Box 196
Galeton, Pennsylvania 16922

Kaufmann's Streamborn Flies
P.O. Box 23032
Portland, Oregon 97223

Bud Lilly's Trout Shop
West Yellowstone, Montana 59758

Marriott's Fly Fishing Store
2700 W. Orangethorpe
Fullerton, California 92633

Murray's Fly Shop
P.O. Box 156
Edinburg, Virginia 22824

North Country Angler
Route 16, Box 156
North Conway, New Hampshire 03860

The Orvis Company
Manchester, Vermont 05254

Reed Tackle
P.O. Box 390
Caldwell, New Jersey 07006

Thomas And Thomas
22 Third Street
Turners Falls, Massachusetts 01376

In addition to having good sources of supply, the fly tier/angler can gain a great deal from joining and becoming involved in fly-tying organizations. Two national organizations with local chapters throughout the United States are

Federation of Fly Fishermen
P.O. Box 1088
West Yellowstone, Montana 59758

Trout Unlimited
501 Church Street
Vienna, Virginia 22180

One other very worthwhile organization, dedicated to the promotion and establishment of fly tying as an art, is

United Fly Tyers, Inc.
P.O. Box 220
Maynard, Massachusetts 01754

All three organizations publish interesting periodicals which are mailed to dues-paying members.

RIFFLE

Perhaps a brief note regarding an individual's association with such groups is in order here. Fly tiers and fly fishermen are a minority in the world of fishing, and yet they take on more than their share of the battle to protect and preserve the waters where fish abound. Though individual efforts in the constant fight and surveillance are admirable, they lack the strength and money which can be achieved only through group effort. To borrow, "united we stand"—to one end, the continuation through all generations of what Charlie Fox has so simply and clearly called "this wonderful world of trout."

Appendix C

Selected Bibliography

*BATES, JOSEPH D., JR. *Streamer Fly Tying and Fishing*. Harrisburg, Pa., Stackpole, 1950, 1966.

*———. *Atlantic Salmon Flies and Fishing*. Harrisburg, Pa., Stackpole, 1970.

*BAY, KENNETH E. *Salt Water Flies*. New York–Philadelphia, Lippincott, 1972.

*BERGMAN, RAY. *Trout*. Rev. ed. New York, Knopf, 1952.

*BOYLE, ROBERT H., and DAVE WHITLOCK. *Fly-tyer's Almanac*. New York, Crown, 1975.

*BROOKS, JOE. *Trout Fishing*. New York, Harper and Row, 1972.

CAUCCI, AL, and BOB NASTASI. *Hatches*. New York, Compara Hatch Ltd., 1975.

*FLICK, ART, ed. *Art Flick's Master Fly-tying Guide*. New York, Crown, 1972.

*FLICK, ART. *Art Flick's New Streamside Guide to Naturals and Their Imitations*. New York, Crown, 1970.

*JORGENSEN, POUL. *Dressing Flies for Fresh and Salt Water*. New York, Freshet, 1973.

*LEISER, ERIC. *Fly-tying Materials*. New York, Crown, 1973.

MARINARO, VINCENT C. *A Modern Dry-fly Code*. New York, Crown, 1970.

*McCLANE, A. J. *McClane's Standard Fishing Encyclopaedia*. New York, Holt, Rinehart, and Winston, 1965.

SHAW, HELEN. *Fly-tying*. New York, Ronald, 1963.

*SWISHER, DOUG, and CARL RICHARDS. *Selective Trout*. New York, Crown, 1971.

*VENIARD, JOHN. *Fly Dresser's Guide*. London, Adam and Charles Black, 1968.

Index

A Note About the Type

The text of this book was set in the film version of Optima, a typeface designed by Hermann Zapf from 1952-55 and issued in 1958. In designing Optima, Zapf created a truly new type form—a cross between the classic roman and a sans-serif face. So delicate are the stresses and balances in Optima that it rivals sans-serif faces in clarity and freshness and old-style faces in variety and interest.

The book was composed, printed, and bound by Haddon Craftsmen, Scranton, Pa. Typography and binding design by Earl Tidwell and Karolina Harris.